Slavery and Frontier Mississippi 1720–1835

Slavery and Frontier Mississippi

1720–1835

David J. Libby

University Press of Mississippi - Jackson

www.upress.state.ms.us

The University Press of Mississippi is a member of
the Association of American University Presses.

Copyright © 2004 by University Press of Mississippi
All rights reserved
Manufactured in the United States of America

11 10 09 08 07 06 05 04 03   4 3 2 1

Library of Congress Cataloging-in-Publication Data

Libby, David J., 1969–
  Slavery and frontier Mississippi, 1720–1835 / David J. Libby.
    p. cm.
Includes bibliographical references and index.
  ISBN 1-57806-599-2 (alk. paper)
1. Slavery—Mississippi—History—18th century. 2. Slavery—Mississippi—History—19th century. 3. Slavery—Mississippi—Natchez (District)—History. 4. Frontier and pioneer life—Mississippi. 5. Frontier and pioneer life—Mississippi—Natchez (District) 6. Plantation life—Mississippi—History. 7. Plantation life—Mississippi—Natchez (District)—History. 8. Mississippi—History—To 1803. 9. Natchez (Miss. : District)—History—18th century. 10. Natchez (Miss. : District)—History—19th century.
I. Title.
  E445.M6L53 2003
  306.3′62′0976209032—dc21   2003010748

British Library Cataloging-in-Publication Data available

TO ANNE

Contents

Acknowledgments

ix

Introduction

xi

Chapter One

French Slavery in Colonial Natchez

3

Chapter Two

Resettlement of the Natchez Region

17

Chapter Three

The Cotton Frontier of Territorial Mississippi

37

Chapter Four

Slaves in the Western Migration

60

Chapter Five

Defining the Boundaries of Enslavement

79

Chapter Six

The Transformation of Mississippi

101

Conclusion: Mississippi, the Closed Society

119

Appendix A: Slaves Purchased by John Randolph, Charleston, South Carolina, February–March 1830

121

Appendix B: Locust Grove Plantation, ca. 1833

123

Notes

127

Index

159

Acknowledgments

This book is the result of years of effort and in the process, I have accumulated debts of gratitude to a number of friends, relatives, teachers, and colleagues. First, I would like to thank my parents John and Patsy Libby, whose support took a number of forms, not least of which was financial. Also my siblings, Joseph, Richard, Rob, his wife Karen, Mary, her husband Patrick, and Charlie, have provided tremendous support and shown remarkable interest in my work.

As a student I developed numerous friendships with professors and fellow students. While pursuing my bachelor's degree at St. Mary's, the late Lee Brown, Daniel Rigney, Charles Cotrell, and Oakah Jones all inspired me to pursue an academic career. I followed Oakah Jones to Purdue to study Latin America, and while my interests soon changed to the South, his scholarship on borderlands regions continued to inspire me, and has made an impact on this study. At Purdue, I learned a great deal about the South from Harold Woodman and Robert May. Susan Curtis and Charles Cutter provided much-needed moral support, as did fellow students Steve Wagner, Jason Przypek, Greg Weeks, Paula Hinton, and Cherry Spruill. Upon completing my M.A. at Purdue, I decided that I needed to be in the South to study the place. I arrived in an amazingly collegial and yet intellectually challenging environment at the University of Mississippi. I had a wonderfully supportive advisor in Winthrop Jordan, who with his wife Cora, made me always welcome in their home. Professors Ted Ownby, Charles Reagan Wilson, Sheila Skemp, Harry Owens, Robert Haws, and Douglass Sullivan-Gonzales all sharpened my skills as historian. The research and analytical skills I learned from them are reflected in this work. Fellow students at Ole Miss also helped create an intellectually refreshing environment by providing constructive criticism in a friendly context. They include LaTonya Thames-Leonard, William Fitzgerald, Scott Holzer, Paul Beezley, Jennifer Beezley, Corey Lesseig, Scott Lish, Anthony James, Paul Anderson, Joe Wojak, Joe Bonica, Steve Rosecan, David Callejo, Ben Wynne, David Ballew, Leigh McWhite, Minoa Uffelman, Alice Hull, and Michael Hawkins.

I have also benefitted from the support and help of library staffs at several institutions. The John Davis Williams Library at the University of Mississippi

Acknowledgments

is perhaps the perfect place to begin research on a book about Mississippi. During my time at Ole Miss, the library's Department of Special Collections and Archives had an excellent staff, including Debbie Landi, and Lisa Speers, who provided helpful assistance. Also helpful were the staffs at the Mississippi Department of Archives and History, the Southern Historical Collection at University of North Carolina, the Perkins Library at Duke University, and the Barker Texas History Center at the University of Texas.

In my years since graduate school, I was fortunate to teach at Wake Forest University, Western Washington University, and the University of Texas at San Antonio. Colleagues at those institutions who provided intellectual support include William Meyers, Richard Zuber, Terence Kehoe, Daniel Pfeiffer, Alan Gallay, Darlene Lake, Patrick Kelley, Kolleen Guy, Wing Chung Ng, and Bill Sutton. Also helpful have been the comments of numerous critics at academic conference sessions. Various panel organizers kept putting Christopher Morris and me together, so in addition to my thanks, he earned the endurance award. Other critics who provided helpful criticism include Steven Stowe, Jay Gitlin, Phillip Morgan, Sylvia Frey, and Light Cummins. After I chose to leave the academic profession for a more stable career in commercial educational publishing, I found a group of colleagues and supervisors who continued to support my research interests. I especially appreciate supervisors Patricia Pederson, Luis Guzman, Brian Vogel, Cheryl Schiano, and Herb Harris, who continued to provide time and occasional travel funds to support my research.

The staff at the University Press of Mississippi has been tremendously helpful. I am pleased to have had the opportunity to work with Editor-in-Chief Craig Gill. The anonymous reviewer provided excellent advice on making my final revisions. Editors Anne Stascavage, editorial assistant Walter Biggins, copyeditor Derik Shelor, designer Pete Halverson, production coordinator Shane Gong, and several others with whom I had no direct contact, all did a great job. My thanks to all of them for turning my manuscript into a book.

Finally, a special word of thanks. On my way out of the history profession and into a new career, a colleague at UTSA invited me to lunch. Since then, Anne Hardgrove provided an important reference point by sharing her own scholarship on India. She has given me encouragement, criticism, and in the process, she has changed my life. In the weeks after our honeymoon, she tolerated my working late evenings reviewing page proofs. For her companionship, friendship, and love, this book is dedicated to her.

Introduction

Visitors approaching Natchez, Mississippi, on a paddle-wheeled tourist steamboat today first approach a section of town called "Under-the-Hill." A gambling boat named *Lady Luck* is moored there permanently, near establishments providing food and drink. Climbing Silver Street, the visitors would in minutes be on the city bluff, near an urban grid platted in 1790 by Spanish planners. Within a few blocks are the historic Adams County courthouse, antebellum bank buildings, offices, churches, and most memorably, the planter mansions from an age of great affluence.

Many of these buildings stood atop the hill in 1835, when proslavery author Joseph Holt Ingraham first arrived as a "Yankee" transplant. Ingraham saw Natchez as the capital of the southwestern cotton kingdom. Under the hill, he described a scene similar to what it is today. The city looked down, both figuratively and literally, on the gambling halls and saloons of the town under the hill. Majestic two-story planter homes stood atop the bluff as monuments to plantation wealth. Bankers, cotton factors, and slave dealers provided the planters with financing and slaves that allowed them to erect their mansions. Slave traders conducted auctions at offices in town, despite worries that the public traffic in slaves introduced cholera, malaria, and other diseases, not to mention potentially rebellious slaves. Concern over civic health and public order could be seen in a system of public works dating to the first decade of the nineteenth century, and in chain gangs of slaves and convicts who marched through town cleaning and repairing the streets.[1] Concern could also be seen in the gradual movement of the main slave mart to the outside of town in the early 1830s. The desire for public order illustrates the Natchez planters' belief that they were the leaders of a great and refined civilization.

Other visitors and migrants arrived from the east during the nineteenth century. Two roads led to Natchez, the Natchez Trace, which came from Nashville, Tennessee, through Jackson and Washington, Mississippi, and another road (today's highway 61), that led north from New Orleans, through Natchez, to Vicksburg. At the intersection of these roads the new slave market informed visitors that the town was nearby. By 1830, Natchez was 43 percent slave. Outlying areas of Adams County had an 80 percent slave population.

Introduction

A visitor arriving in 1817, the year that Mississippi became a state, would have found a smaller but well established town. A public nursery provided chinaberry trees to line the streets. Poor relief was a major municipal budget item. In 1819, the first water system began piping water to the city from artesian wells. A board of health regulated drainage, wells, cisterns, and privy houses.[2] Smaller and somewhat less opulent plantation homes were fast expanding. A slave population in the city of 30 percent contrasted with 74 percent in the county. Fewer streets had been paved (although paved sidewalks were becoming the standard), and fewer of the boats under the hill were powered by steam. But barges still shipped hundreds of tons of cotton to New Orleans, New York, Liverpool, and in finished form to households throughout North America and Europe.

A century earlier, French colonizers had arrived at Natchez and found a much different setting. An Indian village occupied by a people called Natchez was home to a small local civilization. The Natchez were heirs of a culture rooted in the ancient Cahokian civilization that had declined even prior to European contact. The bluffs overlooking the Mississippi River provided a good location for the Natchez to settle. High ground provided security from attackers and flood waters. Thousands of years of spring floods had deposited incredibly rich soil in the region. The subtropical climate offered a lengthy growing season, during which the Natchez cultivated two annual corn crops. Surrounding areas provided ample game. While hardly an Eden, with intense summer heat and humidity, spring floods, and other natural dangers ranging from poisonous insects and snakes to alligators and predatory wildcats, it was one of the best places in the lower Mississippi valley to settle. It is here, under the Natchez civilization, that the history of slavery in Mississippi began.

Although they did not employ it on a widespread basis, Natchez Indians had their own notions of slavery, as did the neighboring Choctaw. American Indian forms of slavery were different from those employed by Europeans in the Americas. The Natchez and Choctaw viewed slavery in terms of membership in (or exclusion from) society. French colonists introduced their own form of slavery, and brought people they thought were well suited to enslavement. The slaves the French brought from Africa also had concepts of what slavery was. The three groups—American Indians, Europeans, and Africans—were strangers to each other and entered into a foreign world. Each spoke a different language, and defined society, authority, family, and slavery in its own ways. Each group used its notions of these and other cultural institutions to negotiate a new world, one in which all were outsiders.³ In this context of negotiation, the evolution of slavery in Mississippi began. As it evolved, slavery in Mississippi was part of an economic system related to European colonization that created a transatlantic marketplace.

Historians have considered slavery and Mississippi together in academic studies, but their connection was always a given; it was assumed that slavery and Mississippi were, and always had been, inextricably linked. This study attempts to answer the hows and whys of slavery's development during the period when Mississippi was a frontier region. It suggests that slavery took many shapes in Mississippi before it became the institution stereotyped in so much scholarship studying the later antebellum period.

To study slavery from its origins in Mississippi is to reconsider the assumptions of several fine studies. For example, believing that other scholarship had already established why and how slavery developed in Mississippi, Charles Sackett Sydnor organized his 1933 study topically, with chapters emphasizing themes rather than chronology.⁴ More recent studies have also assumed that slavery, or race relations more generally, have been static and unchanging, indeed calling Mississippi "a culture frozen in time."⁵

Looking further back in time, and ignoring the overwhelming evidence from the late antebellum and Jim Crow eras, one finds that Mississippi was once markedly different. Most white Mississippians were pioneers rather than planters. In its earliest colonial stages, contemporary observers estimated that Mississippi's slaves comprised nearly half the colony's population. However, throughout the eighteenth century, the presence of various Indian groups made both white and black settlers minorities in Mississippi.⁶ In this early period, Mississippi was more western than southern, and more colonial than "antebellum."

This book is a study of slavery in Mississippi in the colonial and early national periods. Specifically, it studies the plantation society and economy established in eighteenth-century Natchez as it expanded further into the Natchez district, the Mississippi Territory, and ultimately the State of Mississippi. It focuses on issues of cultural exchanges and migrations, work patterns, economic transformations, slave communities, and planter ideology, all in a chronological approach.

Studies of both slavery and Mississippi during the eighteenth and early nineteenth centuries have been in short supply. Historians who have undertaken the scholarly endeavor of colonial and early American slavery have found results that are both fascinating and subtle. Those results undermine previous

Introduction

interpretations of colonial slavery, which frequently projected late antebellum slavery back to the colonial era. Most significantly, these studies suggest that the regions within the South varied widely in terms of economy, society, and slavery.[7] Studies of the lower Mississippi valley in this early period also indicate a variance between the colonial societies of the Chesapeake and Carolina settlements, and that of the Natchez region, for the economy of the Mississippi valley was dominated by exchange networks rather than individual staple crops before the introduction of cotton.[8] As a study of early slavery in Mississippi, this book engages with both colonial and antebellum slavery scholarship, although attempting to study slavery in Mississippi in its own right. Because for much of Mississippi's history the region was situated in a frontier region, this study is also a borderlands study, engaging scholarship on frontiers and borderlands at the same time it engages scholarship on slavery and race. In the process, this study advances our understanding of slavery as a fluid, dynamic social relationship, frequently defined by both masters and slaves and influenced by the environment, by work patterns, and by various cultural influences.

Mississippi was once a remote and obscure corner of New World empires. The French settlement at Natchez was the northernmost outpost of Louisiana. Natchez was the first elevated area north of Pointe Coupée. Its imposing position on bluffs overlooking the Mississippi River appealed to strategic-minded French administrators who viewed control over river traffic as the key to governing the lands they claimed in North America. Rich soil, from annual spring floods in the Mississippi River valley, made the region even more attractive.

The French certainly were not the first to see the defensive and economic advantages of the Natchez area, for its original inhabitants, the Natchez Indians, had lived there for centuries. When the French attempted a precarious coexistence with the Natchez, the first frontier was established in 1716. French settlers attempted to exploit the land's potential wealth and in a few years imported slaves from Africa to provide labor. But ongoing hostile relations between the French and the Natchez provoked the Natchez to drive the French away. In retaliation, French forces with their Choctaw allies destroyed the Natchez, but experience taught the French that the site on the bluffs was too distant for settlement. For the French, Natchez would remain little more than a military outpost for thirty years.

Following the Seven Years' War, the British came to control Mississippi in 1763. They named their colony West Florida. Natchez was once again a frontier outpost, as Spain controlled Louisiana immediately to the west. British authorities parted with convention and attempted to develop an inland, rather than coastal, settlement where the Natchez once lived. Their reasoning for this new type of settlement pattern turned on both the richness of the soil and access to the Mississippi River. British colonists came in droves, bringing slaves and staking out land claims. Their farms and plantations produced lumber, tobacco, indigo, and eventually cotton.

As a result of the hostilities associated with the American Revolution in the late 1770s, Spain conquered British lands on the eastern banks of the Mississippi River. The Natchez district's planters were by this time more loyal to the market than any sovereignty, and the opportunity to sell their products mattered more to them than retaining any nationality. Spain readily obliged, opening access to markets throughout the Spanish empire. Natchez planters rolled their profits into the purchase of more slaves, seeking to increase their productive capacity. The political instability of this era was surpassed only by the economic instability of boom and bust.

By the time Spain peacefully transferred Mississippi to the United States in 1798, Mississippi's residents had devoted their resources to the production of cotton. The planters were committed to a market economy dependent on the fruits of their slaves' labor. Their biggest difficulty would be creating a social structure that controlled the large enslaved population, a population that was growing faster than the white population of Mississippi, owing to the slave trade. Occasional rumors of slave insurrections and acts of individual resistance gave planters pause and at times pushed them to reform slave codes and reconsider the slave's position in society. The passage of these moments of hysteria resulted in little real change for the slaves. The slaves stood subject to the whims of their masters, and often of any white man they encountered. Outside the supervision of their masters, slaves led a much different life, forging families and communities, while fostering the development and continuation of a culture rooted in their African pasts and their experiences in America.

Cotton's position as one of the chief raw materials for the Industrial Revolution made the previously far-flung and obscure settlements in Mississippi suddenly central to the emergent global industrial economy. Large slaveowners became important participants in the international market economy, their business decisions now having a significant impact on the lives of people thousands of miles away. The fortunes of the mill economies in old and New England turned on the success of South's cotton crop, and vice versa.

Introduction

There seemed to be no limit to the demand for cotton, except the planters' own productive capacity, so they brought even more slaves to Mississippi, tapping into the Atlantic trade when it was still open, and later into an emergent domestic trade. At the same time that the demands of the mills disrupted the lives of their workers, the demands of the cotton frontier disrupted the lives of slaves. In search of more productive lands, planters uprooted entire slave communities and replanted them on the frontier. Slave traders readily divided slave families for sale.

The economic convulsions of the early Industrial Revolution had a significant impact on Mississippi's landscape. The increasingly intensive cultivation of cotton depleted nutrients in the land as soil was worn out or eroded. As a result of soil exhaustion, the original counties of the Natchez district lost their position as the state's top cotton-producing counties by 1820. The most productive counties were those to the north and east of Natchez. These counties, in today's central Mississippi, bordered on Choctaw lands; thus, they were the spatial limit of white settlement. The removal of the state capital three times in the early 1820s, from Washington, a few miles east of Natchez, to Columbia, then to Monticello, and finally to Jackson, illustrated the march of settlement northeastward from Natchez.

The 1823 establishment of the state capital at Jackson, at the time a distant and sparse settlement, was symbolic of a grand vision for Mississippi. Jackson was located near the state's geographical center. It was more than a hundred miles from Natchez, the state's economic, if not physical capital. The location represented a future when all of Mississippi would be under the till, a cotton kingdom whose lords ruled their enslaved subjects. Implicit in this future was the confiscation of Indian lands, which both Choctaw and Chickasaw preserved as a kind of managed wilderness. These borderlands provided hunting grounds, and later grazing lands, but the Indians never settled or cultivated the buffer regions.

White settlers concluded that these lands were wasted and that they would be doing the Indians and themselves a favor by bringing the lands under cultivation. The few assimilated Indians (most of whom had some white ancestry) who adopted slavery and cotton cultivation stood as evidence that all of Mississippi's future lay in plantation agriculture. It was ordained, white Mississippians thought, that the Indians should give up the land for white settlers who would put it to proper use.

In opening a huge region to settlement, a disparity emerged between the older, more settled parts of the state, and the new frontier in the north.

Settlers had established plantations before they established towns. Roads existed only seasonally. Most significantly, the civil mechanisms for keeping the population—slave and free—under control did not exist. The first sign of slave insurrection resulted in a radical, hysterical public outrage. Frontier justice prevailed because civil institutions did not exist, and in the process, a pattern was set for the operation of extralegal vigilance committees and vigilante justice that has served the needs of white radicals ever since.

Concluding his observations of slavery in Natchez, Ingraham wrote that "the broad peculiarities of slavery, and the general traits of African character differ not materially, whether exhibited on the extensive sugar fields of Louisiana, or on the cotton plantations of Mississippi. The relative situations, also, of the slaves are so much alike, that a dissertation upon slavery as it exists in one state, can with almost equal precision be applied to it as existing in the other."[9] Ingraham's defense of slavery rejected the experiences and the history of the slaves themselves. To repeat such blanket assertions is dangerous because they suggest that the context in both time and place matters little. Slavery in Mississippi needs to be understood on its own terms and in its own time. This study suggests that things have not always been the way they are remembered, that the past is never static, and that there is always the possibility of change. Mississippi was never frozen in time, for generations of masters and slaves interacted with each other, and with the land, to make their experiences and their history their own.

Slavery
and
Frontier
Mississippi
1720–1835

Chapter One

French Slavery in Colonial Natchez

First Contacts

In precolonial times, Natchez was the name of a people. Among all of the local inhabitants of the lower Mississippi valley, the Natchez were the most highly centralized and stratified. The Natchez believed their aristocracy to be descended from the sun and thus called them the Suns. Highest in this class was the Great Sun, the all-powerful ruler and high priest, who lived in the main Natchez village. The Great Sun's incantations ensured both the rising and the setting of the sun. He also tended the sacred fire in the temple that housed the remains of his ancestors, and one day would house his own remains as well. Beneath the Suns in the Natchez hierarchy were the Nobles, followed by the "honored ones." At the bottom of Natchez society were the "stinkards." The stratification of Natchez society appeared permanent to European explorers.[1]

Upon first contact with Europeans in 1540, the Great Sun, confident in his own power, taunted the Spanish explorer Hernando de Soto. Arriving at Natchez with the greed and confidence typical of an explorer of his age, de Soto demanded that the Great Sun come and meet him, and warned him of the power he wielded. In response, the Great Sun invited de Soto to demonstrate his powers by causing the river's flow to stop; "as to the rest, it is not my custom to visit any one."[2] As a result, de Soto established no relations with the Natchez, and never met the Great Sun. During his visit, he unwittingly contaminated the population with European diseases. The epidemics that followed forced the consolidation of many Indian tribes. The weakened Natchez absorbed the remnants of several other local groups and became one of these amalgam peoples.[3]

Slavery and Frontier Mississippi

French explorers, led by René Robert Cavalier, Sieur de La Salle, followed de Soto to the Natchez region a century later. Subjects of a centralized and autocratic regime headed by the "Sun King," Louis XIV, they felt an affinity for the centralized power structure of the Natchez, who, after all, had their own Great Sun.[4] They attempted to establish more friendly relations with the Natchez.[5]

The French found the Natchez region attractive for many reasons. "The Natchez," as the French called it, was the first well-drained piece of land on the Mississippi River north of New Orleans. Adjacent farmlands boasted some of the world's richest topsoil, producing substantial crops with minimal effort. The hardwood forests around Natchez were parklike in comparison to the surrounding swampy lowlands of the Mississippi valley. An early French visitor wrote that the Natchez region was "even more beautiful than I had realized. There are peach, plum, walnut, and fig trees everywhere."[6] Another observed that there were "flower-adorned prairies, broken by little hills upon which there are thickets of all kinds of fragrant trees."[7] All of these features made the region attractive to the French, and no doubt they had had a similar effect on the decision of the Natchez when they first arrived in the region. Anglo-American settlers who arrived in the 1770s found this environment equally attractive and built their own civilization on the periphery of their world. Still a century later, the lands surrounding Natchez were used for intensive, and often destructive, production of staple crops.

Initially French settlement near the Natchez was part of the French effort to compete with other European powers by staking out New World empires. French explorers attempted to establish outposts on both sides of the Mississippi River, especially near Indian settlements, for the purposes of trade and defense. The first French settlement at Natchez consisted of a small trading post, along with a military installation to protect the settlers. The French hoped for friendly relations with the Natchez, while profiting in the deerskin trade.[8]

Nearby lived the Choctaw, more populous but less centralized than the Natchez. The Choctaw lived in villages spread throughout modern-day southern Mississippi. The Choctaw organized their society into matrilineal clans, and did not have the rigid class distinctions that the Natchez did. Their power structure was divided among male war chiefs and peace chiefs, who achieved their status by merit—either brave acts in war, or displays of wisdom in peace. Chiefs, or Mingos, had little real power in the modern sense, for tribal decisions were made by consensus. The chiefs' opinions carried weight, but they could not force or prevent anyone's actions.[9] As a result, the Choctaw society had no central authority, and was united more by familial bond than political organization.

Choctaw relations with the French were friendlier than Franco-Natchez relations. While the French had little affinity for the Choctaw social structure, they found the Choctaw to be both generous and quite ready to trade.[10] While conflicts occasionally arose between the two societies, the Choctaw proved themselves to be dependable as guides and military allies.[11] The French viewed the Choctaw as a natural ally, perhaps because of English relations with the traditional adversary of the Choctaw, the Chickasaw.[12] In the early decades of the eighteenth century, as the Choctaw fought off the slaving raids of the English and Chickasaw, they found French guns and bullets to be quite helpful. At the same time, the French gladly purchased and enslaved prisoners captured by the Choctaw.[13]

Concepts of slavery among the southeastern Indians differed significantly from European concepts of slavery. Indians defined slavery in terms of membership in a society. Choctaw society extended a series of familial protections to its members through its clan structure. Outsiders—including slaves—had no such protection. A captured stranger might face torture, maiming, or even death, in addition to enslavement. Those enslaved held no status, and had no guarantee of security. Slaves in southeastern Indian societies remained captives, with no social protection. Slavery was a way of defining social otherness rather than an economic activity. Few Indians kept slaves. A slave was something of a luxury and a sign of affluence.[14]

While the southeastern Indians had well-developed notions of slavery, it was not a widespread practice. Indian societies had no place for large-scale slavery. A family might own a single slave, but probably no more. Slaves generally worked alongside their masters. Socially they were scorned and denied the protections of clan membership.[15] The Indians practiced a brand of slavery that ostracized its subjects, and at the same time created opportunities for their assimilation.

As both Choctaw and Natchez Indians viewed the French developing their own form of slavery in the Natchez region, they probably were only half-aware of the kind of social structure that was developing. They were familiar with the concept of slavery, and must have recognized that the slaves the French brought were forced labor. The economic or racial underpinnings of the French slave system were foreign. Initially Indians made little distinction between the French and the African slaves that accompanied them. The French settlers and their African slaves arrived in Natchez together, and they were both outsiders.[16]

Establishing a Colony among the Natchez

French efforts to establish a plantation society in the Natchez district began in the 1720s. In 1717, France had ceded the Louisiana colony to the Company of the Indies, a private concern that promised to develop and populate the colony, in similar fashion to English colonies in British North America.[17] Modeled on the success that the British had achieved in plantation agriculture, the Company of the Indies planned a plantation economy for Louisiana. The French constantly observed the British colonial efforts in Virginia and South Carolina, and either tried the same or attempted to learn from their mistakes.

In Natchez, a small French trading post and military complement lived alongside the Indians. As reparation for their loss in the First Natchez War, the Natchez had constructed a fort for the French in 1716. The French named it Fort Rosalie, after the wife of the French naval minister, Compte de Ponchartrain.[18] The Company of the Indies made concessions, or grants of land, to virtually any Frenchman who would settle. Three hundred colonists requested farm-sized concessions, although the actual number in residence was much smaller. Two large concessions went to Marc-Antoine Hubert and the company itself.[19]

Because the goal of these concessions was to grow staple crops, Natchez faced a labor shortage. The French faced a challenge in recruiting laborers for their colonies, let alone settlers in general. Their difficulty extended from the absence of major population pressures at home, a factor that had helped the British to populate their own colonies. In addition, the popular descriptions of Louisiana in France portrayed an exciting but dangerous land populated by terrifying beasts, bloodthirsty infidels, and lascivious women. Narratives of Louisiana were entertaining, but they hardly convinced prospective settlers to migrate; indeed they probably scared people off. While it was good to have the colonies, for they brought glory to France, they were no place for Frenchmen to settle.[20] Those Frenchmen who came to the colonies in the early eighteenth century were either convicts, outcasts, or from especially impoverished regions.[21] The French resorted to recruiting Germans to populate settlements on the Louisiana coast.[22] Natchez, on the fringe of the colony, attracted even fewer settlers. Seeking a labor force for the Louisiana colony, the Company of the Indies turned to slavery. In keeping with a colonizing tradition established in the sugar islands, the French turned to African slavery.[23]

SENEGAMBIAN SLAVES IN THE MISSISSIPPI VALLEY

Virtually all the Africans brought to French Louisiana came from the Senegambia region of West Africa.[24] Much like the Indians and the French, West Africans were no strangers to slavery. They, too, had their own social construction of slavery. Senegambians defined slavery in terms of membership in society. In Senegambia, slavery took three forms. The first was "trade slavery." Trade slaves were those just recently captured and enslaved through war or slave-raiding expeditions. The children of trade slaves formed a second group that was one step closer to full membership in society. This brand of captivity is best described as "subordinate membership" in society. These two types of slavery were closer in fact to a process of assimilation than to chattel slavery. Indeed, Senegambian slaveowners held no property rights in their slaves, and thus slavery was essentially a social rather than an economic relationship.[25]

A third form of slavery in Senegambia was royal slavery. Royal slaves served regional kings as administrators and bureaucrats, a sort of power conservatory. Their work prevented aristocrats or others from seizing a power base and undermining the king's rule. Other royal slaves served in the military, and in times of peace were the only standing army in a kingdom.[26] One ethnicity particularly prized by both Senegambian kings and the Company of the Indies was the Bambarra. They had a reputation for loyalty in administrative and military slavery. Bambarra loyalty stemmed from their lack of personal interests in regional politics, because they came from the distant interior.[27]

As the French ships carried slaves away from the African coast and toward North America, the captives saw dim prospects for their future. African slave traders terrorized the slaves with tales of cannibalistic Europeans who bought them for food.[28] As they waited in the stockade at Fort St. Louis on the Senegal coast for the arrival of the slave ship, their health deteriorated. The infamous journey across the Atlantic added to their misery.[29] Quite often the slaves in transit rebelled.[30] More frequently, they fell sick owing to malnutrition. By the time of their arrival, weakened by sickness and malnutrition, the slaves were in no condition to be forced into labor. Already enslaved when leaving Africa, they still knew little of the form of slavery practiced by the French. The disjunction between the more assimilative West African slavery and the exploitative bondage of the New World would strike its victims only after they resigned themselves to their fate.[31]

French slavery had little in common with the enslavement practices of southeastern Indians or Senegambians.[32] Three aspects in particular are most notable about French slavery in distinction to Indian and African slavery. First, French slavery was racial slavery. The French never enslaved Europeans, but readily enslaved Indians and Africans. Second, the French practiced a form of slavery based on property rights, known as chattel slavery. The possibility of manumission was much less than in African or Indian societies, for the master-slave relationship was economic more than social.[33] Finally, French slavery was plantation slavery. The chief reason that the French brought slaves to the sugar islands and to Louisiana was to cultivate export crops for the market economy. From its beginnings, the French system of slavery in the New World was intimately related to the mercantilist economy of the French empire, in sharp contrast to the traditional assimilative slavery of both Senegambians and southeastern Indians. The social and legal distinctions were not immediately apparent to the Senegambian slaves upon their arrival. As a result, the slaves could accommodate French slavery, for it resembled the slavery that they had seen and experienced in West Africa.[34]

ESTABLISHING A PLANTATION SETTLEMENT

Soon after their arrival in Natchez, the African slaves fell victim to tensions between the French and the Natchez. In 1722, following a trade dispute, the Natchez attempted to drive the French and their slaves out of their territory. On October 22, Natchez warriors attacked several slaves who were cutting wood near their settlement, beginning what the French called the Second Natchez War. This attack resulted in the death of one slave and the injury of another. Until the French counterattacked, the Natchez fired on anyone who left the safety of Fort Rosalie, and settlers and slaves alike were unable to tend to the crops.[35] The French responded by forging an alliance with neighboring Indian groups, including the Choctaw, and counterattacking.[36] The French-Indian alliance made victory quick and decisive. It weakened the Natchez considerably.

In such moments of instability some African slaves took advantage of the chaos to secure their freedom. For example, in the final settlement of this conflict the French insisted upon and received the return of a slave who had "taken refuge among them [the Natchez] for a long time and makes them seditious speeches against the French nation."[37] The resolution of this conflict and the French show of force in punishment of the Natchez prevented the Natchez from challenging the French presence. The Natchez allowed the French to continue residing alongside them.

Though the first slaves to arrive in Natchez came in the early 1720s, large-scale development began several years later. In the meantime, Natchez languished as an agriculturally unproductive colony. When more slaves arrived in 1724, Governor Jean-Baptiste Lemoyne, Sieur de Bienville, reported that rice, indigo, and tobacco all flourished in the colony. All grew prolifically from "the Natches to the lower part of the river." Tobacco, in particular, grew especially well in the Natchez region, and the crop was the dominant staple during the French era. Bienville suggested the possibility of employing slaves in the winter to "make timber of every sort" if the Company saw the need. Of the fifteen major slaveowners who held more than twenty slaves in Louisiana, two lived in Natchez.[38]

The first major slaveowner in Natchez was the Company of the Indies. The directors of the Company built its plantation "to give an example first and to convince the inhabitants that the Company will not change its determination" to settle Natchez.[39] To achieve this end, the company employed thirty slaves on its tobacco fields. Because of the large number of slaves, the company's local manager recommended that a foreman or overseer be retained to supervise their labor.[40]

Although virtually every French settler in Natchez wanted slaves, the Company soon found that only a few had lands sufficiently prepared for intensive cultivation. Nineteen settlers were named to the Superior Council of Louisiana as "those whom negroes could be given with safety." The scarcity of slaves in comparison to the demand led the company's agent to recommend that "it would be well to oblige them [the settlers] to become partners, three or four together, in order that they may be in a position to form an indigo manufactory."[41] Such assessments suggested that Natchez would soon be a prosperous settlement for the French.

A year after the arrival of the slaves, Natchez seemed to be in chaos. The Superior Council wrote the directors of the Company, complaining that "the plantation of the Company would succeed well if these were good negroes."

Further, fewer than expected arrived, "disgusting the inhabitants who are all asking to return to France." At the same time, "the inhabitants cannot keep their negroes occupied during four to five months of the year" and therefore they needed to be employed "in cutting and dressing timber."[42] The mismanagement of the Natchez settlement continued following the departure of Governor Bienville, as a series of poorly qualified commanders were assigned to Natchez.[43]

Owing to the Company's continued investment in its own plantation, Natchez was not abandoned. In 1728, the Company began construction of a tobacco shed to warehouse the crop as it awaited shipment from Natchez. The plans were slowed, owing to natural obstacles. After cutting timber for the shed, the slaves, upriver from Natchez, floated it down the river on a raft. Company agents reported that "their raft went past that post without their having been able to stop it because of the currents which are violent. This timber ... even went past New Orleans." The slaves had to start cutting timber again for the tobacco shed.[44]

In time, the Natchez settlement began to exhibit potential as a prosperous colony. Notwithstanding the yearly springtime ritual of local company agents predicting that Natchez would finally turn a profit, that potential was never realized. The Company's less than constant attention, coupled with poor local leadership, prevented the colony from achieving any financial success. At the same time the French had worn out any welcome the Natchez extended and were now unwanted neighbors. Misunderstandings, colonial arrogance, and general discontent eventually boiled over into conflict with the Natchez.

Conflict with the Natchez came as a major surprise to the French. The Company considered its treatment of the Indians to be very considerate. For instance, the Company abandoned Indian slavery. Etienne Boucher de Périer, the governor of Louisiana, reasoned that Indian slavery was "the reason that the nations are most often at war." Abandoning Indian slavery bore certain benefits for the French as well. Governor Périer feared that "Indian slaves being mixed with our negroes may induce them to desert with them ..., as they may maintain relations with them which might be disastrous to the colony when there are more blacks."[45]

The Natchez uprising of 1729 and its aftermath illustrated that the relations between the Indians and the Africans were disastrous indeed. The uprising began when Sieur de Chepart, newly appointed commander of Fort Rosalie, granted himself a concession for "one of the most eminent settlements of the whole colony."[46] The existence of the Natchez village of White

Apple on the land in question seemed a minor obstacle. He invited the Sun of the White Apple village to his fort and bluntly told him to "look out for another ground to build his village on."[47] The Natchez bought time by telling Chepart they would leave after the harvest. While offering Chepart as tribute a bushel of corn and a fowl each week to appear cooperative, Natchez elders planned an uprising.

On November 28, 1729, an armed group of Natchez visited the commandant under the pretense of offering tribute. Exhausted from a night of carousing, Chepart neither suspected an attack (despite having been warned), nor was prepared to fend one off. The Indian visitors disarmed the French soldiers by simply borrowing their guns, under the guise of needing the weapons for hunting. The French suspected little, for they readily disarmed. The Natchez slaughtered all the men in the French village and took the women, children, and slaves hostage.

As the Natchez seized power, it might have seemed that the African slaves would again have no control over their destiny. In the Second Natchez War, the slaves had been little more than targets of the Natchez raids. The sole slave defector, whom the French had demanded be returned, seemed to prove a general rule that few slaves took advantage of political instability. The present Natchez uprising followed six years of enslavement, accompanied by annual shortages of food that had increased the slaves' discontent. Africans in the Natchez district seized their opportunity: Some slaves sided with the French and some with the Natchez.

How the Natchez viewed Africans matters because even those slaves not allied to the Indians survived the uprising. The Natchez promised slaves "that they would be free with the Indians, which was in fact the case during the time that they remained with them."[48] Kind treatment of the slaves by the Natchez surprised the French, for experience taught them not to expect it. Governor Périer commented that "the preservation of the negroes is not at all characteristic of the Indians," and speculated that perhaps there were "some Englishmen in disguise with them."[49] But the Natchez accepted the slaves as allies, to weaken French influence in the region.

Those Africans siding with the Natchez were almost all Bambarra, according to the French. Bambarra ethnicity very well may have been a French designation to identify rebellious slaves. This definition seems to have been peculiar to colonial Louisiana. In Senegambia, French slave traders as well as local peoples considered the Bambarra to be singularly loyal, and prized them as military slaves. The Bambarra designation in Natchez is problematic, and it is likely that most slaves in Natchez were not Bambarra. Nonetheless, those slaves that the French identified as Bambarra had been particularly rebellious in Louisiana.[50] In fact, two years after this uprising slaves the French called Bambarra would plot a revolt in New Orleans in which they intended to kill all the French, and then enslave the surviving Africans and Indians.[51] Despite their ethnicity, some slaves supported the Natchez when they planned the attack on the French. In this vein, the Natchez war of 1729 was both a native insurgency and a slave rebellion.

Such organized collective action between the slaves and the Indians was the result of a degree of communication not recorded in the French documents. Although the French quickly established that Chepart had been warned of the attack in advance, the slaves' knowledge of the uprising seemed more detailed, for they expressed no surprise, and most knew which side to take. The Natchez war was a moment when the dialogue between the Indians and the slaves became visible, despite efforts by the French to present the opposite as the case. Yet the decision by some slaves to remain with the French suggests that, as a whole, the slaves would be obligated to no one. They would not simply choose the Natchez out of opposition to the French.[52]

Very quickly, three of the slaves escaped to the French. The escapees reported that the Natchez intended to free the slaves, and to use the temporary disorder of the uprising as a starting point for driving out French colonists. The escapees said that the Natchez offered freedom to slaves who backed their cause and threatened "to take the negroes who were not of their party to the Chickasaws with the French women and children."[53] In short, the Natchez offered slaves who accepted their protection an end to their bondage.

The actions of the slaves among the Natchez illustrate their accurate reading of the crumbling colonial power structure. Most of the captured slaves neither defended the French, nor trusted the Natchez. Instead, Africans awaited the French counterattack. This decision indicates slaves either preferred slavery to freedom—an unlikely conclusion—or had little faith in the Natchez and expected the French to return.

The slaves who did not take up arms with the Natchez also did not take up arms against them. By refusing to take one side or another, the slaves began to negotiate for their future. Such a process of negotiation would not have been acceptable to members within either Natchez or French society, yet the slaves seized on this opportunity to assert their identities. They were not French, they would not become Natchez, but they would negotiate with either side for the best outcome. Ethnic differences among them may have led the slaves to respond in a variety of ways to the tumult. Various antipathies rooted in their African past led some to oppose the Natchez simply because traditional enemies sided with them. The captured slaves accepted the outsider status that slavery assigned them. This acceptance played on the weaknesses of both the French and the Natchez, for both would then make offers to them in exchange for their loyalty.

NEGOTIATING THE TERMS OF SLAVE RETURN

Acting on behalf of the French, an army of five hundred Choctaw attacked the Natchez on January 27, 1730. The Natchez suffered 150 casualties, and the Choctaw recovered 54 French women and children, and between 50 and 150 slaves.[54] In the middle of this battle, the Choctaw were surprised by a group of Africans who "prevented the Choctaws from carrying off the powder and who by their resistance had given the Natchez time to enter the two forts." Indeed, the Choctaw reported that, had it not been for the unexpected interference of these Africans, the "defeat [of the Natchez] would have been complete."[55]

The Choctaw-Natchez-French battle and its aftermath offer further texture to the effect that the Africans had on the course of events in Natchez. During the fighting, as the Choctaw attempted to "liberate" the hostages (only to return them to their French masters), a contingent of former French slaves defended the Natchez' gunpowder stores, allowing the Natchez to return to safety. This unexpected support from apparent hostages illustrates how Africans could influence the outcome of the confrontation. In contrast to the previous Natchez conflict, the slaves offered assistance to the Indians.[56]

The Choctaw inflicted severe damage on the Natchez. In the months that followed, the Natchez abandoned their settlement, as French and Choctaw raids hunted them down and enslaved them.[57] The outcome of the Natchez war turned, in good part, on the participation of Africans, whose assistance prevented the immediate defeat of the Natchez. These Africans acted on their own agendas and in their own interests. African slaves did not simply follow the French out of loyalty or the Indians out of a sense of common cause. Indeed the diversity of their African origins rendered the possibility of any collective action unlikely.

In resolving the issue of the recovered slaves, the Choctaw and the French both acted in ways that they normally would not have to achieve their objectives.[58] Since the French defined their slaves as property, the Choctaw, in their negotiations, also defined slaves as property, despite their somewhat different understanding of what slavery was. While the slaves were the basis for much of the material negotiations between the Choctaw and the French, they never were a party to them. Even so, the slaves had begun their process of mediating their situation. Given these circumstances, the African slaves acted in ways that frustrated negotiations that continued through several months in 1730. In the negotiations, French concerns over the return of the hostages were matched by Choctaw demands that they be paid for their attack. As time passed, some of the slaves were traded to English settlers through the Chickasaws.[59]

The continuing negotiations illustrate the relative weakness of the French bargaining position. The weakness came from the French shortage of supplies for trade. The French had promised rewards, including blankets, cloth, and guns. Compounding the French weakness was their cultural inability to conceive of the matrilineal Choctaw authority structures, which placed little power in the father figure. The French continually asserted a patriarchal authority over the Choctaw. The Choctaw did not object, for in their matrilineal culture, male authority rested in the brother of one's mother.[60] After some Choctaws refused to return African hostages, the French began to make exaggerated demands for their return, at one point asserting that detaining these slaves "was as if they were detaining Frenchmen."[61] The Choctaw understood the French well enough to know that the French would not risk the alliance over a few slaves. They made specific demands that French debts be paid before the return of any slaves.[62]

The actions of the slaves recovered by the Choctaw undermined negotiations for their return. This behavior stemmed from the harsh treatment the slaves received from the Choctaw, which indicated the regard in which the Choctaw held the Africans. Runaway slaves quickly found the French and asked for protection. Some ran away even as they were being returned to the French, as demonstrated by two of five slaves whom Alabamon Mingo was returning to Regis du Roullet. The remaining three asked du Roullet to be returned to the outpost at Mobile, "but they did not want to be taken by the Indians." When du Roullet asked why, they told him that "the Indians make us carry some packages, which exhausts us, mistreat us much, and [have] taken from us our clothing down to a skin shirt that we each had."

One of these slaves had a tomahawk wound in his head that exposed his skull, which, du Roullet wrote, "made me think."[63] Harsh treatment of the slaves suggests that, whatever economic value slaves had, the Choctaw still viewed slaves as complete outsiders, and extended them no social protections.

Another slave ran to the French and told du Roullet that "the Indians do nothing but tell the negroes continually that all those that you trade for are burned on arrival at New Orleans, and the fear that the negroes have causes them to run away when they learn that they are going to be traded for, but when you go to the Choctaws you have only to bring with you a negro from those for whom you have traded to bring you all those who are among the Indians, who would already have come to find you if it were not for the fear that they have of being burned." Du Roullet began keeping a returned slave to explain that the French would not torture them upon their return.[64] Returning to their French enslavers was an act of desperation, as the slaves found the Choctaw unwilling to grant them their freedom. The strength of Choctaw society here is illustrated by their unwillingness to let outsiders—be they French or African—impose the terms of their presence. As a result of the Choctaw unwillingness to compromise, the Africans' position suffered.

In some extreme cases, slaves killed themselves while in Choctaw custody. When discussing the return of some slaves, a council of Choctaw chiefs informed Périer that several of the slaves committed suicide before they could be returned.[65] This act reflected the desperation of these slaves' circumstances. Committing suicide indicates that the treatment they received from the Choctaw must have been incredibly harsh.[66] Although the French and the Choctaw left little record of remorse for the suicides, they stand as evidence that the slaves' efforts to influence the Choctaw-French negotiations were not always successful.

While negotiating with the French, the Choctaw treated the slaves as a valuable commodity; but in their own society the African had no place. The Choctaw seemed to have little use for them, except as hostages for French goods. In circumstances where Africans spent prolonged periods with the Choctaw, their chances for safe return to the French diminished. Only those slaves that the Choctaw adopted as their own—and who effectively became Choctaws—had a chance of improved treatment, for they would soon become accepted Choctaws and were not to be traded. Others received better treatment when they had value, and their value bore a direct relation to the esteem in which the Choctaw held the French.

Choctaw dissatisfaction undermined French efforts to recover their slaves. Besides those who absconded to the French, the Choctaw returned only a few. In March 1731, a slave who had escaped to the French told du Roullet "that there were still thirty-two negroes of the Choctaws, including six negresses belonging to the Company and eighteen belonging to private persons; [and] that seven... had died."[67] Before their return to the French, some Indians gave the slaves the opportunity to be traded to the Chickasaw and eventually the English. Sale to the Chickasaw may have brought a better price, and may also have served some diplomatic function, but there was little benefit for the slave. By May 1731, the Choctaw returned fifteen slaves that had been scattered throughout the villages in the area.[68] The change in Louisiana's administration and the impending war with the Chickasaw Indians made the return of the remaining slaves less important to the French.[69]

Those slaves who were not returned to the French had few options. Had it not occurred already, assimilation with the Choctaw was unlikely, for Choctaw assimilation usually occurred relatively quickly. It was more likely that they would be sold to neighboring Indian groups. The Choctaws had already threatened to sell the slaves to the Chickasaw. Chickasaw slave traders could easily sell the slaves to the British in Carolina.[70]

With their options limited, the slaves still found ways to navigate their circumstances. They sided with local Indian groups. When treated brutally, they ran away to the French. Some established maroon societies.[71] Most importantly, in circumstances that often seemed desperate, the Africans on the French colonial frontier played a role that had a significant impact on the course of events which would effectively end French settlement in the Natchez district.

Chapter Two

Resettlement of the Natchez Region

The British Arrival in the Mississippi Valley

Natchez stood as little more than an outpost defending the European settlements to its south in the remaining decades of the French dominion of the lower Mississippi valley. The French concluded that despite its productive soil, the Natchez region was too distant and isolated for settlement. The Natchez themselves were destroyed, and the region remained exposed to possible attack. All that remained was a complement of fifty French soldiers at Fort Rosalie, along with eight slaves.[1] While the slaves' assignment was to keep the fort in good repair, their duties surely extended beyond the maintenance of the fort, most likely including farming and hunting for food, but also serving as translators and trade agents.[2] Whatever the slaves' duties included, their existence ranged from harsh to unbearable.

France did not entirely abandon this northern frontier after the Natchez uprising. Throughout most of the eighteenth century, the Mississippi valley was home to a network of deerskin trade. The deerskin exchange created nodes of contact between French traders who exchanged cloth and other goods with local Indian traders.[3] Following the French departure after the Seven Years' War and the division of Louisiana between England and Spain, the economic structures of the exchange were disrupted. English trade practices were more formalized, replacing the deerskin trader with the merchant firm. Finally the decline of the deer population portended the demise of the pelt economy.[4] In the context of this economic transformation of the frontier from individual trader to merchant firm, Anglo-American settlers arrived with a much different outlook, a vision for a commercialized agricultural economy.[5] As in other English colonies, English settlers assumed that African slaves would produce staple crops.

In the partition of former French territories, Natchez became part of the British province of West Florida, under the administrative control of Pensacola.[6] British West Florida's Lieutenant Governor Montfort Browne led an expedition to Natchez in 1768, returning with a favorable report. The fields, untouched for thirty-five years, had not simply remained cleared. Browne observed "a whole Field of Asparagus in the highest perfection, supposed to be planted by some of the old Inhabitants before the Massacre," certainly proof of the richness of the land. "The soil," he wrote, "is exceedingly fertile, consisting of black mould, at least three feet deep on the Hills, and much deeper in the Bottoms." Browne rapturously described "the most charming prospects in the World, extensive plains intermixed with beautiful Hills, and small Rivers," not to mention the trees bearing fruit "as good in their kind as any in the World." "For my part, My Lord," he wrote, "I declare I should be happy to spend the remainder of my days in this most delightful Country."[7] Other British visitors were similarly impressed. One characterized Natchez as "the finest and most fertile part of West Florida." "The fences of many of the gardens still remain," as did the fruit trees the French planted there.[8]

Despite all its attractions, Natchez remained exposed to Spanish Louisiana on the Mississippi's western banks. As a result of such defensive concerns, Whitehall preferred settlements along the Gulf Coast. British imperial plans were rendered futile by the "discovery" of richer lands on the banks of the Mississippi River. In 1770, Governor Peter Chester made the case to the colonial office for colonizing the region, writing, "The settling the Interior parts of a Province and neglecting the Sea Coasts, I know is bad Policy where it can be avoided, but such is our situation that the Lands near to the sea are barren and not proper for cultivation."[9] Interest in the lands along the Mississippi became so great that the British attempted to build a canal bypassing the section of the river running through Louisiana, thereby avoiding dealings with the Spanish at New Orleans.[10]

As word of these rich lands at Natchez reached other British colonies, a minor land boom erupted in the far west. In comparison to the French experience, British settlement along the river was less hampered by the presence of Native American groups. Prior to his expedition west, Montfort Browne had already proposed that a town be laid out to encourage settlement in what he described as "a Country destitute of Inhabitants & so worthy of being inhabited."[11] Browne was clearly stricken by the emptiness of the lands.

The British pursued friendly relations with the neighboring Choctaw as well as the Chickasaw (not to mention several other smaller groups). British settlers reinforced these trade alliances by offering high-quality cloth, new weapons, and plenty of ammunition. In addition British traders were able to draw on a constant supply of trade goods.[12] At the same time, the partition of the Mississippi valley weakened the economic and military strength of its Native American residents. The British goods, and their insistence upon trade rather than exchange of gifts, portended the ultimate demise of the Native American economic and political independence.[13]

The British perception of the interior as completely uninhabited was only partially accurate. Indian groups continued to use this land as hunting grounds, and as a buffer region surrounding their villages.[14] The arrival of new European settlers threatened the Indians neighboring the Natchez region. They responded in January 1770, when a group of about thirty Choctaws raided British Natchez, taking "all the Goods away with the horses."[15] Occasional Indian raids may have been disquieting to the settlers of Natchez, but their infrequency prevented Britain from taking steps either to abandon the area or to fortify their presence. The small attachment assigned to Fort Panmure (formerly Fort Rosalie) provided only minimal defense.[16] Despite the potential Indian threat, British settlement at Natchez continued to grow.

The European population in the British lower Mississippi valley grew at a remarkable pace in the early 1770s. The slave population grew quickly, too. New settlers either brought slaves with them, or purchased them on arrival. Settlers took advantage of land policies encouraging the development of a slave economy. British land policy in the Mississippi valley differed starkly from elsewhere west of the Appalachians, where settlement had been prohibited by the Proclamation of 1763. The minimal risk of Indian conflict in Natchez and the economic potential of the lands, along with colonial desire for more western lands, sped migration to the region. Beginning in the 1760s, the British government maximized headrights and offered substantial land grants over and above headrights to settlers, often with the requirement that the land be improved by cultivation within a year or two of the grant. Arriving settlers sought to replicate the plantation society of the eastern seaboard colonies. The nature of the land policy in the west encouraged the development of a staple economy.[17]

Migrants to the Natchez region arrived in large groups. The settler John McIntire led a party of about eighty settlers to Natchez in 1770. McIntire advised Governor Peter Chester "that from the back parts of Virginia and

Pennsylvania is upwards of one hundred Families [who] depends on our encouragement to set out for this place."[18] Another observer reported to Chester that an additional group of seventy-nine settlers included eighteen slaves.[19] The next year, a colonial official reported that the settlers at Natchez "are mostly from Marylan[d] [an]d Carolina, . . . and are in general very laborious good settlers."[20] These reports, along with requests for land and visits from potential colonists, led colonial officials to report regularly on the arrival of settlers. Governor Chester reported in 1773 that "several thousand Inhabitants would emigrate from these Colonies to this Province, provided they could have tracts of land," all in addition to the "considerable number of Families, lately arrived on the Mississippi, who came from the Northern Colonies."[21] At the beginning of 1774, Lieutenant Governor Elias Dunsford estimated that Natchez had "30, or Forty Familys of whom have Grants of Land; and from Information I received 150 Familys who were lately arrived have no Possessions and some of them have considerable Property in Slaves, one of them consisted of no less than 80 Working Slaves[.]" Arriving British colonists saw land as the key to success in the new colony. These settlers came from virtually all of the eastern seaboard colonies. Dunsford estimated that "there cannot be less than 2500 whites and 600 slaves on the Mississippi and parts adjacent."[22]

The settlers who brought slaves along with them could, in a single relocation, significantly expand the slave economy on the Mississippi. Most migrants who brought slaves intended them to be solely for their own use, resulting in the establishment of sizeable plantations as early as the 1770s. Other settlers sold slaves on their arrival, allowing them to purchase additional lands with profits. A settler bringing fifty slaves could provide enough people to work three or four plantations. As migrants continued to arrive, they brought larger and larger groups of slaves with them.

Promoting a New Colony

In addition to incentives provided by British land policy, boosters of settlement in British West Florida also encouraged prospective settlers to bring slaves with them, whether or not they owned any before relocation. The leading advocate of settlement in West Florida was Bernard Romans, who in his *Concise Natural History of East and West Florida* admonished potential settlers desiring to establish plantations "not to forget these useful though inferior members of society"—the slaves. Romans promised that a slave "at the Mississippi is reckoned to bring in his master an hundred dollars per annum." Bringing slaves to the region, for most white settlers, appeared to be an economic imperative for the success of the settler and the region's development. As one promoting settlement, Romans may have exaggerated the degree to which a settler might profit by his slaves, but probably not by much.

Romans provided two examples of settlers relocating to the west. The first was a settler "possessed of two thousand five hundred Dollars in mony [sic], and we will suppose him living in *Rhode-Island*, or in any other part of *New-England*," headed west with his wife and four children. In addition to two house slaves, Romans suggested that "in either of these colonies he may purchase eight good working slaves for twelve hundred dollars," providing labor for his own lands. "About four hundred dollars will buy four young girls or boys, for which he will, in *Florida*, find ready sale, . . . but they ought not be under twelve or thirteen years old," for younger slaves would not be productive. Such an investment could nearly double in value. The planter, after making such a significant expenditure, could still afford to hire a sixty-ton vessel, supply his plantation, and arrive with six hundred dollars remaining—at least according to Romans. Romans's description lured settlers to the Mississippi valley by showing them in practical terms how easily it could be achieved.

Not all potential settlers could afford such outlays of cash to move west, and Romans provided an alternative settlement plan for poorer migrants. By liquidating the livestock on his farm, Romans suggested, the settler could raise four hundred dollars. Such a settler, assumed to have a wife and four children, still could purchase provisions for the trip, tools for clearing and improving his land, and one slave, and still have one hundred sixty dollars.

Romans's how-to advice for settlers indicates the general demand for slaves, as well as the potential for profits from the slave trade. Migrants could be assured that "provisions barely for the voyage will be sufficient, they being always to be had there in plenty," for food supplies in the Mississippi valley were abundant. Above all, Romans wrote that "if the person be able i [sic] would advise him to purchase negroes in the northern provinces, and to carry a few more than he intends for his own use, the profits on the sale of four or five will nearly defray his expences," a reflection of the great demand for slaves. Whether or not one brought slaves, Romans wrote, the settlers should "carry no white servants, unless you have a mind to colonize a large tract of land, and this has never yet turned to account."[23] This comment reflects a strong endorsement of slavery over indentured servitude.

Slavery and Frontier Mississippi

In his descriptions of the potential in settling along the Mississippi, Bernard Romans assumed that slaves were essential to the development of these lands, physically suited to the climate, and socially suited to enslavement. Romans's attitudes were in the mainstream of eighteenth-century racism. Considering the size of the land grants and the soil's productivity, the region's population would not have grown so quickly without a significant labor force. The banks of the Mississippi in the 1770s were as new to the English settlers as the Chesapeake bay was in 1607. Indeed, the genocide of the Natchez Indians allowed two generations to pass before much of this land was tilled even at the subsistence level.[24] While the soil, laying fallow, increased in richness, many of the fields remained clear. Others had grown over with hardwoods, fully matured after three and a half decades. British Natchez remained ideal for European settlers because, even more than when Spanish and French explorers passed through the region, the land was uninhabited.

New settlers brought slaves with them, and they felt they needed more. White settlers in Natchez developed an unquenchable thirst for laborers. Settlers turned to the Atlantic trade to provide labor for their plantations. Slaves came from the Caribbean, and probably from Africa as well. Breakdowns of the geographical origins of the slaves would amount only to educated guesses. The evidence of their import derives from their presence in the colony, but there is little doubt that slaves arrived from the seaboard colonies, the Caribbean islands, and Africa.[25]

Bernard Romans discussed a variety of staples cultivated in East and West Florida under British rule. That list included tobacco, indigo, cochineal, hemp, corn, cotton, and many more.[26] With the Mississippi River as Natchez's chief commercial route and Spanish control of the port of New Orleans, the British settlers feared limits on what they could export. Believing the demand for barrels and hogsheads would prevent the mercantilistic Spanish from limiting their export, planters and their slaves cleared the heavily forested landgrants. To compromise between their economic outlook and environmental as well as political realities, the first staple produced in the Natchez region under British control was barrel staves.[27]

A SCOT IN THE MISSISSIPPI VALLEY: WILLIAM DUNBAR

The location of Natchez oriented the settlement more closely to the Spanish settlements at Baton Rouge and New Orleans than to the British colonial capital at Pensacola. The plantation experiences of William Dunbar illustrate this point. The survival of Dunbar's plantation journal from the 1770s has established him as perhaps the most studied early planter of the Old Southwest.[28] Dunbar settled Spanish Baton Rouge in the early 1770s. Of "proper" social breeding, he had abandoned his aristocratic Scottish future in 1771, leaving for Philadelphia. Rather than remaining in the colonial metropolis, Dunbar made his way to Fort Pitt in the West, then two years later traveled down the Ohio and Mississippi Rivers to Baton Rouge, where he purchased a plantation.[29] Setting a pattern for future planters, Dunbar journeyed to Jamaica to purchase slaves shortly after his arrival at Baton Rouge. In the following years, Dunbar made a living as a planter, merchant, and slave trader, often working in partnership with Alexander Ross. In 1776, Dunbar recorded owning fourteen slaves, "of whom 7 Men & 4 Women work in the field & 3 Women are at present in the House."[30] Like the Natchez planters, Dunbar feared Spanish trade restrictions, and focused his slaves' efforts on clearing land to harvest timber.

Dunbar's Jamaican slaves probably viewed their work as lumbermen as an improvement over the grueling and brutal work of harvesting and milling sugar. Nonetheless, Dunbar's work routine was demanding in its own right. He kept at least half of his slaves working in timber, while the remainder produced food, shelter, and other necessities. His plantation turned out thousands of staves weekly, stacking them up at the river's banks until they were shipped to the sugar islands. In addition to the production of staves, he diversified, planting a variety of crops that included "Corn Rice & a little Indigo, together with peas &c[.]"[31] Such produce provided the currency for an informal economy of staple crops that emerged among the white settlers in the region.[32] One product of this informal agricultural economy, cotton, grew lushly in the region. Because of difficulties in separating the fiber from the seeds, it was cultivated only for use in household economies until a more efficient means of removing the seed could be developed.[33]

As the season required, Dunbar shifted his workers away from the primary work of woodcutting to the increasingly profitable fields. While timber cutting cleared the lands, the constant felling of timber also increased the distances to be crossed. By June 1777, he had his slaves "diging a Canal thro' the Swamp which now serves to transport staves" and also drained new fields.[34]

The work patterns Dunbar recorded in his diary reveal that his vision for the land extended beyond producing lumber. Describing the plantation at season's end in 1777, Dunbar observed the completion of "various works as follos viz, Collected our small Cropt of Corn, finished Diging the Canall up to the high land, cut an Avenue thro' the Swamp about 70 yards broad, opposite the house which has a fine effect in producing an Excellent prospect. . . . Made a good foot path across the swamp by carrying earth from the high land."[35] His plans for immediate production were combined with efforts to prepare the land for staple cultivation by clearing forests and draining swampland. Dunbar saw great possibilities for his land once cleared. Such plans failed to take into account the grim reality that in the course of the year's natural rhythms of labor, beginning with clearing fields, then plowing, planting, and on to the harvest, there were quite a few dangers.

Dunbar's slaves risked two major dangers on his plantation, injury and illness. Dunbar understood the risk of injury, and kept track of those slaves who suffered major injury or came close to it. For instance, "1 girl had her finger almost cut off by a hatchet accidentally." On another occasion, two slaves "employed weeding on the low land, killed two alligators, upon which the Negroes intend feasting," but those same alligators may well have feasted on his slaves had the circumstances been slightly different.[36] It was only owing to the skill of his slaves that Dunbar did not see more injuries on his plantation, especially considering the dangers of lumbering. However, Dunbar never recorded the way a day's work with an axe could leave one's hands blistered and bloody, how standing hip deep in a swamp left one exposed to mosquitoes and other biting insects, and in cooler months subject to never-ending chill.

Dunbar saw more slaves fall to illnesses associated with the environment of his plantation. He seemed to disregard the dangers that the climate presented. For instance, on June 8, 1776, despite his observation "Very rainy all this day," he had "8 Negroes with Mr. Simpson employed falling trees & making staves, 2 wenches sawin logs to make a path towards Mr. Francis'; 14 cutting canes & hoeing rice & 4 sick." On January 8, 1777, when the ground was covered with "a black frost," and Dunbar measured the temperature at "20½ Farenheit's," he "Continued rolling logs with 4 hands—2 hands bolting—3 saws going—Hob & Cato building the Smoke House—Nancy & Aguano carrying staves," imposing a nearly industrial work routine on his plantation, with little regard to the weather.[37]

Entries describing his slaves' work through heavy rain in hot weather as well as cold suggest Dunbar understood the association between the weather and illness. He continued to work the slaves in poor weather because he saw the slaves as dispensable. Dunbar kept the slaves working in the cold until they were sick, as in January 1780, when he recorded that the weather had "been so excessively cold that the negroes have not been able to do much labour & moreover have been almost all sick." A slave by the name of Cato, "the most likely negro upon the plantation," fell victim to colic pains and died before Dunbar could seek treatment. On other occasions, Dunbar ambivalently recorded entries such as "A new negro being a Natural died," succumbing to the dangerous conditions of the swamplands he worked. His concern about the deaths of his slaves was primarily financial, in contrast to more sympathetic entries such as: "Poor Bob, a white Boy an Orphant, died to day," made not long after the "new negro" died.[38]

In his circle of planters, Dunbar operated as a slave trader. He seemed willing, at any time, either to buy or sell slaves if the price was right. Even as he expressed regret over the death of Cato, for instance, Dunbar observed that the slave would have drawn a good price. Dunbar's slaves may very well have been the most traded product of his plantation other than barrel staves. Describing the assets and operations of his plantation, Dunbar wrote that in addition to all of his own slaves, "There are also 23 New Negroes for sale who are employed . . . as occasion requires." Many entries record the sale of slaves solely with "Sold two Negroes." Often Dunbar sold slaves who had been troublesome, or whose health was declining. In January 1777, he "sold a man subject to a Rupture to Escott for 220 Dol.," payable after six months.[39] Because of this traffic on Dunbar's plantation, the slave population was never stable.

If Dunbar's vision for his land turned on the cooperation of his labor force, he depended on a group who did not always share his outlook. His diary reflects his difficulty in dealing with his slaves, who exhibited resistence to their bondage in numerous ways. Their methods of resistance ran the gamut from subtle defiance to plotting insurrection, all of which stood as proof to the Scotsman of their limited work ethic.

The most common form of resistance on Dunbar's plantation was flight. Dunbar constantly battled his slaves' tendency to escape. For instance, Ketty and Bessy took flight on the 29th of July, 1776. Dunbar was confident that he knew their motive immediately; they absconded "because they had received a little correction the former evening for disobedience," and thus he was not terribly disturbed. The next day, Ketty returned "of herself, finding it uncomfortable lodging in the woods." Bessy did not give up so quickly, and answered for her intransigence. On August 3, about a week after she left,

Dunbar angrily "ordered the Wench Bessy out of Irons, & to receive 25 lashes with a Cow Skin as a punishment & Example to the rest." The use of a cowskin whip, which cuts the skin with the first lash, made this punishment particularly harsh. Making examples of runaways did not necessarily put an end to slave flight, but after Bessy's severe punishment nearly a year passed before another slave left the plantation without permission. On May 12, 1777, "Two negroes ran away but were catched & brought back, Wednesday after." Dunbar vented his rage on these runaways, ordering "500 lashes Each at 5 [different] times, & to carry a chain & log fixt to the ancle—Poor Ignorant Devils; for what do they run away? They are well cloathed, work easy, and have all kinds of Plantation produce at no allowance—After a slighter Chastisement than was intended they were set again at liberty & behave well[.]" Dunbar attempted to reinforce an image of his own kindness by reducing the punishment. Dunbar's inability to understand his slaves' discontent contributed to their disaffection. He admitted no reason why they should run away. No matter how brutal the punishments, they continued to leave with Dunbar none the wiser. The slaves began to flee again only a few months later. In August 1777, "Romeo (a negro of Mr. Ross') absconded as he was going out to work."[40]

At times, Dunbar's slaves would run away temporarily, without punishment. On November 21, 1777, Solomon and Murray "did not come home in the Evening, having lost themselves as we suppose." As new arrivals, they may well have been lost, but they also may have left in protest of their relocation. In any case, when Dunbar's search parties recovered them, they received no punishment. Similarly, when Paul ran away, Dunbar "supposed [him] to have gone down to the river to see his wife at A. Ross' " plantation. Dunbar made no mention of punishment.[41] The inconsistency of a master who brutalized some runaways but not others made little sense to the slaves. In response, they continued to take their chances for a few days of freedom.

Like many slaveowners, William Dunbar held his slaves to a higher standard than he did himself, then vented his fury when they did not measure up. As a result, the most minor infractions served as symbolic defiance of his authority. In December of 1777, "Adam was found to be drunk upon wh.[ich] I ordered him to be confined in the Bastile[,] Ordered him 500 lashes next day, in order to draw a Confession from him how he came by the Rum." Adam admitted to stealing the rum. For his crime of drunkenness and theft, Dunbar kept Adam in chains until his leg became swollen, and then made plans to sell him at the first chance. Merrymaking was unacceptable for the slaves, but on other occasions Dunbar had friends over for dinner and drinks. The planters "got merry by the moderate use of Madiera & Claret," behavior that would have merited one of his slaves a brutal chastisement.[42]

Slave resistance often had multiple purposes. First, every instance of defiance was a moment of freedom, a temporary break from a life of enslavement. Here was a moment when Mister Dunbar was not the master, and could not control the activities of his slaves. It reminded everyone that there were ways to preserve human dignity, even if the resulting punishment was painful and insulting. Better yet, there was a chance that such activities might go unpunished. Defiance also registered grievances. A slave's running away after an unusually harsh or undeserved whipping made the point that there were limits to subordination. The form of resistance often related to the injustice. For example, skimping of food allotments might be countered with a raid on the pantry or the unauthorized slaughter of a pig. Whether the slave registered a specific grievance mattered less than Dunbar's understanding discontent. Rarely did such incidents conclude with any true resolution, but they provided a means for slaves to mediate their position within slavery when by definition such negotiations should not even occur.[43]

Flight and disrespect were relatively mild forms of resistance. Dunbar's slaves on occasion displayed more open defiance. In June of 1776, they organized a insurrection conspiracy. As Dunbar plotted his strategy in a stave-making competition with several of his planter neighbors, the slaves in the neighborhood, apparently discontent with increased workloads, organized a conspiracy to rebel. The involvement of slaves from several plantations illustrates the social networks within slave communities. Dunbar learned of this plan in late June, when his neighbors visited to inform him of its discovery. Three of the four leaders turned out to be Dunbar's slaves. Dunbar was astonished when confronted with news of the conspiracy: "Judge my surprise! Of what avail is kindness & good usage when rewarded by such ingratitude; . . . two of the three had always behaved so well that they had never once received a stroke of the whip."

The planters immediately questioned the slave leaders. Bound, but "still ignorant of the Discovery we had made," Dunbar's slave "seemed to know nothing of the matter, & when confronted by Mr. Ross' Negroes (the Informers) who had the story from himself, he still persisted in his Innocence & Ignorance & mentioned as an argument why it must be impossible; that he had now b[een] Considerable time with his Master, that he had fed & clothed him well, & had never once struck him & of course it was absurd to suppose him guilty." The committee took one of Dunbar's slaves (whom Dunbar did not name) and confronted the other slaves involved. "My Negro was sitting in the bottom of the Boat with his armed pinioned; He was 'tis supposed stung with the hegnousness [sic] of his guilt, ashamed perhaps to look a Master in the face against whom he could urge no plea to paliate [sic] his intended Diabolical plan; for he took an oppy. in the middle of the River to throw himself overboard & was immediately drowned—This was sufficient evidence of his guilt."

The committee of planters continued to investigate. The remaining three leaders, two belonging to Dunbar, were apprehended and tried. "Notice was sent to the neighbouring settlements to be present on so solemn an occasion." Following the trial, the planters executed the chief conspirators by hanging. Others received whippings.

This incident is striking for its orderliness. The planters involved understood, with little discussion, the workings of "so solemn an occasion." Every planter in the group understood the procedure necessary to try and punish the slaves, while sending a message that order would be maintained in the region. Understanding that "Masters of Negroes executed by order of a proper Court" were entitled to reimbursement, "The Gentlemen settlers, have therefor thought it equitable, that they should all bear a share of the burthen as these executions were for the general good of the Country: a Subscription hath been opened" to compensate the planters. Compensation of the planters united the planter community by giving each planter a stake in the price of maintaining order and plantation discipline.

Meanwhile, and adding no small irony to this affair, Dunbar's "trial of skill," a competition with neighboring planters to produce the most staves, and possibly the cause of the uprising, failed miserably. "These accidents hath occasioned such fatigues both of body & mind, that Stave making hath been discontinued till the present time."[44] Most likely all slaves were restricted to their quarters during the trials.

The events on Dunbar's plantation attracted widespread attention, as the merchant John Fitzpatrick of Manchac reported it to a friend in Pensacola.[45] At the same time, they illustrate a planter community that was united and ready to respond to reports of slave insurrection, despite wide distances separating them. The procedure of organizing a planter committee, examinations with the lash, and reimbursement for executed slaves parallels similar reactions by planter communities throughout the British colonies, as well as in the antebellum South.

The Localized Economy

Trade patterns in the lower Mississippi were facilitated by itinerant merchants such as John Fitzpatrick of Manchac. Fitzpatrick, a Scot like Dunbar, was a trading agent for the Pensacola firm of Miller, Swanson and Company. He provided commodities, slaves, and luxury items to planters and other settlers along the Mississippi River, with contacts that extended from north of Natchez to New Orleans and Pensacola. As a supplier of household goods to settlers in a very remote region, Fitzpatrick did not always have access to every item his customers needed. Rather than supplying slaves to the region, Fitzpatrick usually arranged the sale of slaves from one settler to another, for many settlers along the Mississippi brought more slaves than they needed, and traded the remainder for food and other supplies.

Merchants such as John Fitzpatrick were crucial to the traffic of slaves in the Mississippi valley. Fitzpatrick used his connections with settlers and traders to facilitate West Florida's internal slave trade. Occasionally he sold slaves on behalf of his firm, such as the "Old Negro Wench that I sold for Mr. Dunford for $150," a fee that Fitzpatrick applied to his client's account.[46] On another occasion, Fitzpatrick, attempting to sell an associate's multilingual slave, observed that "had he not been Indowed with the Faculty of speaking so many Languages I should have been able to have Sold him for the Sum of 300 drs. But I am in hopes Ere long to get that sum for him," and promised to keep the slave busy until that time.[47] Fitzpatrick later commented on his inability to "dispose" of the slave "unless I had given him on Credit which I would not without your Positive Order," thus the slave remained in his hands.[48]

Fitzpatrick's slave transactions indicate that he assisted in many aspects of plantation operations. When a slave belonging to Natchez settler Jesse Lum ran away, Fitzpatrick apologized that "I have not in my power to acquaint you that I had heard some thing of your Negro;—But I Promise you that I have made all the enquiry possible; Both here at Orleans the point Coupée; and have sent Advertms. to Sundry parts on the Mississippi; where I thought he might have Got too."[49] Fitzpatrick offered a fifty dollar reward for the slave's recovery.[50] On another occasion, Fitzpatrick informed Isaac Johnson, the justice of peace in Natchez, that "David Williams & Docr. flowers are arived with 80 prime slaves half for sale and the other for there plantation," as a tip for where slaves could be purchased.[51] Fitzpatrick also offered to purchase, on a client's behalf, two slaves "for two hundred and forty Dollars each payable in Indigo" a year later.[52] Upon hearing that

Natchez planter Alexander McIntosh's slave ran away, Fitzpatrick promised that "should either of 'em come this way, be assured I will have 'em secured, and advise you of the same per first conveyance."[53]

Fitzpatrick's activities in the emerging plantation economy reflect his position as planter and a merchant. Over the years, Fitzpatrick struggled to accumulate land and a small slaveholding. In 1776, Fitzpatrick, requesting a land grant larger than a mere headright, told an advocate in the colonial capitol of Pensacola that "I now have 8 Negroes, self, & Wife, therefore think I am entitle to have some & leave it to you to Mention the Quantity I may reasonably expect," citing his years of service to the British empire.[54] Fitzpatrick often shared information with fellow planters, and called on them to do the same. He was engaged in the slave economy, but not primarily as a trader. Like most participants in the frontier slave trade, Fitzpatrick bought and sold slaves as part of the plantation economy. The ready acceptance and participation in the slave market of migrants such as Dunbar, Fitzpatrick, McIntosh, and Ross illustrates the links between the Mississippi valley and other English colonies, ranging from Jamaica, to South Carolina, to Rhode Island.

NATCHEZ IN THE AMERICAN REVOLUTION

Despite the speedy resettlement of Natchez and the rapid growth of a slave economy, the town remained economically insular as long as a foreign government controlled the port at the mouth of the Mississippi River. Spanish control over exports from the Mississippi valley fostered the production of such items as barrel staves over tobacco and indigo, crops that the British hoped one day to cultivate at Natchez, and which seemed to Anglo-American settlers the most logical use for the rich lands.[55]

British settlement of Natchez coincided with the independence movement in the Atlantic coast colonies. Settlers at Natchez seemed hardly interested in these broader colonial politics, yet owing to its position on the Mississippi River, West Florida would be affected once civil relations between England and the colonies broke down. The events at Boston and Philadelphia seemed of little concern in the summer of 1776, especially as the planter community reacted to the slave conspiracy on William Dunbar's plantation. Indeed some seaboard colonists saw Natchez as an attractive haven from the instabilities of the Revolution.[56] Perhaps the most numerically significant migration was led by South Carolina planters and war refugees Col. Tacitus Guillard and

Dr. Benjamin Farrar. They led an exodus of "about thirty or Forty white men, and Five hundred Negroes" to Natchez.[57] Despite the planters' ostensible political indifference, two years later, a group of raiding patriots forged opinion along the river in favor of the British.

In the winter of 1778, the American Revolution arrived in Natchez when a former Natchez settler, James Willing, led a raid on the lower Mississippi River. Willing, commanding a small force of under one hundred men, "penetrated into the Colony, by the Channel of the Mississippi, and laid waste almost the whole western part of the province." After establishing a presence at Walnut Hills (today's Vicksburg), Willing and his men swept into Natchez on February 19, plundering the town and its outlying settlements. As Natchez planters negotiated with the raiders, a group of Willing's men "proceeded down the River Mississippi carrying off with them, the Slaves & other property of Anthony Hutchins, Esqre. a magistrate in that district & himself a Prisoner." To protect their slaves and other property, Natchez's planters swore their neutrality in the conflict. Meanwhile, Willing's force continued down the river, attacking "most of the settlements . . . burning several Houses, and Seizing upon all the Slaves and other property of the Inhabitants." Known loyalists lost all their possessions. Others, ambivalent about the war, saw only half of their slave populations taken.[58]

Savvy planters such as William Dunbar, with few deeply held convictions, relocated their slaves to inland positions on the Spanish side of the river, and eventually to New Orleans.[59] As these slaves languished in their temporary hiding places, where they must have known of the instabilities within the white community, they did not rebel, perhaps owing to the memory of the recent and very brutal suppression of their plans to overthrow William Dunbar.[60] When the British vessel *Sylph* arrived in New Orleans to evacuate British subjects and their slaves from the region, most planters declined. In a letter to the *Sylph*'s captain, fourteen planters explained that, by evacuating to Pensacola, planters in the West would abandon their property. Their slaves, "numerous, and scattered about in the Country," would also be left behind. "The alternative least fatal to our Interests appears to be that of remaining on the Spanish Territories untill an opportunity presents itself of disposing of our effects to some advantage, or untill Government by affording us sufficient protection Shall enable us to return to our Habitations."[61] Planters' decisions to remain in the region suggest they valued their property more than protection from the British empire, for they chose to take refuge in Spanish lands rather than abandon their property in slaves.

Willing and his men swept through the region, sacked and pillaged, then moved on. While the loss of life was very limited, the immediate confusion of plundered farms and kidnaped slaves shook Natchez. The British commander at Manchac requested that the Spanish lift their trading ban and allow the sale of fresh provisions and livestock on the eastern bank of the Mississippi.[62] Meanwhile, the raiders sold the booty and the 680 kidnaped slaves at an auction conducted by Oliver Pollock in New Orleans.[63]

In the aftermath of the brief hostilities, Natchez and the lower Mississippi grew increasingly vigilant. At one particularly anxious point, sentinels spotted a group of migrants on the river and assumed them to be a raiding party. Relatively defenseless, Natchez braced for another invasion, only to be met by the group of settlers. Britain attempted to shore up defenses in the Natchez region, but was frustrated for want of volunteers and by the demands of war in other areas.[64]

Following the Spanish entry into the colonial struggle, the Spaniards invaded West Florida in 1780, hoping to expand their own territory at the expense of Great Britain. At an engagement on the Mississippi River south of Natchez, a Spanish force routed the British at Manchac so soundly that the terms for peace included the surrender of Natchez.[65] Thus Natchez fell into Spanish hands without a drop of blood spilled on its rich soil, and Spain took title to the town.

Spanish Natchez

The wartime instabilities and political turnovers affected slaves in the region in various ways. Natchez planters thanked British troops who surrendered to Spain for sparing them from further hostilities.[66] Spanish rule appeared promising because it would protect their property in slaves and grant them access to world markets. British settlement had brought significant elements to the area, namely settlers with an eye for intensive cultivation of the lands, and substantial numbers of slaves. The new arrival of the Spanish, whose control of New Orleans dictated what could and could not be traded from the lower Mississippi valley, provided Natchez planters the opportunity to turn the area into a major, staple-producing plantation region.

The Spanish rulers of Natchez took several steps to attract more settlers. First, they recognized the existing British land grants. Spain attempted to make settlement in the Natchez district economically attractive with the hope that English settlers would provide a buffer between the United States and Spanish colonies in Mexico. Second, Spain's King Charles III had offered to purchase all tobacco produced in Louisiana, which he sold in Mexico.[67] This offer now extended to Natchez. Spain also extended a royal monopoly on sugar boxes to Louisiana's lumbermen.[68] These mercantilistic policies served Spain's interests as well as those of the planters by guaranteeing access to markets.

British settlers initially found Spanish rule acceptable because of the economic opportunities it created. The Spanish style of ordered, hierarchical government was a much better prospect than the radical equalitarianism of the United States. However, before long, the settlers changed their minds about the advantages of Spanish rule. Their disaffection for Spain fulminated into rebellion. In May 1781, a group of settlers took control of Fort Panmure and attempted to reestablish English control.[69] The attempt failed, and many fled to the new United States. Others, captured by the Spanish, went to New Orleans to face trial. Following their conviction, Spain liquidated their assets and imprisoned them.[70]

Despite Spain's suppression of the planters' 1781 insurrection, many English-speaking settlers still found Natchez attractive. The promise of fortunes made from tobacco and indigo were incredibly appealing. The rate of migration continued to grow, as Spain readily handed out land grants to prospective settlers. A group of nine families traveled from "the two Carolinas" in 1780, braving the Ohio and Mississippi Rivers in the spring and losing forty people in an Indian attack.[71] In 1785, one observer surveyed the Natchez district, counting the residents of the town, as well as the settlers along Cole's Creek and Second Creek. He estimated that, in addition to the eleven hundred settlers, nine hundred slaves lived in all of the settlements, "which makes a total of two thousand persons, among whom it may be judged that there are one thousand laborers," indicative of who carried the significant portion of the town's workload.[72]

The growth of the slave population, especially after the tumultuous years of the Revolution, owed much to the Spanish control of Natchez. Spain opened a direct connection to the Atlantic slave trade. The Atlantic trade accounted for heavy infusions of slaves at a time when the settlers from the United States brought fewer and fewer with them.[73] Despite such limited migrations of slaves from the newly formed United States, between 1787 and 1792, the slave population of Natchez more than tripled because of the Atlantic trade. By the later date, there were two African-born slaves for every African American.[74]

Such heavy infusions of saltwater slaves invigorated the African culture in the creole slave community at the same time as the trade alienated its victims.[75] Often planters purchasing slaves expressed a desire for African slaves. Planters took advantage of the specialized skills Africans brought with them. In 1794, one planter's wife was returning from New Orleans with boxes of china and glass dishes. Cognizant of the West African method of carrying large parcels, the planter suggested that these boxes "ought to be carried on the heads of Negroes to prevent breaking" and sent his neighbor's slaves, apparently African natives, as "help to carry the brittle things."[76]

Natchez planters were financially prepared to purchase African slaves because the Spanish price for tobacco was favorable and the demand virtually unlimited. Further, the crop itself depended on a heavy investment in human labor. Tobacco growing involved intensive and extensive labor. Grown on a fifteen-month calendar, annual tobacco crops overlapped. The care involved in hoeing, worming, and topping the plants, as well as its constancy from initial cultivation to harvest time, regardless of weather, increased the demand for slaves in Natchez. Planters desired field hands to tend to the plants, as well as specialists, who supervised to the curing and packing of the leaves into hogsheads for market in New Orleans.[77] Often, while still in New Orleans, planters purchased more slaves with the profits received from the tobacco.

One such transplant to Natchez was William Dunbar, who in 1787 moved from Baton Rouge upriver to Natchez to grow tobacco.[78] In the 1790s, while Dunbar still viewed his slaves as "a set of worthless servants," he relied upon their efforts, and apparently their specialized skills, more than ever.[79] On one occasion, while away in New Orleans, Dunbar left his wife, Diana, and a trusted slave, Harry, in charge of the plantation, instructing Diana that the slaves would be obedient to Harry's leadership.[80] Dunbar advised his old Baton Rouge partner, Alexander Ross, of the wealth to be gained at Natchez. Responding to Dunbar's invitation, Ross relocated to Natchez, traveling first to Providence, Rhode Island, to purchase fifty slaves.[81]

In the hinterland of the Natchez district, new settlers continued to come to Mississippi seeking economic opportunities. While eking out a living with a few slaves and a guaranteed market for their tobacco, they also traded with the local Indians and generally lived a rustic pioneer lifestyle. The deerskin trade between Anglo-American settlers and southeastern Native American groups was declining during the final two decades of the eighteenth century, but such exchanges still fostered regular contact and established relatively peaceful coexistence among white settlers and Indians.[82] Surprisingly, Spain moved to make settlement more attractive to virtually any settler in the region by guaranteeing religious freedom and suspending some of its most rigidly mercantilistic policies. Specifically, Spain dropped the import duties previously collected on African slaves, as well as those charged on many staple crops.[83]

By the middle of the 1780s, tobacco faded (but never disappeared) as a cash crop, owing to the combined forces of nature, economics, and Spanish colonial policy.[84] Slaveowning residents of the Natchez district looked for a new staple. Initially that crop would be indigo.

Highly valued for its blue color, indigo was one of the great staples of the early modern Atlantic economy. In the hopes of cornering the market on this dye, the British crown heavily subsidized its production. In the Mississippi valley, it had served as a currency throughout the eighteenth century.[85] While a census taken shortly after the 1781 British rebellion at Natchez showed no commercial production of the dye, by 1792 Natchez produced 35,006 pounds of indigo.[86] This rapid increase is all the more dramatic considering the highly involved and specialized method of indigo production.

The cultivation of indigo plants was only the first step in the production of the blue dye. The plants, mature at about three feet tall, were harvested with a scythe, then immediately steeped in a large vat. Twenty-four hours later, the liquid with the dye particles suspended in it was drained into a second vat. Slaves constantly churned this mixture for eight hours or more, adding lime or vegetable mucilage (often derived from okra) to aid in the precipitation of the dye particles. The precipitate settled after the churning, then the slaves drained the liquid. The mud-like dye was transferred to draining boxes and, once solid, cut into cubes or tiles. The process produced ten to fifteen pounds of dye. Depending on the grade of the dye and the market demand, indigo brought between fifty cents and dollar and a half per pound. The rich Natchez soil could produce about seventy-five pounds of indigo per acre, rendering the crop remarkably profitable.[87]

Indigo, a staple that grew well and turned a profit, was short lived as the primary crop in Natchez. Because the process of refining the dye from the plant was both capital and labor intensive, it attracted only the wealthiest planters. Moreover, as one observer stated, "the whole process was of the most disgusting and disagreeable character. Myriads of flies were generated by it which overspread the whole country." The process produced poisonous waste water. Indeed, the fish that once filled Second Creek reportedly died from indigo byproducts. Further, grasshoppers thrived on the plant, and eventually destroyed entire indigo crops in the early 1790s.[88]

Natural circumstances and market pressures ultimately made indigo a crop that would not create great prosperity in Natchez. By the time the planters of the Natchez district realized the crop's various difficulties, they had invested significant capital in their land and forced thousands of slaves to the region. None of this was accidental. In the second era of colonization, from the 1760s to the 1790s, the planters of Natchez had consciously chosen to plant a staple-producing economy on the banks of the great river.[89] They expended considerable energy and cash to tame a distant and uncultivated environment for their own profits. These efforts served the mercantilistic interests of Spain and England. Without some sort of staple crop, the economy and society of Natchez would collapse. The economic development of this small district is nothing short of amazing. In the lifetime of many of its elite planters, Natchez grew from uninhabited wilderness to a heavily invested economic unit dependent on the Atlantic market for its livelihood. Just as all of the wealth invested and generated in this region neared collapse, a piece of machinery called the cotton gin was invented. The cotton gin made a minor subsistence crop grown and used chiefly in household economies the premier staple of the Natchez district. With cotton's arrival, the system of slavery in Natchez was revived. The world of the slaves would be transformed radically as they organized their daily existence around the demands of this cash crop.

Chapter Three

THE COTTON FRONTIER OF TERRITORIAL MISSISSIPPI

NATCHEZ: BOOMTOWN IN THE MISSISSIPPI VALLEY

The Natchez District presented an attractive destination for enterprising planters from the new United States. In 1794, the first commercial cotton crops began to turn a profit owing to the cotton gin. The cotton gin mechanized the process of removing seeds from cotton, making the crop profitable when cultivated by slaves on southern plantations. United States designs on the region would soon be realized when Spain relinquished the territory in 1795. Following the formal exchange of power in 1798, the United States established a government for the Mississippi Territory.

Overlooking the political formalities, southeastern planters on the make had begun their migration a decade before. They arrived in a place whose natural and cultural landscape was much different than that of their old homes on the Atlantic seaboard. The region's slaves were involved in a process of cultural mixing, or creolization. They had more in common with other slaves in the lower Mississippi valley than those of Virginia or South Carolina. Further, they were steeped in a tradition of resistance.[1] In 1795 that tradition flared again in the failed insurrection conspiracy at nearby Pointe Coupée, Louisiana. Natchez area slaves were almost certainly involved, as some Natchez planters were reimbursed for slaves executed in the conspiracy's aftermath.[2] Executions following the Pointe Coupée conspiracy reflected the vindictive nature of the planter elite of the lower Mississippi valley.

Tobacco and indigo proved to be dead ends in Mississippi's search for a staple, but cotton was a boon. From the 1770s on, white migrants to Mississippi had brought with them slaves for some undetermined future need. Early planters worked their slaves, clearing the forests, then growing tobacco for the Mexican market while it lasted. They invested heavily in indigo only to see two entire crops devoured by locusts in successive years. At this crisis point in the 1790s, when the economy of the Mississippi valley faced an uncertain future, the cotton gin made cotton a viable staple.

John Steele was a planter on the make who departed Staunton, Virginia, in the summer of 1798 for Natchez. Steele illustrated the transformation in planters' attitudes as he relocated to the west. He took his personal servant, George, with him, leaving behind his family and some slaves. Following his departure he frequently asked his brother Samuel "how or what is the situation of my black people. George enjoys good health but is impatient to hear from Milly and his Children." Steele also made sure that his brother provided them warm clothes for the winter.[3] After nearly a year in Natchez, John pressed Samuel about the slaves: "you have never said a word about them in your letters whether they are well or not. And I have been anxious to know. . . . I must soon make some sort of arrangement to take them all into my own employ."[4] Steele's benevolence indicates he held many of the values of the old Virginia planter elite.

As Steele settled into Natchez, he saw firsthand the impressive cotton crops. His host, "a very hospitable Irishman," owned eighteen slaves expected to produce thirty thousand pounds of cotton in 1799 "like the driving Snow as it comes from the Gin." At twenty-five cents a pound, cotton was lucrative, and the income was almost pure profit. "If you could draw such a product from your own labour, you would feel yourself amply rewarded, for independent of this, the same people make all his Corn, Potatoes &c., &c., &c., in great Abundance." It still bothered Steele that he separated George from his family. "Keeping him so long from them, has been a source of uneasiness to myself—it is what I did not intend or expect when I left home."[5]

By the end of 1799, Steele's attitude had changed. His curiosity regarding the cotton crop was replaced by cotton fever. He urged his brother "to loose [sic] no time in sending on my servants and furniture with my Library. I will make my arrangements for the summer under an Expectation of their being here in time to Commence a Crop of Corn, and a Garden." If Samuel wished to join them on the trip, "I will make it worth your while." Discussing some property he owned in Richmond, Virginia, John offered to "take two Negros for it. They would sell here for 1,000 or 1,200 Dollars. Some planters will make 500 Dollars to each hand this year."[6] Only to the personal servants such as George did John "feel bound from humanity" to preserve an enslaved family.[7] Steele discovered that the limits of his benevolence extended only to household slaves. Otherwise he sought to bring as many slaves as possible to Natchez.

John Steele stood as an example of the transformation in attitudes of planters who migrated west. Newly arrived to Natchez, he brought with him a few slaves and in a short period rose to the heights of Natchez society. He became involved in local politics. In coming years he would hold the office of territorial secretary before being elected to the territorial legislature. By the mid-1820s he was wealthy enough to diversify his investments into such ventures as a leather tannery opened by the artisan merchant James Foster.[8]

Stories of cotton magnates such as John Steele are emblematic of the first cotton boom in the Mississippi valley. In the process they set off an outbreak of cotton fever among all the planters in Natchez. Territorial Governor William C. C. Claiborne described the situation to Secretary of State James Madison. "The fact is," he wrote, "that Labour here, is more valuable than in any other part of the United States, and the industrial portion of the Citizens [i.e. planters] are amassing great fortunes[.]"[9] Planters seemed unable to find enough slaves to work their crops. Such a demand explained the purchase, en masse, of forty-six slaves, all of African origin, for the price of $30,750, by Joseph Pannell in 1807.[10] The willingness and the ability to invest huge sums of money in slaves indicates the faith that planters had in cotton.

The cotton plant had been cultivated by humans for centuries. Its place in Mississippi agriculture long predated the invention of the cotton gin. Throughout the 1700s, European settlers in Mississippi grew small amounts of cotton for local usage. The meticulous work of removing the seeds by hand passed the time during evenings and on rainy days. The fiber, once carded, spun, and woven, clothed entire households of farmers and slaves.[11] Other cotton producers employed primitive gins, whose closely spaced twin rollers allowed the fiber to pass between them but prevented seeds from passing through. The process was time consuming and difficult.[12] Cotton could not be produced on a massive scale as long as the removal of its seeds was so slow and labor intensive.

The difficulty in removing the seed from the fiber was specific to the short staple strain of cotton. Planters in the Sea Island region of Georgia and South Carolina grew long staple cotton, and their slaves removed the seed easily with roller gins.[13] Similarly, Caribbean islands such as Barbados grew long staple cotton and processed it the same way. The basic design for the roller gin dated to 300 B.C. in cotton-growing regions of India. Such processes benefitted from the smooth seeds that were easily separated from longer fibers. Mississippi's climate could not sustain long staple cotton cultivation, for it required nearly 300 frost-free days; the Natchez district could only guarantee about 210.[14]

Short staple cotton only called for growing seasons of 200 frost-free days. But the shorter cotton fibers clung tenaciously to their seeds, and so the difficulty lay in the extraction of the seeds from the bolls. Various contraptions had been developed to resolve this difficulty, and each was a step closer to the eventual solution. Ultimately, an itinerant tutor and inventor, Eli Whitney, patented his cotton gin in 1794. Several explanations have been offered as to how the Whitney gin arrived in Mississippi.[15] What is certain is that by 1795 a gin operated at Natchez, where a committee of planters evaluated its performance. They reported it cleaned eight pounds of cotton in fourteen minutes, at a point when "the machinery was very incompleat, work'd by a bad horse and none of us understood attending properly." The committee predicted that when completed and properly attended, the machine would clean a thousand pounds daily, or more.[16]

The inner workings of the cotton gin are remarkably simple. Then, as now, the gin consisted of two circular rollers that turned in opposite directions. One roller, as Whitney designed it, was a cylinder covered with metal wires, which whisked the fibers away from the seed and pulled them through a sheath of metal ribs closer together than the width of the seed. The other roller (sometimes called a fan) held brushes that pulled the fibers off the wires and blew them into a separate container. The seeds came out of one side of the machine, and the fiber out of the other. Soon after the machine's invention, metal teeth took the place of the wires on the first cylinder, increasing the efficiency of the machine and reducing the damage to the fibers. The rollers, or saws, as they came to be known, could be cranked by hand, powered by horse, as the first Natchez planters did, or, as would become increasingly commonplace, turned by steam engine. The underlying concept for the cotton gin remains essentially the same today.[17]

The gin made the cultivation of short staple cotton profitable. Short staple cotton, or *Gossypium hirsutum,* is one species of an herbal tribe of over three hundred known types. It is also one of only four that botanists term, rather ironically, "slave" species, owing to their intensive cultivation by humans.[18] Natchez planters grew several different strains of *G. hirsutum* initially, but the introduction of a Mexican cotton and its resistance to an infectious rot resulted in its being the most commonly grown in Mississippi.[19] Over time, scientific-minded planters in Mississippi developed hardier and more productive strains.[20] To the slaves cultivating and harvesting the cotton, the exact strain mattered little, for the work was the same.

THE COTTON CROP

Assuming the land had already been cleared of trees and other naturally occurring plant life, the process of cotton cultivation began not long after the previous year's harvest. The first step in planting a new crop involved beating down the old plants.[21] Generally, women and children did this work early in the spring. This gendered division of labor assigned duties to slaves based on assumptions of their physical abilities. Prior to the realization that decaying stalks fertilized the fields, many planters burned the stalks to prepare the soil for planting.[22] The men then ploughed the field, creating furrows between the previous year's furrows, ploughing those over, and then running a third line of furrows. Such heavy ploughing, intended to break up the soil for cultivation, called for a plough drawn by two mules or horses. Finally, the field was ploughed with a one-horse plough to create furrows for cultivation.[23]

With the field cleared and fully prepared for cultivation, the slave women sowed the cotton seeds. Then as now, the cultivation rarely commenced before April 1, to avoid frost, and it often ran into mid-May. The women pulled the lower end of their aprons up with one hand to form a pouch in which they kept the seed. The swing of an arm spread several seeds across the furrow. After seeding, the men plowed a light harrow to cover them.[24] In the early years of Mississippi cotton cultivation, planters varied the distance between rows according to their estimation of the soil's productivity.[25] Over time, however, the distance became standardized. The rows were set roughly three feet apart, measurable by the width of the back end of a mule. Modern agronomists now advise that cotton rows should be closer together to maximize productivity, but the distance remained the same until very recently, and indeed, many Mississippi planters still follow the old standard.[26]

As seedlings sprouted, gangs of slaves "scraped" the fields, using a hoe to prevent weeds and grass from growing on the sides of the ridges. Once the cotton plants reached a few inches in height, the hoe gang thinned the crop, "chopping" or cutting out the plants to the distance of about a foot, measured by the length of a hoe's flat end. On richer bottom lands, the plants were thinned to about twice that, allowing space for the branches to extend. In later times, slaves on some plantations thinned the crop by running a "bar-shear" plough through the rows.[27]

The next significant stage in the cultivation of cotton followed thinning with minimal delay. The slaves ran ploughs through the rows with an attached "mould board," which threw the dirt (mould) onto the plants. This process, called "moulding" or "dirting," usually began by mid-June. Immediately afterward, the hoe gang took to the field and chopped the cotton again, cutting down any plants knocked down by the moulding. Moulding freed the plants of grass and weeds, and ensured that only the strongest made it to harvest. In the subsequent scraping passes, slave gangs hoed loose soil around those remaining plants for their support. At this stage (usually completed by July), the cotton crop would only need occasional scraping passes by the hoe gang to be safe for harvest.[28]

Having completed the initial rounds of establishing the cotton crop for the year, the slaves' attention turned to the other crops. In the downtime between the seasonal bursts of energy focused on cotton, the slaves tended to the corn crop, vegetables, livestock, and other plantation operations. Chief among these, however, was corn. Corn required less attention than most staples, which explains, in good part, why its cultivation passed time between other crops. Usually the corn had been planted rather hurriedly immediately before the cotton. Despite six to twelve weeks of neglect, corn stalks grew high. Slaves spent much of their time in the cotton lay-by collecting the blades from corn stalks for fodder. After drying them in the field, the slaves tied the blades in bundles for storage until they were fed to the livestock.[29]

Many planters had their slaves harvest the corn in August before the cotton bolls opened. An early harvest ensured a food supply during cotton picking, and once the cotton crop was in, preparations for the next year's crop could begin immediately. Others left the corn in the field, to be harvested after all the cotton was in. When doing so, the planters had their slaves bend down the corn stalks to make the ears point to the ground, believing that in the downward-facing position the husks protected the corn from rain, mildew, and possible sprouting.[30]

Whether before or after the corn harvest, the cotton picking commenced as soon as the bolls opened. The first bolls opened in September, and most were open by October. At this point, hailstorms, early frost, or other extreme weather could destroy the entire year's harvest. Once the cotton harvest began, it consumed the slaves' efforts for the remainder of the year. Each boll had to be carefully picked by hand, with the cotton fiber separate from the locks of the boll. The locks dried as the boll opened, creating sharp edges that cut all but the most heavily calloused skin. As each plant had dozens, even hundreds of bolls, the process moved slowly. Slaves walked through the rows of cotton plants, picking bolls and depositing them in large sacks suspended from the neck and shoulder. As the bags filled, the slaves emptied them in large baskets at the end of the row.[31]

During the peak of the cotton harvest, the slaves began their day one or two hours before sunrise, working until dark. The picking season ran from early fall until all the cotton was in. In three passes slaves picked the bolls at the bottom, then the middle, and finally the top of the plant, in the order that they opened.[32] Often the harvest ran into January. The peak of the harvest often fell at a time of year when temperatures varied greatly between morning and evening, forcing slaves to work in extreme temperatures.[33]

Throughout most of the picking season, the expected daily amount of cotton picked was not very high. One planter estimated that during the early weeks of picking season, as at the end, each slave was expected to pick about fifteen to twenty pounds of cotton. On the other hand, at the apex of picking, planters expected larger returns. Individual slaves brought in daily totals of over one hundred pounds only during a two- or three-week period at the highpoint of the picking season. Planters usually kept track of the individual performance of their slaves during the harvest. Each slave had his or her own cotton basket at the end of the field. The driver or overseer weighed the cotton in the field, usually at noon and at the end of the day before having it loaded onto a cart and taken to the gin.[34]

There appears to be no set amount by which a slave missed his or her total to merit the overseer's attention. Often, punishment resulted from picking "trashy" cotton, containing leaves, dirt, and rocks. At weighing time, the overseer called those slaves whose performance had been lacking to step forward. One at a time, each explained the shortage of cotton in his or her basket. "[I]f his reasons are insufficient, he is ordered to lie down upon his face, with his back exposed; when he receives ten, twenty, or fifty stripes with the whip, according to his deserts. In this way the overseer goes over the list, punishing only those who have idled away their time."[35] The other slaves watched the whippings and saw random assaults on the dignity of their family and friends. Certainly such events bred contempt for the overseer, a contempt that flourished in the slave quarters, creating a breeding ground for a subculture of defiance and resentment. This subculture exposed itself rarely; its manifestations were hidden in the ways that the slaves worked and interacted with their masters and overseers.

At the same time, because weighing time involved such anxious moments, the slaves looked for ways to protect themselves from the overseer's wrath. As each basket was weighed, the slave who did not excel experienced much trepidation waiting before his or her cotton was measured. Some replaced their baskets with others already weighed. Others added cotton from other slaves' baskets. Still others, aware that their work would fall short of the overseer's expectations, put dirt or rocks in the bottom of their basket. Experienced overseers, with near fiendish sadism, extended the weighing session, reweighing every basket and checking for inconsistencies, with the hopes of catching slaves who filled their baskets from others. Such sessions, which generally occurred at the height of the harvest, surely terrified all but the most proficient pickers.[36]

At the ginhouse, the process of cleaning the cotton, separating the seeds, and packing it into bales began at the same time as harvest. Unless the season ended dry, the cotton had to be laid out in the sun to dry before ginning. While on the drying scaffolds, the children, the elderly, and other slaves unable to work in the fields, picked the cotton over, removing trash such as dirt and leaves.[37] Once dried and cleaned, the cotton went into the gin.

In the early years of cotton cultivation in the Natchez district, planters employed public toll gins. Soon, planters began to construct their own gins, for their own cotton as well as for consignments from smaller planters and farmers. The manufacture of gins lagged behind the cultivation of cotton so long that some gins "were kept running unceasingly for several years; cotton being brought to them continually from every quarter."[38] Eventually, owing to the wealth produced by the cotton, virtually any planter who desired one owned a gin.

After ginning, the cotton needed to be baled for shipping. The earliest packing efforts involved little more than stuffing the ginned cotton into cloth bags. In 1801, William Dunbar used an iron screw press to shape the cotton into square bales. As his press cost one thousand dollars, it did not become the standard. The square bale did. Another planter, David Greenleaf, designed a wooden press for the baling of cotton in the early 1800s. This press had screws at both ends of a wooden box. To press a bale of cotton, the box was first lined with hemp bagging. Then the box was filled with the proper amount of cotton. On top of the unpressed cotton, the attendant placed another piece of cloth bagging. By turning the two screws, the press formed the cotton into a bale. With the press still holding the bale together, slaves stitched the two pieces of bagging together, then ran rope through grooves on the inside of the box to bind the cotton tight. Finally, a side door on the box was opened, allowing the bale to be taken out.[39]

The ginned cotton awaited bailing several days or even weeks. The operation of a cotton press involved the labor of four or five men, as well as a horse or a mule. Since their labor was more profitably spent in the fields, the press operated only on rainy days on all but the largest plantation establishments. On a single rainy day, a full crew could press and bale ten to twelve bales of cotton.[40] Toward the end of the harvest the number of rainy days grew more numerous, and thus even the most mechanical aspects of cotton production readily fell into the seasonal rhythms of plantation labor.

With the cotton picked, ginned, and baled, all that remained was shipment to market. Planters handled the transport of cotton with the help of an overseer and a few trusted slaves. By late December or early January, the cotton crop had been completed. A few days' rest usually coincided with Christmas, or marked its celebration in early January. Then the slaves tended to plantation maintenance, repairing fences, clearing new fields, rolling logs, and cutting timber. Within a month, preparations for the next cotton crop would begin, repeating the same cycle. The constancy of work instilled in the slaves an industrial work pattern, regulated by modern conceptions of time, all of which would on the surface seem incompatible with the agrarian nature of cotton growing.[41] Such a juxtaposition is hardly surprising, since cotton, the product of their labor, fueled the Industrial Revolution.

The labor patterns on plantations in the frontier regions of the cotton South changed little once the routine described here was established. Agricultural historians believe that the era of experimentation in cotton cultivation techniques had ended as early as 1800.[42] Variations from plantation to plantation dealt with discipline, timing, and the work that filled the time between high-demand periods, but the cultivation and processing of the cotton crop was essentially the same everywhere. In reality, the stages of cultivation were not as rigidly segmented as this description would imply; rather, they ran together, seamlessly forming a fabric of labor that was constant, unrelenting, and arduous. As time passed, little changed in the patterns of work until mechanization in the middle of the twentieth century.[43]

COTTON AND MISSISSIPPI IN THE MODERN WORLD

Cotton's ascendancy accounted for further change in the lives of Mississippi's planters and their slaves. In the eighteenth century, Mississippi's plantations had been ordered for numerous modes of production. By contrast, the cycle of cotton cultivation was altogether different. Unlike other New World staple crops, cotton was closely tied to the Industrial Revolution. Most other New World staples fostered a kind of premodern work culture that allowed the slaves to preserve many aspects of their African heritage through their work. The methods of rice cultivation in South Carolina, for instance, were the same methods by which Africans had cultivated rice for themselves.[44] Similarly, Virginia's tobacco culture fostered a mind set among Virginia planters that resisted the intrusions of market forces, credit, and other aspects of the emerging economic system.[45] The outlook of Virginia planters allowed their slaves to hold on to many aspects of their African heritage. Sugar cultivation in the Caribbean islands, Brazil, and Louisiana also ensured the survival of Africanisms in the slave culture. These regions imported many more Africans than the South, because of the high mortality rate on sugar plantations.[46] By contrast, cotton assimilated slaves into an African-American culture based on African cultural traditions, but those traditions did not shape the work patterns on cotton plantations. Rather, the labor routine on cotton plantations was heavily imbued with certain modern industrial features.

What separated cotton from other New World staples were the work patterns required to cultivate the crop. Cotton growing and processing were, in modern industrial terms, unskilled labor. Indeed, blacksmiths with the most rudimentary of skills easily fashioned the first cotton gins in Natchez based on simple instructions that were most likely verbal. While the cycle of cotton cultivation appeared agrarian and pre-industrial, the labor patterns in the cotton regions of the South were quite modern.[47]

Cotton plantations organized slave labor into the "gang system," which for slaves used to a task-based work system, had no precedent. There is no record of any slave in Mississippi or elsewhere asking the overseer for the rest of the day off after having picked the requisite hundred or more pounds.[48] Instead, masters assumed they owned their slaves' work *and* their time, punishing slaves for wasting their time in the fields. In his description of whipping, John Monette asserted that the overseer punished "only those who have idled away their time."[49] In exchange for a week's labor, the slaves received food and clothing rations. Under the task system, in varying degrees, the slaves used the time not spent on their task assignments to tend to providing food and other necessities for their families.[50] Not so with gang labor. In short, there was nothing traditional about gang labor, and given the opportunity after the Civil War, African-Americans attempted to adopt more traditional modes of agricultural production, such as subsistence agriculture.[51]

The regime of cotton cultivation doubly exploited the slaves. It used the product of the slaves' labor to fuel an industrial revolution, while imposing a nearly industrial regime on the slaves, without the rewards of wages. The relationship between cotton and industrialization in the United States is critical to this connection. Southern cotton planters and northern mill owners were business partners in the economic transformation of the early nineteenth century. Culturally, the slaves were alienated from both industrial America and traditional Africa. Enslavement systematically deprived them of their African cultural heritage while it exploited their labor for commercial profit. The labor patterns in Mississippi, which at first glance seemed to preserve the culture of the heavily African labor force, by their nature suppressed many aspects of that culture. This suppression resulted from the imposition of modern labor patterns onto an agricultural labor force. Because cotton cultivation appeared agrarian, observers never questioned assumptions that it was essentially so. But the assumption that plantation life was "premodern" or agrarian overlooks both the unrelenting constancy of labor, in contrast to the seasonal breaks in most other agrarian regimes, and the relationship between its product, cotton fiber, and the Industrial Revolution.[52] In this regard, the division between agriculture and industry is a false dichotomy. Because the slaves were alienated from industrial processes, it follows that planters were complicit in their alienation. Frontier planters in Mississippi welcomed modernization, because their prosperity derived from the modern world's desire for cotton.

Modern life was not necessarily the good life. While efficiency and prosperity opened the world to new possibilities which smashed older certainties, they created all manner of new uncertainties. Slaves lived in an uncertain world where planters made rash decisions and imposed harsh rules about labor. This experience created a sense of fear among many slaves. Planters, for their part, feared what the slaves did—and what they might do. Indeed, the greatest fears that each had were related to the seemingly irrational decisions the other made. Certainly planters also feared for the performance of their cotton on the world market. While for planters economic uncertainties involved acceptable risks, the uncertainty of the slaves' activities were unacceptable risks.

Maintaining Order in a Slave Society

American society in the decades straddling the turn of the nineteenth century had grown ever more tense and insecure about its racial composition and social order. The language of the American Revolution had contributed to the uneasiness, for some considered that liberty and equality should extend to all men, regardless of race or social position. Anxiety grew stronger following the outbreak of the Haitian Revolution in 1792 as slaves secured their freedom, inspiring American slaves to seek or expect the same.[53] In anticipation of revolt, planters responded with brutal suppression. As one historian has stated, "violence perpetuated itself, permitting brutalities which contrasted anomalously with humanitarian amelioration."[54] Instances of slave resistance met harsher punishment, which contributed to greater disaffection among slaves, manifested in resistance. In response, white Americans determined that, in addition to the considerable economic benefits of slavery owing to the invention of the cotton gin, there was a social imperative to hold African Americans in slavery, and to limit both the activities and the very existence of free blacks.[55]

In this atmosphere of racial mistrust and inequality, the United States created the Mississippi Territory out of the old Spanish Natchez District. There seemed to be little doubt that Natchez would retain slavery when it became part of the United States. The first government agents to arrive there noted how widespread plantation slavery had become by 1798, the year of the territory's creation. Despite their own humanitarian reservations, the agents felt the government should be compelled to allow slavery to continue in Mississippi.[56] Rather than violate the Northwest Ordinance, the existing legal framework for the creation of new territories and states, Congress passed a separate bill, copied nearly verbatim from the Northwest Ordinance, but banning only the introduction of slaves from foreign lands.[57] The creation of the territory invited more settlers to move there.

As cotton slavery expanded in territorial Mississippi, it continued to resemble both industrial labor on the one hand and the agrarian "way of life" on the other. The law of slavery, grafted from the harsh codes adopted in other Southern states as a means of increased vigilance, very strictly limited the activities of slaves, tightening their boundaries and formalizing previously assumed strictures.[58] Although an act adopted in 1805 promised that "no cruel or unusual punishment shall be inflicted on any slave within this territory," 1807 legislation specified punishments for noncapital offenses. Outlaw slaves would "be burned in the hand by the sheriff in open court, or suffer such other and corporal punishment as the court shall think fit to inflict." Slaves who presented false testimony against other slaves would have "one ear nailed to the pillory and there stand for the space of one hour; and then said ear to be cut off; and thereafter the other ear nailed in like manner at the expiration of one other hour; and moreover to receive thirty-nine lashes."[59] Strict legislation did little to mollify planter concerns, and anxious moments cluttered the planters' lives, owing to real and imagined threats.

When a group of artisanal slaves led by a man named Gabriel conspired to rebel in Virginia, Mississippi planters took note. Gabriel's ideology owed much to the Haitian Revolution, combined with a mistrust of commercially oriented employers.[60] In response to the news, Mississippi's territorial governor, Winthrop Sargent, issued a circular letter to Natchez slaveowners informing them of the plan, stating that "this alarming Business *probably* had its origin in *foreign* influence" but warranted their attention nonetheless. Sargent emphasized that while the agitators must have been outsiders, the threat to Mississippi should not be ignored. Many Natchez slaves were foreign, and some of the slaves had arrived with planters who were refugees from Haiti. Sargent asked the planters to become more watchful personally (as opposed to instructing their managers to be vigilant) of their slaves. To avoid alarming (or perhaps instigating) slaves, he advised them to attribute the scrutiny to recent attacks on slaves by overseers.[61]

The next spring, speaking before the militia, Sargent addressed the issue of potential slave insurrection again. "That we deprive them of the sacred Boon of Liberty is a Crime they can never forgive—Mild and humane Treatment may for a Time Continue them quiet, but can never fully Reconcile them to their situation." Sargent identified the underlying conflict between slavery and freedom in the United States. In these early and unsteady years of the Republic, Sargent observed that the slaves were a potential ally for any enemy in a war, "irresistably stimulated to Vengeance." He called on the militia to enforce the laws restricting the activities of slaves, "not unnecessarily to harass the Men, but *more* strongly to impress the Negroes that we are never off our Guard." Sargent's identification of the slave population as a potential enemy illustrated the insecurities of the planter society he led. Rather than inciting random violence against slaves, Sargent communicated his disapproval of "cruel and Barbarous usage practiced towards slaves" by patrols.[62]

While such vigilance cropped up regularly, the chief issue for planters remained profits. They continued to look for more efficient ways to produce cotton. Owing to William Dunbar's correspondence with Thomas Jefferson, Mississippi adopted contoured ploughing, to limit erosion, at a very early stage.[63] Another early innovation was the use of a plough to speed the process of moulding.[64] Others looked for more productive strains of cotton. Once the Mexican cotton became the standard, Dr. Rush Nutt, an early agronomist at Port Gibson, selectively bred and cross-bred cotton strains. He ultimately developed what became known as the Port Gibson strain of cotton, which became very popular throughout the South because of its resistence to disease. Others developed uses for unused cotton seed, which before that time had been discarded.[65] Indeed, William Dunbar, considered by his contemporaries a scientist more than a planter, when necessary, put his plantation operations above his scientific observations. On one occasion he rued to Isaac Briggs that, "having no overseer," his own time investment in plantation operations deprived him of "time to calculate a single one of your observations."[66]

The tendency toward agricultural innovation so early in cotton's ascendency belies the perception that southerners—especially deep southerners—resisted agricultural reforms and innovations.[67] Indeed, the rapid advance of agricultural innovation seems almost contrary to the image of the rustic frontier planter. Early planters in Mississippi embraced these kinds of agricultural reforms for the same reason that they readily imported tens of thousands of slaves and forced them into a virtually industrial labor routine. The frontier was dominated by cotton capitalism, a component of the Industrial Revolution.

The avarice of the territorial slave market, the brutality of the labor scheme, and the willingness of planters to embrace agricultural reforms and think scientifically concerning their crop all suggest that the underpinnings of society on the cotton frontier of territorial Mississippi were much different than those of later decades. In good part the difference lay in Mississippi's colonial past. West Florida's distance from other slaveowning British colonies was illustrated by the fact that Natchez was closer to New Orleans, for instance, than to Charleston. The Mississippi Territory's planters were in closer proximity to a culture foreign to that of the United States.[68] The settlement of Mississippi by chiefly Anglo-Americans and its ultimate cession to the United States grafted the region onto a social and legal tradition that defined slavery differently than did the civil law and multihued society of Louisiana.

The ideas and theories about exactly what slaves were and how they fit into to social landscape of Mississippi, and indeed America's society and economy, certainly influenced the daily lives of the slaves as much as the cultivation of cotton. Since planters considered the enslaved investments as much as people, slaves often felt the impact of the economy as it resonated through their masters' account books and onto the cotton fields.[69] In the unstable frontier economy, it was the slaves who suffered the mistakes and misfortunes of slaveowners. For example, financial disaster for a planter was minuscule compared to the separation of slave families and communities as planter holdings were liquidated to settle debts.

Planters often used slaves as collateral to secure loans, for slaves were often the most valuable properties on the frontier. As a result, planters risked their credit and even their honor on investments in slaves. Such was the case with a planter named Colonel Morehouse. Unable to repay his debt to William Dunbar when it came due, Dunbar wrote to inform him that "the slaves will be delivered back to my order & hire paid for them at the rate of 12 dollars each pr. month." Dunbar heard "a vague report" that Morehouse had sold one of the slaves, "but this I cannot believe as you possess no absolute property in either" before they had been paid for in full. Dunbar's letter threatened his customer's reputation, but of course the greater threat was to the slaves, who stood to lose their homes if returned to Dunbar.[70]

Others attempted to avoid falling dangerously into debt by liquidating their slaveholdings. While liquidation preserved the master's reputation, it destroyed slave families and communities. Such was the case of a friend of John Willis, who wrote, "I must now beg you to dispose of the Boys Tom and George . . . for the best price you can, for cash, as the Gentleman I ow[e] it to is now awaiting for it." He added that if he could not "make up the balance other ways," he would be $190 short.[71]

Thus when debt befell one slaveowner, the slaves suffered the most, and some other planter benefitted. The master's worst-case scenario was merely the recovery of the slave, whom the creditor might keep, or more likely, resell. The slave, on the other hand, stood to lose family and community if resold. Even when slaveowners worked out transactions that essentially negated debts for other debts, the situation often involved the transfer of slaves as well.[72]

Many planters found themselves greatly in need of labor but unable to get enough slaves. Such was the case with Jesse Hunt, who had his brother

Slavery and Frontier Mississippi

Abijah, a Natchez merchant, write an associate stressing the "importance of your hiring some negroes for [Jesse] Hunt he will require two good ploughmen and three or four for the hoe. I will add that the Salvation of our crop depends on it being worked at this time & I am concerned unless different arrangements are made the cotton will be greatly injured before it is thined & cleaned."[73] Generally, in Mississippi, the need was more for slaves, as anyone with slaves and some land could within a few months have enough cash to cover his debts. Some laid out large sums for combinations of slaves and land. The partnership of Barcly and Sackeld purchased the Bayou Pierre plantation of Abijah Hunt for sixty thousand dollars in 1808. In addition to "one thousand to twelve hundred arpens of land," a cotton gin and press, and livestock, the transaction included "the negroes on the said plantation amounting in number from sixty one to sixty five."[74] Exchanges of this sort indicate the kind of cash available on hand for such investments.[75]

The demand for slaves in the Natchez District fostered the reopening of the African slave trade in the first decade of the 1800s. While the ordinance creating the Mississippi Territory banned the import of slaves from foreign ports, frontier planters ignored it before the federal ban on the Atlantic trade became effective. Barely coming in under the wire, E. Frazier advertised for sale "twenty-five very likely CONGO NEGROES" in November 1807.[76] William Dunbar wrote to Tunno and Price, a Charleston slave-trading firm early in 1807, requesting "assistance to procure a Certain number of african slaves" for his plantation. He was willing to spend £3,000 sterling. He desired slaves between twelve and twenty-one years old, "well formed & robust; & the proportion of females about ¼ to ⅓ of that of males." Dunbar's desire for a predominantly male population reflects the productivity of enslaved men, but the inclusion of women in his request illustrates the preference that women perform certain tasks in the cycle of cotton production. Dunbar requested that none be Ibo, and that all be from "nations from the interior of africa, the individuals of which I have always found more Civilized, at least better disposed than those nearer the Coast."[77] In requesting the Ibo be excluded, Dunbar illustrates the power that African ethnicity continued to wield in the Americas into the nineteenth century.

As planters busied themselves so much with their financial affairs, gambling their slaves' futures on the value of cotton and paying little attention to the slaves' needs, their actions bred discontent. Slaves voiced dissatisfaction through a variety of subtle and overt acts of resistance. Acts of sabotage, especially arson, were ideal forms of resistance because the perpetrators were so hard to catch. A wooden ginhouse filled with cotton was extremely flammable. A small fire would travel quickly, and probably never be traced. Such a fire erupted in William Dunbar's cotton magazine in December 1806. Dunbar expressed no suspicion of arson, attributing the fire to "some inexplicable cause." The ginhouse had yet to gin what Dunbar estimated would have been seventy thousand pounds of cleaned cotton. The fire also destroyed the gin, two presses, the year's corn crop, and all the farming implements. Virtually every building on Dunbar's plantation except the dwellings burned. He estimated his loss at twenty thousand dollars, an astronomical sum for that time.[78] A similar gin fire in 1814, "the act of some malicious incendiary," at the plantation of Stephen Minor prompted him to offer a two thousand dollar reward for the discovery of those responsible.[79]

Acts of sabotage were effective forms of resistence because they had an impact on the planter's livelihood. Destructive acts that targeted property, but not people, paralleled the defiant acts of other workers forced into a modern labor system. By destroying the means of that modernization, namely the ginhouse, the cotton press, and other machinery, the arsonist hoped to return to the earlier, nonindustrial means of production. Other forms included work slowdowns and stoppages. Often, the performance of slave ineptitude provided a mask for the defiant activity of machine-breaking. When George Rapalje's mill needed repair, he was at the mercy of a friend's blacksmith, "who is intoxicated" and twice failed to repair it. "I will take it as a favor if you will let your Negro boy mend it and in the mean time spare me a bushel of meal" for the slaves.[80] Protests such as arson, machine-breaking, and negligence expressed a working-class conservatism in the face of radical economic changes that devalued the slaves' work and fostered their dependency upon the very means of production that they resisted.[81] In the case of slavery, protests against the means of production hardly implied that slaves accepted their bondage. Instead, it suggests that they directed certain types of resistance against the kind of work they did. Slaves discontented with their work regime destroyed their tools. Slaves in personal conflict with their masters usually chose flight.

As settlements in Mississippi were quite isolated, most instances of flight were a temporary form of resistance. Slaves turning up in New Orleans might have disappeared into urban anonymity, but they may also have ended up the slave of someone else. Neighboring Indian groups had little to offer strangers, especially as Anglo-Americans encroached on their resources and lands.

Running away appears to be a way to escape the immediate environment. The first decade of the nineteenth century offers the best window through which absconding slaves can be observed, through runaway advertisements. Unlike most later advertisements, the announcements in the early nineteenth century offer relatively thorough descriptions of the slaves, along with bluntly honest clues as to why they escaped. Within a few years, planters were less likely to advertise their runaways in newspapers, and when they did, their descriptions were less thorough, and riven with racial stereotype.[82]

According to runaway advertisements, runaway slaves were mostly male, usually in their twenties, and often bore physical and emotional scars from the savagery of plantation life. Of 101 escaped slaves advertised in the *Natchez Mississippi Messenger* between 1805 and 1808, 85 were male. By far the most, 48, were aged twenty to thirty, while 28 were nineteen years old or younger, and 15 were over age thirty.[83] Perhaps most compelling were the descriptions of the physical injuries the slaves bore. A common disability was missing toes.[84] In most cases, slaves lost their toes to frostbite, owing to poorly made or absent shoes in the coldest part of the winter.[85] Missing toes may also have been a sign of the African origins of the slaves. The Guinea worm, a parasite native to West Africa that burrowed into the flesh of the toe, could cripple its victim. The delicate procedure of extracting a Guinea worm sometimes resulted in a gangrenous infection that would result in the loss of the toe.[86] Other runaway slaves suffered disabilities resulting from a poorly mended broken bone or other injury. Advertisements describing turned feet, scars from broken bones, and liming also were rooted in accidents.[87] Often the damage was the result of the poor state of medical care, and the unwillingness of planters to provide injured slaves ample time to heal before returning to work. The advertisements for runaways offer many other descriptions of scars inflicted by the masters. Scars between the shoulders, on the side, and slaves "very much marked with the whip" testify to the damage caused by the lash.[88] Such candor about whipping in runaway advertisements should not indicate that whippings were the limit of plantation discipline. Numerous runaways had burn scars, facial scars, and disfigured appendages.[89] Even more alarming are the descriptions of slaves with cropped ears and brand marks.[90]

If the slaves' physical appearance revealed something of their treatment, it also offered insight to the ways in which they asserted their identities through their appearance. Appearances, from hair to fashion, often are cultural artifacts of identity.[91] Mississippi slaveowners noted markings which provide evidence of slaves projecting their identities onto their bodies. Slaves wore earrings, or unique hair styles, and some were still identified by "marks of distinction ... received in his own country."[92] In a society that allowed a master to change a slave's name, slaves seized control over their physical selves through external markings.[93]

Slaves who escaped also communicated subtle messages about why they took flight, and of what mattered to them. Running away was at times a family affair. In one case, a group of eight runaways included two men and their wives. Women ran away with infants, and in some cases with several older children.[94]

Slaves also bore psychological scars resulting in characteristics that helped masters to describe their slaves. The most common were speaking disorders. Numerous slaves were described as quiet, or having speech impediments, resulting from the psychological effects of abusive treatment.[95] Masters interpreted talkative slaves as potential threats. Conversely, masters were often frank about defiant runaways, describing slaves who were "confident," "bold," and "impudent."[96] One in particular, Jim, was "talkative and has a good address, but is much marked by the whip, is a great thief, can read and write, may forge a pass as a free man."[97] Published announcements that such dangerous slaves were at large served to undermine planter authority in a public way, for it provided evidence of the planters' inability to keep their slaves under control.

Heightened Tensions and Conspiracies

As Mississippi planters continued both avaricious in their economic decisions and insecure about their slaves' insurrectionary activities, the prevailing fears of possible slave rebellion would be visited upon them again. No resolution had been achieved for the perceived trend of increased rebelliousness in Mississippi. Vigilance could ameliorate planter fears, but it still reflected their anxiety, and never changed the perception that the slaves were unhappy in their situation, or plotting rebellion. As a result, the planters' fears grew alongside their wealth. The planter Stephen Minor would not even transport a few slaves alone. He asked his brother John if he "or some trusty white person" would accompany him, "as it will not do to trust the negros by themselves"; some would undoubtedly run away, or worse.[98] Flight and subtle resistance reminded planters of the dangers of a discontented labor force.

In the summer of 1812, the speculation concerning the risks of insurrection suddenly became very real to the planters of Mississippi. When requesting arms for the local militia, Territorial Governor David Holmes advised the region's military commander, James Wilkinson, that, while the Choctaws "are not at present unfriendly," they may, upon learning of the war with Britain, attack. However, "of the slaves," Holmes continued, "I entertain much stronger apprehensions. Scarcely a day passes without my receiving some information relative to the designs of those people to insurrect. It is true that no clear or positive evidence of their intentions has been communicated; but certain facts, and expressions of their views have justly excited considerable alarm amongst the citizens. For my own part, I am impressed with the belief that real danger exists, and that it is my duty to loose [sic] no time in procuring arms for the defence of the Country."[99] Holmes's growing concern over the threat the slaves presented indicated his awareness that a conspiracy was afoot.

The next day, Holmes noted to planter David Pannell that a slave had been incarcerated on suspicion of planning a rebellion. The slave was from the Second Creek area, to the southeast of Natchez, and Holmes said that "an examination," or interrogation, of the slaves involved would be conducted the next day. He asked Pannell "to send to this place on tomorrow the slaves who gave the information you have communicated," along with the slave they implicated.[100] The hearing would be conducted in the presence of a judge, therefore ensuring the legality of all the proceedings.

While little else is known about the nature of the slaves' plan, it clearly raised the ire of the planters, as they conducted hearings and requested armaments for their militia, which often functioned as a slave patrol. The fact that the nation was at war with Britain, and the location of the Natchez district along a major river, but far removed from the rest of the country, must have made its residents feel vulnerable and exposed. The presence of hostile Creeks and potentially hostile Choctaw and Chickasaw Indians added to their fears. Planters began to assume the strong likelihood of open conflict. A New Orleans planter advised Benjamin Farrar that "the dangerous situation of the country renders it necessary for you to instruct me what to do in case of invasion or insurrection."[101] As British naval vessels waited offshore to invade the Mississippi valley, a rumor circulated through New Orleans "that the British squadron just arrived, had loaded 3 to 4,000 Troops at Pensacola to co-operate with the Creek Indians[.]" Although the report was soon discounted, word reached Natchez very quickly.[102] Rumors and planter fears may well have inspired the slaves to strike while their chances were best.

Reacting to such threats, planters toughened their slave codes, as if to prepare themselves to deal with an insurrection plot in their midst. Meeting in December 1812, the territorial legislature created a new process to make more expedient the trial of slaves charged with capital offenses. A group of three judges, which could include a justice of the peace, would be competent to hear a trial "without presentment, or indictment and pass sentence and order execution thereof, in a manner prescribed by law."[103] Perhaps to clarify, additional legislation specified that all participants—regardless of race—in slave conspiracies to rebel, murder, or even assault a white person, would suffer death. Slave patrols were reorganized under the authority of the militia.[104]

Despite the threat of harsher penalties, some slaves seized on the opportunity created by the instabilities and planned to abscond. They probably heard the rumor from New Orleans, as Willis Vick wrote to William Willis that "the Negroeos [sic] are plotting a general escape to the British and Indians; I have been to day collecting informations." Vick found that some "calculated on going by the way of the Creek nation of Indians; others are preparing to descend the River. A white man is at the head of it."[105] Each conspiracy the planters uncovered reinforced their fears, contributing to the tension between masters and slaves.

These social strains ultimately provoked a realization among planters that to reduce the slaves' discontent efforts had to be made to ameliorate their condition. Mississippi's planters at this point had not yet entertained notions that the slaves were content. Winthrop Sargent warned of the discontent that harsh treatment would breed in his speech to the militia at the turn of the century. His warnings amounted to a call for increased vigilance and a caution against excessive abuse. However, few Mississippi planters heeded this call at the time, for they did not sympathize with the slaves. Instead, planters set out with the goal of finding wealth by brutally working their slaves, frequently trading them, and generally making their lives miserable. Following the anxious moments of the 1811 Louisiana slave insurrection and the 1814 Battle of New Orleans, along with the uncovering of plots to overthrow the slave regime or abscond to the enemy, Mississippi planters began to reform the slave regime.[106]

The transformation in attitudes leading to the reforms appears to have accompanied the fears associated with the War of 1812. Planters came to understand that coercion alone would not keep their slaves under control. An 1814 law limited the number of lashes administered to slaves to thirty-nine, which could be extended to one hundred if two "respectable slave holders" concurred with the ruling. Courts could choose not to execute slaves found guilty of capital offenses, by substituting "stripes or burning, as the case requires." Such "reforms" were limited, but they spared lives and limited corporal punishment only a few years after the legislature adopted draconian measures such as prescribing that lying slaves have their ears nailed to the pillory. In addition, the new code continued to register the fears of white Mississippi, reaffirming executions for slaves who committed capital crimes such as murder and rape against white women. Added to the list was a new crime, arson.[107] The addition of these new offenses indicates that a new set of planter insecurities informed some of these changes.

The reforms in the slave regime also affected the actions of the masters. Some planters began to listen to their slaves. A merchant at the Choctaw trading post on the Natchez Trace, having captured a runaway slave, informed the owner that he "would wish for to purchase the Boy," although the slave "told me that he belongs to you and that he wants to get back to you, & the sooner the better."[108] The merchant listened to the slave and clearly communicated his preference to be returned to the master. In 1814, John Willis informed a friend that if he "wanted to hire Tom for the present year" he would be able to, "in consequence of his not being satisfyed with" his current employer. Sensitive to Tom's disaffection with his assignment, Willis actively sought a new employer.[109] On another occasion, Daniel Burnet, a courier sent to escort a hired slave named Jacob to the Barnes plantation, found Jacob in poor physical condition. Jacob convinced Burnet to transport another slave, Frederick, in his place. Burnet assured his employer that "if Mr. Barnes after trying him should be of the opinion that he is not as good a hand as Jacob, I hope he will let me know it," but this offer came after extending an act of kindness to a slave.[110] Barnes actually placed the health of Jacob above the orders of the planter. In 1817, the overseer H. A. Huntington wrote to his employer, William Christie, concerning the fate of a slave named Beck. Huntington wrote that he "dislike . . . to displese [sic] her by removing her from her husband—and it is equally as unpleasant to have her sold." At a loss as to what to do, he "concluded to leave it alltogether to you to do with her as you please either to hire her or sell her." Either option, distasteful to the plantation manager, would have to be handled by Beck's owner.[111] Incidents such as these reflected a sensitivity to the feelings and needs of the slaves not found in earlier years.

The subtle changes in relations between slave and free in postwar Mississippi suggest that the experience of the War of 1812 altered the plantation regime. The slaves' concerns, which had been voiced all along, were now being taken more seriously by planters. Moreover, the planters occasionally attempted to accommodate them. To a certain degree, the evangelical notion of reciprocal obligations between master and slave had achieved a broad acceptance among slaveowners.[112] At the same time, such efforts toward the amelioration of slavery served to quiet many antislavery critics who emphasized the brutality of the masters.[113] Masters who reformed their slave regime were better able to defend their practices. Furthering the change in master-slave relations, many planters better understood the slave population, and their attempts to communicate their concerns, by 1815 or 1816. The international slave trade had officially ended in 1808, thus the African-born slave population had become more conversant in English, and more familiar with their masters.[114] Still, the reduction in runaway advertisements suggests that planters were less likely to acknowledge their slaves' discontent publicly.

Planter sympathy amounted to a sense of humanitarianism, which is to say it did not constitute any planter paternalism. Measures to limit or reduce cruelty to slaves were intended to prevent future instances of slave rebellion.[115] In adopting this new outlook toward their slaves, planters now played on the human characteristics of their slaves. Planters who empathized with ill or tired or lonely slaves could expect future loyalty. Masters who made appeals to sentiment among the slaves developed a new tool in the subjugation of slaves.[116] Children of planters often developed special friendships with favored slaves, for instance, but the planters still expected the slaves to keep up with the workload.[117]

Efforts to reform the slave regime had to be backed with appearances of empathy and acts of humanity, or the slaves would see through the pretense.[118] In this respect, the treatment of slaves was probably better at the end of the territorial era in 1817 than at the start of the cotton boom in the late 1790s. The society had stabilized by the second decade of the nineteenth century, and once the planter elite in Natchez had emerged, they held political dominance over the state. Their power was built on the slaves' labor, but the planters understood the relationship between their own security and the well-being of the slaves. They had forged an ordered society that took into account the slaves' need for decent treatment, but which still was imbued with a desire to generate wealth through cotton cultivation. The end of the War of 1812 and the creation of the state in 1817 encouraged expanded white settlement in Mississippi. In the following years, planters, and planters on the make came to Mississippi, and they, along with slave traders, brought a massive population of slaves with them. The planters' economic interests would again be directed away from the interests of their slaves in the cotton boom of the 1820s. The result would be another cycle of struggle as slaves and planters would again attempt to redefine the boundaries of enslavement.

Chapter Four

SLAVES IN THE WESTERN MIGRATION

The domestic slave trade of the United States never closed before emancipation. It met the growing demand for slaves in the southwest that blossomed in the years following the War of 1812. As it grew, forced separation from family and community became a certainty for many slaves. Those who could interfered to ensure an outcome they could live with. Not long after moving to Natchez, Vermont native Isaac Farnsworth observed "Negroes going round to sell themselves. There is one right now whilst I am writing making a bargain" with Farnsworth's employer, "selling himself, wife, and six children."[1]

The slave who bargained with a potential new master negotiated for the preservation of his family. A visitor to Natchez observed his host purchasing a coachman named George at a Natchez slave market. The purchaser asked, "Have you a wife?" George replied, "Yes, master, I lef' young wife in Richmond, but I got a new wife here in de lot. I wishy you buy her, master, if you gwin to buy me." The purchaser agreed to buy George for $975, and seeing the deal close, George interjected, "But—beg pardon, master—but—if master would be so good as to buy Jane." On meeting her and discussing her price with the attendant, the planter agreed to take her home, "and if the ladies were pleased with her, he would purchase her." Only at the agitation of George did the buyer consider purchasing Jane.[2]

Slave agency intended to influence the decisions of purchasers in the slave markets of Mississippi should not be surprising. More than anyone, the slaves understood that the westward migration of planters involved the separation of slave families, the destruction of slave communities, and the deaths of slaves owing to accidents, climatic changes, and dangerous travel conditions. Try as they might to influence the outcome, the enslaved who bargained for their future merely acquiesced to the reality that the decision would be made by someone else.[3] This uncertainty was surely one of the worst brutalities of American slavery. Between Mississippi's admittance as a state and 1835, a significant slave population grew into a black majority owing to the migration. In its various forms, the slaves' migration to the Southwest had a tremendous and disruptive impact on African American culture.[4]

Slave migration to Mississippi took three different forms.[5] The most visible means of slave migration was the slave trade. Slaves also moved westward by migrating with entire plantation communities, led by their masters. Lastly, many Mississippi planters, wishing to increase their slave holdings, visited the eastern states, or sent agents, for the express purpose of purchasing slaves. Each form of westward migration affected slaves differently.

THE DOMESTIC SLAVE TRADE

Without question the slave trade was the harshest mode of migration. The product of population pressures in one region and demand in another (from the planters' perspective), the trade was dominated by speculation and greed. Slave traders purchased "excess" slaves from planters, and after accumulating numbers sufficient to transport them west, sent these slaves either by overland coffle or by ship. As the trade involved significant amounts of cash and credit, slave traders grew much more affluent, if not genteel, than the popular contemporary image of them would indicate.

The origins of the domestic slave trade lie in two important events: the closing of the African trade in 1808, and the opening of the southwestern frontier. While a land speculation scandal, Thomas Jefferson's embargo of 1807, and the War of 1812 combined to inhibit the domestic trade for a decade, the slave trade had considerably expanded by the time Mississippi achieved statehood in 1817.[6] Although it is difficult to guess the proportion of migrant slaves brought by the traders, they comprised a great part of the African American population in Mississippi before 1835.

The slave sold to a trader in the East must have suspected that sale was imminent. Many lived on plantations that no longer required intensive slave labor, having converted from tobacco production to wheat. The growing slave population, combined with the reduced need for field hands, pushed the planter either to abandon his lands and move west or to get rid of some slaves. Slave traders preferred to purchase slaves in the "prime" productive years of their late teens or early twenties.

The marital status of the slave mattered little to the planter, but if married, the slave family may have been sold together. Frequently the slave's spouse lived on a neighboring plantation, and the union was not preserved. E. A. Andrews, a northern observer of the slave trade during the 1830s, recounted speaking to a servant in the East who was about to lose his third wife to the trade. While "accidental circumstances had prevented the accomplishment of this purpose," the slave, having lost two other wives to the trade viewed the third reprieve "to be but a temporary respite." Slave traders professed a desire to preserve families, but their insistence merely promoted a humane image for their customers. Andrews encountered a slave trader riding a steamer on the Potomac River and transporting a cargo of "young mothers, from eighteen to twenty-five years old, with their children, many of them infants," along with a few young men, who "do not appear to be the husbands of the females on board." Despite outward appearances, the trader assured Andrews that he did not separate families himself, "but that in purchasing them he is often compelled to do so."[7] Such assurances aside, a slave observing the eastern trade described the plight of a mother of seven whose family was about to be divided by auction. "She knew that *some* of them would be taken from her; but they took *all*. The children were sold to a slave-trader, and their mother was bought by a man in her own town." Her new master refused to let her say goodbye to her children the night before they left. "Why *don't* God kill me?" the woman cried.[8]

Various travelers visited the Alexandria, Virginia, stockade of the major slave-trading firm Franklin & Armfield at the height of its operations in the mid-1830s. In July 1835, Andrews posed as a potential purchaser at Franklin & Armfield. He reported that the slaves stayed in a stockade with an enclosed yard. Andrews arrived shortly after the slaves had eaten, and noted that their meal, "judging from what remained, had been wholesome and abundant." Approximately one hundred slaves (sixty men, forty women) awaited transit to Natchez. They passed their time, "some amusing themselves with rude sports, and others engaged in conversation, which was often interrupted by loud laughter."[9] A critic of slavery, Andrews was deceived by images of happy slaves in the trade. His impression of the trade was one that the trader worked to make, ironically turning his antislavery polemic into proslavery propaganda. As one escaped slave suggested, "if you want to be fully convinced of the abominations of slavery, go on a southern plantation, and call yourself a negro trader. Then there will be no concealment."[10]

Franklin & Armfield's effort to present a palatable image of the trade was unusual. Contemporary observers considered Franklin & Armfield among the most humane slave dealers of the era, a reputation that reportedly elicited requests from slaves aware of their impending sale that it be to Franklin & Armfield. With such a distinction, it is not surprising that the firm allowed visitors to inspect their operations. Their effort to cultivate an image of themselves as benign and respectable was for the most part a success. Many other slave traders preferred to hide their operations from public view. A Washington-area Quaker observed "that it is difficult to obtain much information" on the slave trade, "as its operations are in some degree concealed from the public eye." One slave trader loaded his transport ships under cover of night to avoid any observers.[11] Still others, dealing in free blacks abducted into slavery, conducted their operations almost entirely out of public view.[12]

Slaves accumulated in eastern states traveled westward in one of two ways. Many went by overland coffle, shackled in human trains often of over one hundred slaves, and forced to walk to their destination. Others were increasingly sent west by way of coastal ship.

Slave coffles generally traveled to the southwest in the late summer and early fall. Travel conditions at this time of year were best, and the climate change was least noticeable, lessening the chance of slaves falling ill and possibly dying. George Featherstonaugh, a British traveler, observed John Armfield escorting a coffle encamped on the New River in Virginia in September 1834. The men, he reported, remained in chains overnight. The next morning he watched the caravan cross the river. "The female slaves," he reported, were "sitting on logs . . . whilst others were standing, and a great many little black children were warming themselves at the fires of the bivouac. In front of them all, prepared for the march, stood, in double files, about two hundred male slaves, *manacled and chained to each other*."[13] As soon as the coffle was ready, and a spot found to ford the river, the wagons crossed with white passengers and slave children, followed by flatboats with the slave women. Featherstonaugh reported that at river crossings the traders were at their most vigilant, for the slaves knew "that if one or two of them could wrench their manacles off, they could soon free the rest, and either disperse themselves or overpower and slay their sordid keepers, and fly to the Free States."[14] Even during river crossings and delays the chance of flight was slim, as the slaves did not know the landscape. The trip from Virginia to Mississippi took about seven to eight weeks.[15]

On such a rough and lengthy trip, slave traders made some effort to make the slaves comfortable, and therefore both less repugnant to prospective buyers and less prone to uprising. The same British traveler who noted the possibility of rebellion during the river crossing mentioned the slave trader's "endeavor to mitigate their discontent by feeding them well on the march, and by encouraging them to sing 'Old Virginia never tire,' on the banjo."[16]

In contrast to white observers, free blacks abducted into slavery from the northern states experienced the trade firsthand. One free man reported sitting in the hold of a ship in irons "for about a week" as they traveled away from his home in Philadelphia. Landing at an unknown place, his captors marched him "30 miles a day, without shoes; when they complained of sore feet and being unable to travel they were most cruelly flogged." Such mean conditions contributed to the death of one of the captives.[17] Another man in a similar circumstance reported that on the journey the prisoners "were not permitted to talk to anyone they met" and received a severe whipping "for saying we were free."[18] The reports of those who experienced the trade reveal a harsh and abusive experience not fully captured by any white observers.[19]

During the 1830s, transit by ship to the Southwest became increasingly common. The slave traders Franklin & Armfield owned several ships to transport their slaves from Virginia to New Orleans, where steamboats picked them up for the trip to Natchez. Coastal slave brigs transported 150 slaves, and generally traveled in the months between October and May, when temperatures were more bearable. During these months the slave ships operated on a regular basis. Franklin & Armfield, for instance, in November 1831 shipped 371 slaves to New Orleans, including 291 on their own vessels, and the remaining 80 by other means. By 1835 one of their ships departed Alexandria for New Orleans every two weeks, an indicator of the scope of the trade as well as the demand for slaves in Mississippi.[20]

Not every shipload of slaves arrived safely in New Orleans. In some cases, shipwrecks provided the means for escape. In January 1831, the *Comet*, in transit from Alexandria to New Orleans, wrecked in the Bahamas. Among the 164 slaves it transported were 76 belonging to Franklin & Armfield and bound for Natchez. Other ships rescued the crew and survivors, taking them to Nassau. As they awaited repairs to the *Comet*, eleven slaves escaped into the city. They were returned by local authorities, but before the ship could leave the British colonial governor declared all the slaves free. Franklin & Armfield collected $37,555 from two insurance companies, who assumed the claim against Great Britain.[21] Such a turn of events was very rare, and slaves could not count on shipwreck as a way to win freedom.[22]

Upon arrival at New Orleans, slaves bound for Natchez were quickly loaded aboard steamboats on the Mississippi River. Owing to the humanistic concerns of some Natchez planters, Isaac Franklin advised a junior partner, Rice Ballard, to "be sure to have them Cleaned out for Natchez Mississippi" before loading slaves on a river boat in Louisiana.[23] Then they made the final leg of their journey. Arriving at Natchez, traders unloaded the slaves and brought them to the stockade where they would be sold. Before the middle 1830s, slave firms sold their merchandise at offices throughout the town, while some maintained their stockades away from town at the market that became known as "Forks of the Road."

The differing characters of the Natchez slave markets is conspicuous. Slave markets in town generally had a more exciting, though disturbing, feel about them. Traders auctioned their slaves, and for white visitors the spectacle seemed to be some kind of entertainment. Most local residents had grown used to the auctions, and paid them little attention. Joseph Holt Ingraham saw a slave auction within moments of arriving at Natchez. His description relates the intensity of the episode:

> Upon a box by the door stands a tall, fine-looking man. The auctioner descants at large upon his merits and capabilities—"Acclimated, gentlemen! a first-rate carriage driver—raised by Col.——. Six hundred dollars is bid. Examine him gentlemen—a strong and athletic fellow—but twenty seven years of age." He is knocked off at seven hundred dollars; and with "There's your master," by the seller, who points to the purchaser, springs from his elevation to follow his new owner, while his place is supplied by another subject.[24]

In stark contrast to the commotion of the frontier town slave auction is the same newcomer's description of the stockade at Forks of the Road. Situated about a mile outside Natchez, Forks of the Road was becoming, by the time he visited, the chief point of sale for slaves in Natchez. Ingraham described it as "a cluster of rough wooden buildings, . . . in front of which several saddle-horses, either tied or held by servants, indicated a place of popular resort." The visitor entered the establishment, and saw a "line of negroes, commencing at the entrance with the tallest, . . . down to the little fellow around ten years of age, extended in a semicircle around the right side of the yard. They were in all about forty."[25] The exciting yet rapacious slave auction in town contrasts sharply with the orderly lining up of slaves and service of an attending slave seller at Forks of the Road. That such auctions were going out of vogue at the same time that the remote, more service-oriented stockades were becoming more popular indicates that Natchez desired to hide, to some degree, and also to gentrify the slave trade. Traders who changed their image did so for the benefit of their customers—the planters—and slaves received little real benefit from these alterations.

The public image of the slave traders hid the brutal reality of life in a slave stockade. Private correspondence between Isaac Franklin, John Armfield, a third partner, Rice Ballard, and Franklin's nephew James depicts slave traders operating in a moral vacuum, equating slaves with their market values, counting deaths as business losses, dumping the bodies of dead slaves, and raping attractive female slaves, or "fancy girls." Massed together in large stockades after a trip that, whether by land or sea, had weakened them, large proportions of the slaves often fell victim to epidemics of measles, cholera, and other diseases that frequently broke out on the frontier. "Sales are very dull indeed," Isaac Franklin reported in 1832, with one third of the ninety slaves at Natchez having suffered measles. "Having our Negroes crowded in the Brig we have had a great many sick, but only lost one an old diseas'd man" whom the other slaves properly buried.[26] A year later a cholera epidemic struck many more slaves in the Southwest, infecting an entire shipment of slaves. Though Rice Ballard claimed to feel "very much for the shipment," he observed that the firm's loss was not total, for "the more Negroes lost in that country, the more will be wanting if they have means of procuring them." Even when large numbers of his slaves succumbed to disease, the slave trader read the deaths as future business opportunities.[27]

Such rosy predictions about future sales appeared misplaced, for Isaac Franklin found that in Port Gibson "the people were so much alarmed that they would not purchase." The general concern about the cholera epidemic of 1833 was such that Franklin had to camp outside of towns for fear that he and his slaves might infect the residents. Franklin lost nine adults and six or seven children (his count), with more suffering from cholera. The spectacle of carrying out corpses of slaves who succumbed to the disease struck even Franklin as a "sin tolerated," yet his attitude was equally one of concern that the firm ran the "risque of our Credit suffering."[28]

By the end of December Franklin could report "No cholera here," but the threat of disease always loomed. Only four months later the city council of Natchez required slave traders to leave the town limits to avoid the spread of sickness.[29] The firm's ambivalence toward the well-being of their slave merchandise was indeed matched by their hopes that even diseased slaves may turn profits before succumbing to cholera. When the cholera outbreak turned out worse than expected, Isaac Franklin's nephew James, who had joined the business, expressed a hope that "all the fools are not yet dead and some one-eyed man will buy us out yet."[30]

Speculators stayed in the slave-trading business, risking their own health and that of their slaves, not to mention considerable financial investments, for the sheer profit to be made from it. Isaac Franklin observed at the end of one trading season that he had "sold all of our negroes for Good prices & Good Profits accept some old negroes say 18 in number," on some of which he took a loss, others he retained to sell the following "Spring if they do not Die before that time." Always observant of the possibility of even greater profits, Franklin felt he "could have sold . . . more if we had the right kind." Men sold for $800 to $900 in the boom year of 1833, while women went for about $600 to $650. On the other hand, tapping into a demand traditionally associated almost exclusively with New Orleans, Franklin sold "your fancy Girl Alice for $800. There are Great Demand for fancy maid[s]. I do believe that a likely Girl and a good seamstress could be sold for $1,000." Indeed, Isaac and James Franklin, John Armfield, and Rice Ballard all took advantage of the sexual vulnerability of attractive female slaves, or "fancy girls." When Isaac Franklin referred to slave women as "your Girl Minerva" and "your fancy Girl Alice," he expressed his recognition of Ballard's forced intimacy with them. Franklin's disappointment "in not finding your Charlottsvill[e] maid that you promised me" illustrates his own desire to engage in coerced sex with slave women.[31]

Planter Migrations

The westward movement of planters to new lands in the Southwest brought more slaves to Mississippi. The relocation of large slave holdings was often the least demanding manner of slave migration. Planters who forced their slaves west tended to preserve some families because their slaves often were married to one another. Further, slaves migrating with their masters did not experience the sense of loss, rejection, and insecurity that accompanied being sold. Although they were unwillingly uprooted, often from a broad slave community much larger than their home plantation, these slaves retained many of their primary social relationships after their departure. Slaves with spouses and children on neighboring plantations saw their families divided, and retained only the security of remaining in the same slave community, and even having the same master.

Contemporary observers noted that the migrations of entire plantation populations to the Southwest were quite common. A British traveler returning from the Southwest in 1835 reported that on a single day "we passed at least 1000 negro slaves, all trudging on foot" as they accompanied their masters to the frontier.[32] Another, on his way to Natchez, reported similar scenes over a decade earlier.[33] Such heavy migrations of planters and their slave populations in the early decades of the nineteenth century created conditions in later years which called for heavy activity by slave traders. It follows that before 1835, planter migrations rather than slave trading was the preponderant means by which African Americans migrated to the Deep South.[34]

Not all slaves who migrated as a part of a plantation cohort went with their master. Some planters merely shipped their slaves to newly acquired lands on the frontier, never experiencing the migration themselves. The forced migration of absentee plantations to a new plantation was handled by overseers, a group whom planters tended to rely upon and to distrust in equal amounts. James K. Polk was such an absentee. In 1834 he ordered his overseer of a Tennessee plantation, Ephraim Beanland, to relocate to Mississippi. On the rich lands to the south, Polk's partner Silas Caldwell wrote, "we can make from 12 to 15-Hundred pounds of cotton to the acre."[35]

In January 1835, the first party of settlers left for the new plantation. Transit during the dead of winter—after the harvest but before spring planting—may have been profitable, but it was also treacherous. Polk's slaves moved about one hundred miles in an eight-day trip. Upon arrival, the early party set about building new cabins, clearing land, and establishing the basics for a large plantation operation. Polk's partner reported as he departed that "Mr. Beanland is very much pleased with his situation, the negroes only tolerably well satisfied." The migration did not merely leave the slaves disgruntled, for later in the same report Caldwell said that he "lost while I was down a negro woman named Juda," and as a result advised Polk that "it will be necessary for you to buy another hand as soon as you can," for "Negroes are very high here" and Caldwell lacked sufficient funds to replace the slave.[36]

Planters who migrated with their slaves often professed a desire to preserve slave families. When the Virginia planter Thomas Dabney decided to migrate to Mississippi in the early 1830s, despite professed efforts to preserve the family ties of his slaves, he left some behind. The rest of Dabney's slaves were uprooted by the migration. Indicative of this dilemma is the case of Mammy Harriet, a favored house slave. Harriet recalled quite clearly when Dabney assembled the slaves and "tell 'em dat he did not want anybody to foller him who was not willin'. He say, all coud stay in Figinny, an' dey all could choose dey own marsters to stay wid. Ebery one o' he own, and all who b'long to de odder members o' de fambly who was wid him, sy dey want to foller him, 'ceptin 'twas two ole people, ole grey-headed people, who was too ole to trabble."

Harriet's recollection illustrates the choice each slave faced, for they had a master who treated them well, but who was leaving. She remembered the sorrow of those left behind, saying that "dey cry so much I did feel so sorry for them. I couldn't hep cryin' I feel so sorry." Harriet left her own husband behind, for his master would not sell him. He would buy Harriet, "and two odder people dyer wanted to buy me too. But I say 'No, indeed! Go 'long! I shall foller my marster.'" Harriet's reasoning—and that of all Dabney's slaves—was simple, "Our people say, 'Ef you got a husband or a wife who won't go to Mississippi, leff dat one behind. Ef you got a good marster, foller him.'" The move separated children from their parents as well. Harriet recounted Dabney telling their father, "'Billy, your children shall not lack for father and mother. I will be both father an' mother to them.'" Even as he divided families, and headed for profits on the frontier, Dabney played the paternalist well enough to convince Mammy Harriet.[37]

The actual journey westward illustrated to the slaves, perhaps for the first time, the very real implications of a decision to part with one's family and community. Mammy Harriet described the journey as a relatively pleasant affair (in which Dabney provided umbrellas to all the slaves when it rained). Other planters committed the feelings of their slaves to paper. Sarah Sparkman, on her way to Mississippi, wrote to her sister that, on the journey, "the Negroes are all in high Spirits, they run and Play like children along the road" as they walked to the frontier. While they traveled over fifteen miles a day, the slaves found energy to sing and entertain themselves.[38]

These descriptions of slaves entertaining themselves while migrating west are by no means signs that they enjoyed the prospect of removal. Rather, the slaves were trying to keep their spirits up while coping with the destruction of their communities.[39] On the rare occasion that a master allowed communications between uprooted slaves and their families back east, the slaves expressed a profound sense of loss and the hope that some kind of message could get through. Sarah Sparkman, later in her journey, wrote to her brother Richard Brownrigg that "the servants request me to send Many Messages to all their Friends and Relations, and your Dave requested me to write a letter to his wife. . . . You will see what a medley I have written for the

Negroes." A series of messages by various slaves to the family they left followed. Dave wrote to his wife, "I should be quite happy to get My Master to say something for you and in his Letter for it would comfort Me to hear from you all." Rose wrote to her husband Hardy, "I wish to let you know that I think of you often and wish to see you very bad. . . . I hope yet to see you."[40] After they arrived and settled in, Sarah Sparkman could report to her sister Mary Brownwigg that the slaves "are better satisfied than at first." The slaves' words relate the reality that they were less than content. "Anis says she never will be so untill you are all come out. She desires her love to her children." India asked, "please let her know how her Mother and children are."[41] Other slaves, able to express their feelings more fully, told their relatives back east of their utter sense of loss since removal. Phebe Brownrigg wrote a lengthy and poignant letter to her daughter Amy Nixon:

> *My dear daughter—I have for some time had hope of seeing you once more in this world, but now that hope is entirely gone forever. I expect to start next month for Alabama, on the Mississippi river. Perhaps before you get this letter I may be on my way. As I have no opportunity of sending it now I shall leave it with Emily to send.*
>
> *My dear daughter Amy, if we never meet in this world, I hope we shall meet in heaven where we shall part no more. Although we are absent in body, we can be present in spirit. . . .*
>
> *My Master, Mr. Tom Brownrigg, starts the middle of next month, with all the people, except your sister Mary, she is———, and not able to travel. . . . Your father and myself came down to see our grand children, brother Simon and all our friends for the last time. I found your children just recovered from the measles. They all send their love to you. . . .*
>
> *Fare well, my dear child. I hope the Lord will bless you and your children, and enable you to raise them and be comfortable in life, happy in death, and may we all meet around our Father's throne in heaven, never no more to depart.*[42]

As with the relocation of absentee plantation groups, new resident planters needed to set up their establishments immediately. A heavy workload, including the clearing of land and building of cabins and other facilities, occupied the relocated slaves before the planting season began. Shelter for the planter and his family took precedence over that for the slaves, who lodged in tents until their quarters had been constructed.[43]

A new region called for revamped work schedules to acclimate the slaves to the Mississippi weather and patterns of laboring in cotton. In much the same way that slave traders protected their investments by transporting their people when the weather was most favorable, planters allowed their slaves to adjust to the new climate slowly. Mammy Harriet recalled that "When we fust come out to dis country, Mississippi, marster made the ploughers tik out de muck at eleven o'clock. An he didn't 'low 'em to put 'em back 'fore three o'clock, and nobody worked in dem hours. I s'pose dat was to get us used to de new country." Not long after, their midday break was shortened by one hour.[44]

Mississippi Planters in Eastern Slave Markets

Once migrant planters had established their operations, their desire for more slaves increased. While many purchased slaves from slave traders, others wished to handpick their slaves. They preferred to go east to make purchases, though some sent sons or other trusted agents, such as relatives or longtime overseers. In bypassing slave traders, planters saved money as long as they purchased a large contingent. Some met their expenses and turned a profit by acting as an agent for their neighbors.

The slaves involved in such transactions must have been as confused, or even more so, than those who migrated with their plantation cohort or those sold to traders. A British observer described the slaves awaiting sale in South Carolina, "with most melancholy and disconsolate faces, and others with an air of vacancy and apathy." One woman, who with her children was up for auction, "expressed a strong desire to be purchased by some one who lived near Charleston, instead of being sent to a distant plantation." After her purchase, the observer reported, she had no idea whether her request had been honored, only that she had a new master.[45] As with the slave trader, the planter or his agent, while assembling a new population, often left his slaves in a stockade or jail as they awaited transport west. Planters or agents assembling a new plantation cohort paid little attention to the families or community ties of the slaves they purchased.

The slave traffic had a tendency of increasing the demand for slaves back east as well as in Mississippi. The resulting demand undermined the security of all southern slaves, for planters looking to buy would not return until they had purchased enough slaves to meet their needs. When planter Abram Barnes wished to increase his slaveholdings, he sent Samuel Cobon to Virginia to purchase slaves for his estate. Cobon experienced difficulty in purchasing any slaves, owing to the high prices.[46] In July 1828 Cobon observed that in the Richmond area "there are very large sums to be invested in negroes this year which will keep prices up until late"; still, he thought, "they will certainly decline in the fall." Fearing that "my last purchases will be the worthless," Cobon promised to stay until September, since "traders generally try to get off by 20th August at the latest," lowering the competition and prices.[47] Bery Smith, a young planter on the make from Maryland, wrote to Natchez nabob Abram Barnes of his plans to move to Mississippi and join Barnes. Smith reported that "negroes is very high here, & am doubtful whether I shall obtain as many as I want[.]"[48]

Some Natchez planters on the make went to Virginia themselves to purchase slaves. Stephen Archer traveled east in 1833 for the sole purpose of buying slaves. He wrote to his brother Richard that "I think this will be a good time to buy as cotton is selling high a prospect of its advancing which will make negroes sell much higher." Acting as an agent for friends, Stephen asked Richard to tell a friend that "we will try to get the Smith for him. Tell him also if he does not want the woman & family I will stake them of what they cost him with interest up to the time I get them," suggesting, again, that the division of slave families was an action taken lightly by planters as well as by traders.[49] Two years later, Clinton, Mississippi, planter John Faulkner encouraged the Virginian William Powell to follow a similar path into the planter class. "If you could buy 20 to 30 Negroes" financed over several years, once in Mississippi "you and John could pay for them & never feel it." With rich lands on the Yazoo River, now was the time to get in the business. While prices for slaves were indeed high, "you and John have the lands and If [you] could get the negroes at a fair price and pay for them," they would never "face it again."[50] Apparently, Bery Smith had that plan in mind, as he wrote to Abram Barnes to report that, while he had "been using every exertion to purchase negroes," he had only bought a dozen. He intended "to get ten or twelve more and start them down the river in September and expect to find you have got A Green's place for me to put them on." Upon arrival, Smith planned to "carry on a good stroke at Clearing this winter," in order to be prepared to plant a twenty-bale cotton crop the next year.[51] The new plantation cohort traveled via riverboat to Natchez while their owner took a coastal steamer. Expecting that they would arrive before him, he asked Barnes if "you will please have the goodness to take charge of them and set them to work" clearing the land at his new plantation.[52]

While slave traders preferred to purchase valuable young adult slaves and migrating planters took with them all but the oldest slaves, less is known about what kinds of slaves planters purchased to ship west. One might assume that their purchasing patterns were similar to those of traders, perhaps with closer attention paid to the preservation of families. On the other hand, the planter on the make might have had even less consideration for the slave family and community. The available evidence is only suggestive. A single purchase of thirty-eight slaves by Mississippi planter John Randolph offers some insight into the ways planters purchased their slaves (see Appendix A). His records reveal what kinds of slaves he looked for.[53] Less than a fourth were in the supposedly "prime" years between eighteen and twenty-one, while a third were younger than eighteen and a fourth were between twenty-two and twenty-nine. Three were aged forty; one had lived sixty years. No mention of price or value is given on these bills of sale.

Randolph purchased thirty-eight slaves from twenty different private owners. There would be little point in traveling to Charleston to purchase from a slave dealer, since one could do the same in Natchez. Further, the names of the sellers and the fact that there were several indicate that they were not slave traders. It seems unlikely that people named "Miss Keith," "Ann Coburn," and "Mrs. Rodgers" were in the slave-trading business, as the realm of women in the South (and perhaps especially in South Carolina) was limited, and by 1830 those limits were increasing.

In purchasing his slaves, Randolph and his sellers seem to have paid little attention to family ties. Only two family units are readily apparent. Sally, twenty-two years old, came with a child named Isaac, and Rudy, aged twenty-nine, came with two children, Phillis and Nancy. Rudy's former owner did not sell Randolph any male slaves, but Sally's sold Randolph a twenty-six-year-old slave named George. It is unclear whether George was the father of Sally's children, but it is entirely possible. Of the other sellers, only two sold male and female slaves to Randolph, and in only one case were they less than ten years apart in age. At best, Randolph bought one or two complete families; even this is unlikely.

Randolph, in addition to apparently ignoring family units, readily purchased unmarried teenagers. The most common age for a slave in these bills of sale was fourteen. In fact, one seller, B. Jenkins, sold Randolph four fourteen-year-old male slaves. Hugh McDonald sold Abraham, who was "about" fourteen, suggesting that Abraham may have been younger. Bowing to social conventions against the sale of children, the slave's age may have been estimated to be appropriate for sale.[54] In addition to these four fourteen-year-olds, Randolph purchased slaves aged fifteen, sixteen, and seventeen.

The high proportion of teenagers in contrast to the paucity of slaves in their early twenties suggests that Randolph was purchasing for future production rather than immediate output. His six fourteen-year-old slaves, all of them male, would in five years be prime field hands well acclimated to Mississippi. Although he could not have known, they would reach their prime at the apex of the cotton boom. On examination of the general breakdown of his slave population, it appears that Randolph's reasoning extends further. His purchases of many older slaves, those in their late twenties and early thirties, assured current production. His purchase of a handful of much older slaves—including Patsy, who at age sixty was elderly for her time—suggests that he desired to build a slave community on his plantation. The age differences suggest an effort to establish a variety of experiences, with older role models and a large number of slaves who within the next few years would be very productive and quite valuable.[55]

The gender division of the Randolph purchase only slightly favored male slaves. Closer examination of the purchase divided by age indicates that Randolph's purchases were prejudiced towards men in two very significant age groups, those under eighteen and those over twenty-one. Randolph appeared to want men with their most productive years ahead of them or those just beyond their prime. Still, the absence of men in their late teens and early twenties indicates either that such slaves were prohibitively expensive, or that Randolph preferred not to deal with slaves who were physically mature but still quite rambunctious. If Randolph was attempting to create a community of slaves, he certainly did not want any disruptive slaves on his plantation. Probably price and demeanor combined to deter Randolph from such purchases.

The typicality and representativeness of Randolph's run of bills of sale is certainly open to debate. The preference for young men and the paucity of "prime" slaves seem to be the reverse of the types of slaves that slave traders purchased.[56] Randolph was not a slave trader, and above all this example tells us that planters who assembled slave communities through purchases in eastern states followed different patterns and had different preferences than slave traders and their clients.

Mississippi's Slave Majority

The growth of the frontier slave population in the period between 1817 and 1835 was nothing short of massive. Through the various ways discussed, planters and slave traders imported slaves at a higher rate than white pioneers migrated. By 1835, Mississippi had a black majority. This outcome is hardly surprising; the earliest plantation settlement patterns suggested that this would be the case. In 1810, for instance, the section of the Mississippi Territory that became the State of Mississippi was 46 percent slave. Two of its eight counties had slave majorities (map 1). Ten years later, while the overall state population had dropped to 43 percent slave, four counties were majority slave, including Adams County, whose 66 percent slave population rose to 74 percent when Natchez was excluded (map 2). Every county in the state was over 15 percent slave. By 1830, the proportion of slaves in Mississippi had risen to 48 percent, including the remarkably high 73 percent slave Adams County, whose slave population rose to 80 percent when Natchez was excluded (map 3).

The "Flush Times" of the early part of the 1830s saw a high rate of slave importations to Mississippi, contrasting sharply with the depression of the later years. A state census taken in 1837 indicated that by that year, Mississippi's population was 53 percent slave, suggesting it had achieved a slave majority two or three years earlier. The first half of the 1830s illustrates the remarkably fast growth of the slave population and, as a result, the plantation economy. By 1837, eight of fifty-six counties had populations that were more than 70 percent slave, and eighteen were over 50 percent slave; in sharp contrast, only ten were less than 25 percent slave, and only two less than 10 percent slave (map 4).

The massive influx of slaves to Mississippi illustrates the scope of slave migration. Every slave forced to the frontier had a story of someone, a close friend, a parent, a spouse, or even a kind master, lost in this migration. While those arriving slaves no doubt found ways to fit into and create a new community, their lives were never truly the same.

A move that separated husband from wife, parent from child, and even slave from master battered the primary social relationships that defined the slaves' position in society. The slaves lost their sense of belonging, not to mention their sense of security. Slaves became more defensive, they grew prone to rebellion, and they were more likely to risk flight. At the same time,

Slavery and Frontier Mississippi

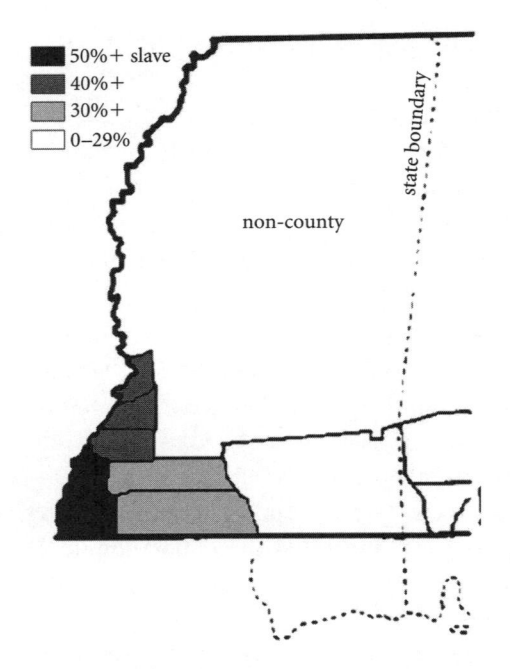

Mississippi Territory 1810

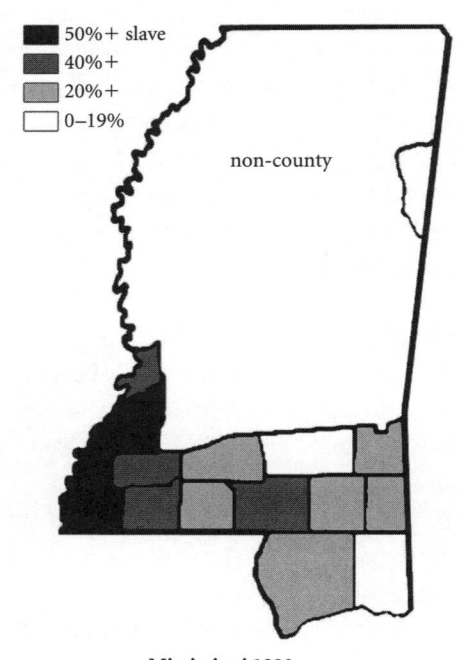

Mississippi 1820

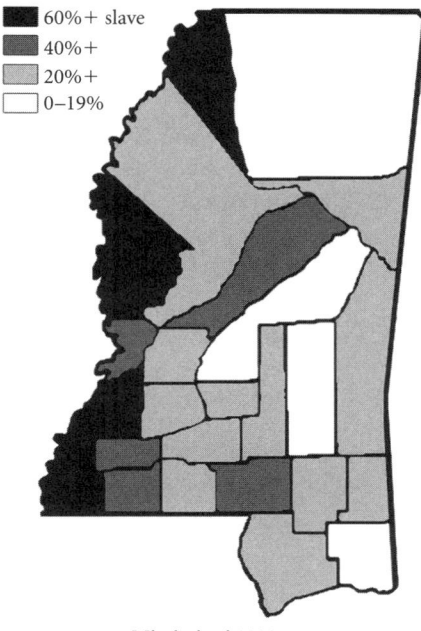

Slaves in the Western Migration

Mississippi 1830

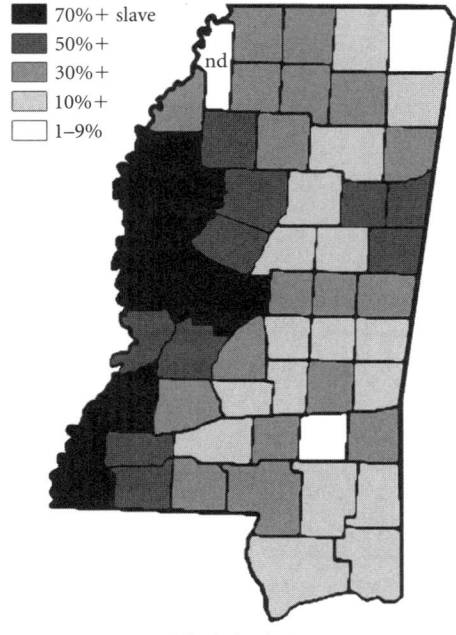

Mississippi 1837

the slaves did their best to relocate themselves in their new society. They took new spouses and made connections in their new slave community. The descriptions of slaves singing, telling stories, and laughing during their migration are doubly deceptive. Few accounts describe the crying, the attempts at escape, and the physical resistance that went on daily at the slave markets. Indeed the singing and laughing recorded was just as painful for the slaves, for it reminded them of home. It also provided a momentary escape, an opportunity to reminisce. Descriptions of slaves singing in the markets and stockades allowed masters to justify their actions, for the slaves appeared content. The enslaved were not happy, nor did they willingly adapt. Given the reality of their new surroundings, slaves faced an option (not chosen by all) to form new communities with others displaced in Mississippi. The effect on slave communities uprooted and relocated to Mississippi is not unlike that of Native American peoples decimated by colonial incursions and European diseases. Communities that lost various and often important members had little choice but to amalgamate and create new societies—which is precisely what many slaves in Mississippi did.

Even those that did adjust faced one of the most traumatic of experiences related to slavery. With limited options, uprooted slaves chose to develop new community ties, and form new families.[57] At the same time they accommodated new working conditions. Fictive kin relationships, always important in slave society, took on even greater meaning following separation. Such adjustments grew more difficult as slaves faced the reality that they would never see home or kin again. Further, following such an ordeal, slaves would never feel as secure in their new locations as they once had. In this respect, the slave migration of the early nineteenth century was an important turning point in African American history.

Chapter Five

Defining the Boundaries of Enslavement

The Struggle to Define Enslavement

When an overseer named Staunton discovered a runaway slave, the slave appeared nearly starved. Absent for several weeks, he remained in hiding nonetheless. Staunton "took him hom[e] and gave victuals which he eat upon the steps" by the door of his cabin. The overseer prepared to saddle up his horse for a trip to Natchez where he would turn the slave in. As he did so, "the Negro asked Mr. S.' wife to give him som[e] more food. While getting it the Negro took Staunton's gun & Pistols and made off. Mrs. S. called her husband who advanced towards the fellow and rec'd. 1 whole charge in his heart—fell dead. The Negro fled."[1]

Little public notice was given to this incident. No hysteria broke out, and no furious mobs proceeded to lynch dangerous looking slaves. This event can be explained in part as an indication of the generally violent social atmosphere in Mississippi. The region was still frontier, as much "western" as "southern." Yet the absence of hysteria or outrage over this crime indicates the confidence among white Mississippians that their control over society was firm and not in question.

Mississippians did react to threats to their social order. At almost exactly the same time that the runaway committed this murder, Natchez residents tarred and feathered the planter James Foster for murdering his wife, Susan. Foster threatened white Mississippi's understanding of elite masculinity; rather than protecting his wife, he killed her. He paid with a ritual stripping of his manhood, although thanks to his status he escaped with his life.[2] The runaway also threatened society, but his offense did not seem to threaten the

79

fundamental social order of Mississippi. A rogue slave might occasionally run away and even kill, but most were loyal to their masters—indeed, Staunton was not even a member of the master class.

Mississippi's planters harbored no illusions that their slaves were completely content. Instead planters worked to establish a level of interaction between them and their slaves that would be harsh enough to ensure their superiority, but mild enough to avoid rebellion. Planters desired their slaves to be fully cognizant of the force a master wielded. They also wanted slaves to perceive them as allies, someone to turn to in times of need. For their part, the slaves attempted to work a system that was stacked against them. They did not rise up because they recognized the master's power. Aside from the threat of physical punishment and possible sale, the masters provided slaves with food, clothing, and shelter. Weekly food rations, semi-annual distributions of clothing, and monthly inspections of slave quarters reminded the enslaved of the master's presence in their everyday lives. Slaves also understood that the masters dictated the terms of their labor. While slaves may have challenged the plantation labor regime, the threat of increased labor, or the promise of days off, reminded them of the planter's control over their workload, and the point was driven home by whippings, isolation, and sales of unproductive bondsmen. At the same time that they recognized the planter's power, slaves engaged in a daily struggle to define the parameters of their enslavement. The planter's authority was never absolute, and slaves took advantage of opportunities to slow down their work, provide their own food, secure a break from the labor by temporary escape, and most important, add meaning to their existence through the formation of family and community bonds. The larger goal of this struggle was to maintain some degree of dignity and identity in the face of such an overwhelming opponent. In short, both masters and slaves strove to define the boundaries of slavery in Mississippi.[3]

Planters found the struggle particularly difficult. To protect their egos, and to maintain order on their places, they felt they had to win every time. They employed brute force as well as much more subtle measures to keep their control.[4] Planters had a desire to think themselves good people, kind masters who cared about their slaves, and whose slaves, given a choice, would remain loyal.[5] Such a belief could be difficult to reconcile with the brutalities that lay at the root of slavery. However, as a cult of domesticity emerged in the United States during the first decades of the nineteenth century, notions of affection and control became interrelated. It stands to reason that planters expressed affection for their slaves in part by imposing a strict discipline.[6] Domesticity venerated the family, and planters who attempted to gain their slaves' loyalty extended privileges that ensured the formation of slave communities and the propagation of a slave culture in Mississippi. The formation of such communities undercut the master's authority as often as it shored it up.[7] Ultimately, the existence of the communities was, by their very nature, subversive; they provided a forum for protesting the master's authority and organizing lines of communication across plantation boundaries.

Planters were deliberately ambivalent regarding the slave community. It could be an asset when viewed in moralistic terms, but a liability when slaves used it to resist planter authority. Despite their desires to be good masters, most set as their main goal the profitable production of cotton. Successful harvests and content slave populations went hand in hand and thus planters kept a close eye on their account books, filling them at times with both production totals and slave family trees.[8]

Southern planters' concerns for profits related to their slaves because they invested a great share of their financial resources in slaves. Planters acted with their own interests in mind, and when those interests were in agreement with those of slaves, they appeared kind. Slaves took advantage of these shared interests to form families and propagate their culture. To maximize planter investments, the slave had to be content enough to be productive and not take flight or rebel. Such was the ideal, at least. The sheer domination of slavery played out in a much more brutal reality. Mississippi was a violent place in the early years of its statehood. Aside from the genteel classes in Natchez—whose gentility certainly had limits—a great many of the state's residents were rough frontiersmen who moved there, as one wrote, to "live like a fighting cock" with fellow ruffians.[9] Many of Mississippi's frontier slaveholders employed brutality while attempting to improve their slaves' lives out of their skewed sense of humanitarianism. The Mississippi planter John Monette's discussion of whipping, written primarily for a northern audience, illustrates the conflicting ideas involved in punishing slaves:

> *It may not be improper to make a remark or two relative to whipping. This is generally performed with as much care and humanity as the nature of the case will admit. A person standing at the distance of two hundred yards, being unacquainted with the mode, and hearing the loud sharp crack of the whip upon the naked skin, would almost tremble for the life of the poor sufferer. But what would be his surprise, after hearing fifty or one hundred*

> *stripes thus laid on, to go up and examine the poor fellow, and find the skin not broken, and not a drop of blood drawn from him!*[10]

Informed by such reasoning, planters' "care and humanity" ran the gamut from harsh domination to paternalistic condescension. Monette's words were an attempt to illustrate that popular images of slave whippings were not so harsh as commonly believed in the North. Contemporary movements to reform asylums and penitentiaries, often viewed as well-intentioned, if misguided, were similarly cruel.[11] Monette's own view can be read in much the same way. He emphasized, for instance, the adoption of a lash with a soft buckskin "cracker" to replace cowskin whips, which sliced the skin. "One hundred lashes well laid on with it," he wrote, "would not injure the skin as much as ten moderate stripes with a cow-skin."[12] The point is not to defend the way planters treated their slaves, but to illustrate their willingness to classify brutal punishments in reformist terms as humane means for slave control. Mississippi planters believed that their brand of slavery was quite humane, a belief that vindicated the planters, in their opinion, for they chose to allow family and community activities in the slave quarters. Yet family and community could just as easily become a target for punishing slaves who transgressed the boundaries of plantation discipline.[13] Fifty to one hundred lashes for picking too little cotton was considered a standard, one that reminded the entire community of slaves of the importance of getting the harvest in. While individual practices varied from plantation to plantation, masters still spoke a language of dominance that obscured the harsh realities of their slaves' existence.[14] If the struggle in the planters' minds to define slavery as humane was little contested, the effort by both planters and slaves to define the boundaries of slavery was a greater challenge.

Cotton, Slavery, and the Atlantic Economy

While by most antebellum standards Natchez was quite a small town in the 1820s, it was the largest in Mississippi, and second only to New Orleans among lower Mississippi River towns. Natchez had become something of a metropolis for Mississippi, the center of wealth and population, although no longer the capital. A decade after Mississippi became a state, frontier counties to the east produced more cotton than those of the Natchez district.[15]

The expansion of plantation empires reflected the growing connection between Natchez and the larger Atlantic economy. Regular visits to the cotton mart at New Orleans provided firsthand information about the market, information that was supplemented by frequent dispatches from cotton factors. Benjamin Farrar, for instance, was among the first to know of the coming Panic of 1819, having heard in January of a "rather dull" demand in Liverpool, and declining prices in New York which were expected "to be lower owing to the pressure for money. Many failures are taking place in Atlantic ports."[16] The leading planters of Natchez made it their business to have the best information about the state of the cotton markets where they made their fortunes.

By the 1830s, the cotton markets had improved, and the nabobs remained closely connected with their business partners abroad. The Liverpool firm of George Green & Son spelled out many of the intricacies in dispatches to the planter William Newton Mercer:

The consumers had confined their purchases to their actual wants & materially reduced their stocks, in expectations of obtaining a decrease in price. . . . When they did attempt to come forwards [sic], they were met in the market by both speculators & buyers for export, which has been productive of considerable animations & an improvement in price. . . . The state of things here aided the demand for yarn &c in Manchester Market on Tuesday & higher prices were demanded.

    The preliminary treaty with Holland has been ratified & the embargo on Dutch vessels removed—This will aid our export trade.[17]

The planters understood their connections to markets, industry, and international politics. Aware of the volatility of the outside world, they attempted to create an illusion of stability at home. Illusions notwithstanding, market reports from New Orleans, New York, and Liverpool reminded them of larger economic forces at play. Inspired by the promise of greater income, they expanded their world, and moved into newer, more fertile, and (for their purposes) uninhabited lands.

Planters in the frontier counties purchased more slaves, investing their profits and expanding their productive capacity. Until the early 1830s, much of this settlement was limited to the southern half of the state, for Choctaw and Chickasaw Indians still inhabited the northern part. By 1830, one observer stated that planters controlled and cultivated "all the high lands" and established operations "in the swamp scattered about wherever they find land that does not overflow. Every year they make as much in one year on the Bottoms if not overflown as they do on the highlands in two."[18] Little surprise that John Faulkner, purchasing 1,638 acres on the Yazoo River for $2,000, expected an income of eight to twelve thousand dollars on the 800 acres he cultivated. "You will be more than paid by selling steam boat wood," he urged an eastern investor.[19] Dense forests prevented the flat, rich lands lying in the delta between the Yazoo and Mississippi Rivers, from Vicksburg north to Memphis, from being cultivated before the 1850s.[20]

As the frontier moved eastward, the planters in Natchez consolidated their position as the state's economic and social elite. The growing frontier population took charge of the state's politics, a change formalized by the movement of the state capitol to Jackson in 1823. The Natchez "nabobs" who controlled Mississippi's high society and still owned the most slaves pursued their interests in other ways by the creation of an idealized plantation world.[21] Their landed and slave property holdings grew in size to the point where they considered a man who owned twenty slaves to be a smaller planter.

As the political voice of the nabobs declined, they expressed their vision for the region in more ostentatious ways. Many of the huge plantation houses standing today in Natchez were built during this era. In keeping with a tradition begun in the 1790s by early English and Spanish settlers, Natchez planters emphasized both scale and detail in the construction of their houses, modeling the architecture on the plantation homes of Virginia and South Carolina. Planters continued to erect and expand their mansions up to the beginning of the Civil War, employing the labor of their own slaves as well as skilled artisan slaves hired in Natchez. In constructing such luxurious and aristocratic expressions of wealth, Natchez planters set themselves apart from and above not only their slaves, but their fellow slaveholders who worked to carve a place out for themselves in the Choctaw cessions. Upon achieving any level of prosperity, smaller planters also pretended to be an aristocracy in the cotton kingdom.

The nabobs envisioned their plantations as islands set apart from the larger world. Despite their business dealings with cotton brokers and slave traders hundreds of miles away, planters strove for self-sufficiency, or at least the perception of such.[22] Cotton was foremost in their production plans, but the larger plantations all produced corn, livestock, fruits, and vegetables for their own use. The main house, surrounded by dense greenery, presented itself as the headquarters for business and social undertakings. Slave quarters were situated away, and preferably obscured, from the main house. The house and the

Defining the Boundaries of Enslavement

plantation shared the same name in "organic union," for indeed the plantation represented what the masters thought an organic society.[23] Planters were conscious of the appearance of their places as they established and maintained them. From New Orleans, John Dick advised Benjamin Farrar of some improvements needed at Farrar's Poplar Grove plantation:

1. It appeared that the [live]stock of the adjoining plantations had extensive ranges on Poplar Grove, which it was very desirable to prevent[.] Some considerable *fencing* was therefore wanted.
2. The *negro houses* were without chimnies—Badly covered in[,] were too low[,] wanted their eves to be extended[,] were too few in number. In regard to the police of the quarter, the hen houses & other erections of the negroes to be placed back, or removed altogether—the houses themselves to be white washed inside once a month &c.

Although he claimed to "merely throw out" the suggestions "to be used according to their expediency," John Dick revealed the ideology of a plantation as home to an organic society, a place that presented visitors, neighbors, slaves, and even livestock with the image of a planter firmly in control of his place.[24] The creation of this outward appearance obscured the underlying brutality and emphasis on profits, in the same way that the planter language of humane treatment obscured the cruel and frequent abuse of slaves.

As planters on the make filled in the frontiers east and north of Natchez, the theoretical underpinnings of slavery in Mississippi had not been resolved. Race may have defined who was slave and who was free, but no strict pattern of social separation had developed yet. Some planters saw the good in slavery as they made profits from cotton, while others held a view that slavery was a "necessary evil" that kept order in a biracial society. There was still a great deal of fluidity as young parvenus matured into first planters and occasionally blacks crossed the line from slave to free. Slaves and free blacks were seen in gambling halls, saloons, churches, and revivals.[25] They had a great deal of latitude in propagating their culture and forming families.

Spiritual Equality and Social Inequality

Christianity was often a dangerous thing in slave communities, for it promoted a message of brotherhood and equality that was dynamite in the quarters.

Regardless, many masters allowed their slaves to practice Christianity, with some restrictions. It seemed to matter little to masters if their slaves were religious.[26] Perhaps they were aware that suppressing the slaves' faith would be even more explosive than allowing its practice under close supervision. Some planters, as professed Christians, feared the moral consequences of suppressing the faith that their slaves shared with them. What is clear is that planters instructed their overseers to pay close attention to what went on in slave services. Joseph Johnson instructed the overseer George Comer that the slave preacher Edmond "is not to be permitted to go from the plantation to preach, without express permission," although "he may execute his preaching gifts on the plantation if he chooses, but that must be in your presence & hearing[.]" Further, such events could not occur on Sundays.[27]

The religion of the Second Great Awakening had reached Mississippi at its very earliest stages. The Awakening was not exclusive to any race, for it was a highly equalitarian movement. Evangelists targeted the slave population as ripe for conversion.[28] In the revivals, Mississippi's slaves worshiped alongside free men. Increasingly in the 1820s, slaves organized their own independent congregations into African churches affiliated with the evangelical denominations. These churches did a better job of attracting slaves to the faith.[29] Yet evangelical blacks and whites continued to worship together. The seating arrangements at these services usually were segregated, but at times slave ministers preached to mixed-race congregations, conferring an elevated spiritual and social status on a member of a supposedly inferior race. In an era when the evangelicals' discussion of the morality of slavery had not yet concluded, such visible signs of equality contrasted sharply with the acts of Christian slaveholders who enslaved their brethren.[30]

Among nonevangelicals the image of free and slave worshiping alongside each other at camp meetings and revivals substantially challenged the emergent racial order of Mississippi. In response the state took steps to prevent interracial religious fellowship in an 1822 law banning biracial religious services and unsupervised black religious meetings. Such meetings in Mississippi were commonplace, and the planter elite considered them dangerous.

In response to the new law, the Methodist itinerant William Winans challenged the popular governor, George Poindexter, when he ran for Congress in 1822. Winans's candidacy suggests that the evangelicals believed interracial religious worship was something worth voting over. However, his poor showing in the election, followed soon by evangelical concessions on matters of slavery and interracial fellowship, suggest that such conviction was not essential.[31] The legislature quickly revised the law, allowing slaves whose masters so desired to have access to religious instruction and services. By closing the door on African-American denominations, the law ultimately brought more slaves to biracial churches while segregating the congregations.[32]

The compromise of eliminating African churches was the first of a series of concessions by which evangelical church organizations slowly abandoned their black members. Revisions to state law added limits to the practice of religion by slaves, an interference that was effective only because the denominations allowed it. In 1831 the state legislature banned slaves from preaching, with no major challenge from evangelicals.[33] The next step was the organized effort at colonization. In the late 1820s, evangelical ministers and wealthy planters organized Mississippi's colonization society. This society began transporting free blacks back to Africa in 1831. Throughout the 1830s, Mississippians donated the substantial sum of $100,000 to the "cause" of transporting free and recently freed blacks away from the United States. As racial and political attitudes in the late 1830s turned against any effort that might be perceived as abolitionist, the movement faded. Rather than an antislavery movement, colonization in Mississippi was a sign of what one historian of religion termed "the seeds of compromise with slavery and racial separation, with its implicit inequality," which had begun to permeate Mississippi's evangelical churches.[34]

As evangelical religion became more mainstream and adopted the values of planter society, the slaves turned to folk religion. This form of spirituality was infused with the richness of their African-American culture, as well as a Christian morality that harshly condemned their masters for holding slaves.[35] Masters continued their attempts to restrict or regulate the religion of the slaves by preaching to their slaves themselves, hiring preachers who delivered messages amenable to slavery, and monitoring the services that slaves conducted. The masters' awareness that folk religion informed slave insurrection conspiracies raised suspicions of slave preachers.[36] Slowly, the prospect of a condemnation of slavery by southern established religion faded until southern evangelical churches split away from their national organizations on the issue of slavery.[37]

As the religious culture of slaves withdrew into secret meetings on weekends and late at night, this form of their culture would leave little historical record. This absence of records of slave culture hardly indicates nonexistence, for there is a clear record of how and why slave religion became an underground institution in Mississippi. Evidence from later antebellum years and beyond illustrate the cultural continuities through this period.[38]

FAMILIES AND COMMUNITIES

In contrast to religion, Mississippi's planters viewed other aspects of slave society as beneficial to themselves and their slaves alike. Family was essential to the propagation of the slave community. While it had no legal basis, the slaves' families preserved their culture through kin and fictive kin relationships. Much of the record of the slaves' forced migration illustrates its destructive effect on slaves' families. Yet upon arrival in Mississippi, families that survived the migration took in new members, and those who lost their families worked to create new ones.

Locust Grove plantation, located near Natchez, was home to a growing slave community during the 1820s and 1830s.[39] At one time or another the home to eighty-four slaves, Locust Grove's community consisted of nineteen families; only thirteen slaves had no formal relations. The structures of the families at Locust Grove, reconstructed from a plantation logbook, varied from married couples with no children to extended families (see Appendix B). Eight couples had no children. Others had several children. The couple Green and Charity had two daughters, Beck and Charlotte. In 1832, Beck married Isaac, a slave purchased that same year.[40] They had two children: Willis, who died in infancy in 1834, and Rawsby, born in 1834. Green and Charity's other daughter, Charlotte, married Adam, a much older slave in 1834, the year after his arrival. Green and Charity's was the most extended family at Locust Grove, but not the only large one.

Armstead married Louisa, probably in 1827. They had four children: Eliza, born in 1828; Harriet, born in 1830; Betsey, born in 1832; and Polly, born in 1834. A similar family was that of Leven and Mary. Their first child, Sarah Ann, was born in 1827. Andrew was born in 1829, Emiline in 1831, and Pleasant in 1833. The existence of two families which, despite the horrors of slavery, could establish seemingly stereotypical nuclear families on the Mississippi frontier suggests the degree to which these slaves clung to their values of family and kinship.

Most slaves on Locust Grove were not in such stable family circumstances. Some couples were separated because they belonged to different masters. For instance, Maria was purchased in 1830 or 1831. She had two children. With no mention of a father, it is likely that he resided on another plantation, or was a white man. Jacob, purchased around the same time, found his name changed to Peter to avoid confusion with another Jacob. Henry and Lewis, the sons of Marie, were orphaned in their infancy. Several children died in their infancy, quite a common fate for slave and free in the nineteenth century.[41]

Despite such difficulty in maintaining family and identity, the slaves at Locust Grove continued to form families. Childless couples chose to spend their lives together, even if their unions risked destruction at the hands of an angry or cash-strapped master. Children married as young as sixteen or seventeen. Rose, whose husband Phillis died in 1831, remarried to Jim in 1833. Many slaves married within months of being purchased. Family was something that the slaves at Locust Grove valued, and thus they sought to form familial unions at the first opportunity. In ideal circumstances, they attempted to form families which were very stable and long-lasting. Significantly, in less than ideal situations, slaves still sought to make familial connections with other slaves.

By making note of such families, planters recognized the social need to establish family ties in their slave communities. Indeed, some attempted to reconstruct families separated by sales. Minna, for instance, asked her master, L. R. Starks, to purchase her son, and thus he wrote the slave trader Rice Ballard to let him know that "I therefore will take him if you will send him." Even though Starks had little cash, he assured Ballard that, having planted 130 acres in cotton, he could "make the money sure upon time. . . . I want the boy & the mother is much pleased at the idea. You will therefore send him to me."[42]

Once family connections had been established, slaves risked all to preserve and cultivate their marriages. Quite often slaves felt that they simply had to be with their spouses, with or without a pass. The issue could have been a fight, a sick child, or simply loneliness. The Natchez planter John Nevitt's slave Jerry, for instance, "went over the river yesterday to see his wife without a pass," earning him "a light flogging for it."[43] Jerry visited her on other occasions with a pass, but in October ran away. Nevitt advertised for him, and heard quickly that "Jerry had been shot by Mr. Minors overseer[.]"[44] On the next day, "Jerry came home with [a] note from Mr. Minor's overseer (Mr. Hyner) who had not shot him as reported yesterday but shot at him and missed," a fortunate turn of events. Nevitt gave Jerry "a severe whipping" before putting him back to work. Jerry's brush with death illustrates the risks slaves willingly took to maintain their familial connections.[45]

Master and Slave in Microcosm: Claremont

John Nevitt's Claremont plantation in Adams County provides a good case study of planter-slave relationships. Nevitt kept a diary from 1826 to 1832. His notations on the cultivation patterns illustrate the annual cycle of cotton and corn crops. In contrast to the more tyrannical and efficiency-minded William Dunbar, Nevitt was a much kinder master to his slaves. Still, his entries tell the stories of a constant push and pull between Nevitt and his slaves. The slaves' defiance at times was outright, but at other times it was very subtle.

Nevitt suffered a great loss on a cold January night in 1827 when "my gin was destroyed by fire." He immediately attributed the fire to "an incendiary," although he had no clue as to whom. All his slaves that night were "Employed puting [sic] out fire and saving what cotton possible," yet he estimated his loss at four thousand dollars. He also reported that "the Boy Gusty was Burnt in the gin[.]"[46] The gin fire may have been some sort of protest, perhaps of the slaves' workload, or perhaps a protest by a relative or friend of the slave Sarah, who had recently been sold as part of a deal settling a lawsuit.[47] Nevitt had erected the gin only a year earlier.[48]

Nevitt's slaves took on additional workloads that year to construct a new ginstand and cotton magazine. He still assigned them the same amount of work cultivating crops and tending to the plantation's maintenance. A week after the fire, while Nevitt had already begun plans for constructing a new gin, he had slaves clearing the fields and building and repairing fences.[49] Corn planting began on schedule late in February.[50] Almost all his slaves took time in mid-March "raising [the] gin frame Except 3 ploughing and a small gang pulling and beating down stalks[.]"[51] In early April, as cotton planting began, some of his slaves worked "raising the rafters on the gin[.]"[52] Where the efforts of some slaves were focused on building the gin, other slaves made up the difference in work for their absence in the field. Nevitt's increased workloads were assigned for reasons that were apparent to his slaves, rather than being arbitrarily imposed.

Slaves not only had to construct and maintain the physical plants of their masters' establishments, they also had to make sure a crop was in the field. Daniel Willis's slaves, for instance, in 1825 planted cotton before his fences enclosed the crop, "so you see," he wrote to Abram Barnes, "I am ploughing in an open field, but there is not much stock to tread it down," and all but three of his slaves were constructing the fence.[53] One overseer warned his employer that "With Respect to building the Negro Cabbins it is impossible to do that at the present moment and to carry on the farm in a propper manner as I find evry thing out of fix[.]"[54]

Having incurred an increased workload, Nevitt rewarded his slaves for their efforts. He gave them a half day off on a Saturday in August (he normally required them to work all day on Saturdays), "and gave them a dance at night for the good conduct during the making and laying by the crop."[55] The festivities reminded his slaves that extra work would be rewarded, shoring up their understanding that even within the slave system, the master could only demand so much without additional reward. While the dance may have represented sincere appreciation, Nevitt did not consider it any kind of insurance. He had purchased a policy on his gin back in June.[56]

Major acts of defiance such as arson were occasional events on Nevitt's plantation.[57] Minor acts of defiance seemed unending. In April 1830, "Jerry and one or two others got a flogging for misconduct last night[.]"[58] On another occasion, Nevitt "found that Kate was put in Jail on suspicion of having stolen meat[.]" She said she got it from Bill, and thus Nevitt and the constable "apprehended Bill who after a little flogging confessed that he & Mr. Campbell's Sandy had broke open Mr. Lyle's warehouse and taken from it Bakin & liquor[.]"[59] On another occasion, Nevitt sent his trusted slave Bill to purchase "sundries articles" in town. Nevitt "found on my return home he had been stealing the greater part of a Demijohn of molasses," apparently an unforgivable offence. After "a good whipping," Nevitt "sent him to Jail with a determination to sell him," endangering Bill's marriage as his wife lived on a nearby plantation. Bill was relatively fortunate, as his wife's master purchased him.[60]

These forms of resistence were quite dangerous undertakings for the slaves. Even simple acts of theft, which may not have undermined the entire slave regime, were nonetheless acts of rebellion and seen as such. In committing such acts of rebellion, the slaves were assaulting the master's authority, whether he knew about it or not. When such resistance was successful, it was not even recorded. But the stolen molasses was money out of Nevitt's pocket, and when he found out about it, he cut his losses by selling the slave.[61]

Nevitt's slaves frequently ran away. Claremont's closeness to Natchez— only a day's walk to town and back—must have proven too great an attraction for an adventurous or dissatisfied slave. Peter had run away for nearly three months before being returned for a reward. Nevitt whipped him as punishment.[62] When Cinthia ran away overnight, on her return she "had a light whipping and went to work[.]"[63] Ruben and Maria each received a similar "light whiping" upon their return.[64] When the slave Jerry convinced "Old Edmond" to return, Edmond also got a "light whipping."[65] On another occasion, the same Jerry, after returning "was corrected and set to work[.]"[66] Dan, too, for running away and being caught rather than returning, was whipped "twice severely," and sent back to work.[67] On Albert's return, Nevitt "gave him a severe whipping" as well.[68] Oddly, a month earlier, when "Rubin came home having been runaway for two or three months," Nevitt "*did not punish him*[.]"[69] Nevitt's judgement must have seemed even more erratic to Jerry and Albert when they returned, for he "gave Albert a flogging and forgave Jerry," markedly different punishments for similar offenses.[70]

On all plantations, highly valued slaves such as Jerry, aware of their status, were bold in their defiance. Such boldness made little sense to the planter Thomas Hill, as he complained about six slaves who had run away. Some had "never been whiped on this plantation and are the very best nigroes on the place."[71] The skilled artisan slaves of the plantation world had an advantage over the others and their masters. While planters sold their field hands readily, skilled slaves were more secure. Planters viewed them as greater investments to be sure. They also held skilled slaves in higher regard. A skilled slave was crucial to some aspect of plantation operations and thus a more important part of the planter's world. They received a degree of trust from the planters that could be used as license to run away. The trust planters gave skilled slaves also allowed them opportunities to explain their actions and possibly escape punishment. In this light, it is hardly surprising that Jerry ran away more frequently. He was forgiven when others were not.

Running away bore risks besides punishment for Nevitt's slaves. The "fellow Edmont," who had run away in October 1829, was discovered dead at a nearby plantation the next January. Nevitt, concerned about the loss of a valuable slave, wrote to the sheriff of Adams County "informing him of the circumstances" and requesting an inquest. The coroner determined "that he came to death by the visitation of God" (possibly a euphemism for lynching).[72]

Recognizing such threats, Nevitt went to great measures to protect his investments in slaves. In 1828, Bill, Peter, and George all disappeared, apparently having run away. When he received a letter from Bill, "stating himself and the other two . . . to be at Columbus Stolen away by Rubin Burdin," in July, Nevitt "Got ready immediately to go after them," leaving by steamboat the same day. He went to Columbus, Ohio, but while there "Saw nothing of the negroes."[73] The slaves were in Columbus, Alabama, not Ohio, and in August Nevitt "recd. a letter from the Jeailor of Perry County Alabama stating my negro Bill to be in that Jail[.]" There would be a trial to determine their ownership.[74] Nevitt did not recover his slaves until March of 1829, after almost a year's absence.[75]

Despite the trouble in which Nevitt quite often found his slaves, they never became openly defiant. Other slaves in the neighborhood did, and his slaves must have known about it. In 1827, two slaves from a nearby plantation were hanged at one of the gates of Nevitt's plantation for trying to kill a

Defining the Boundaries of Enslavement

soldier.[76] The hangings reminded Nevitt and his slaves of the possibilities as well as the consequences of violent resistance.

Nevitt seemed to avoid outright resistance from his slaves through a combination of sympathetic treatment during heavy workloads and seasonal rewards at Christmas and the Fourth of July. During the harvest, he hired additional workers to supplement his labor force, which eased his slaves' efforts noticeably. He commonly hired local Indians—probably Choctaws—as well as free blacks to help bring in the harvest.[77] By employing what amounted to a migrant labor force to help at the end of the season, Nevitt presented himself as a master trying to keep his slaves from being overworked, a gesture which probably went a long way in keeping them content with their workload.

The slaves at Claremont also could expect the celebration of certain holidays. Nevitt celebrated Independence Day more regularly than his slaves did, but in some years he "gave Holliday to the negroes" while he went to a neighboring plantation for his own celebration.[78] The irony of slaves celebrating independence perhaps became clear, as he usually did not include them in July Fourth celebrations. He did give them occasional breaks when he (or perhaps they) felt their efforts deserved it. The most notable such celebration followed the increased labor associated with the gin reconstruction, but Nevitt on several other occasions gave his slaves half-days and passes into town, and must have used them to reward faithful service while withholding them for disciplinary purposes. Such rewards indicate that when Nevitt sensed discontent among his slaves he attempted to boost morale with celebrations and breaks. These events, like the dance that followed the gin-raising, reminded the slaves at Claremont that their master cared about them.[79]

One celebration which was not open to negotiation was Christmas. The holiday lasted three or four days. Christmas festivities began on December 24, when Nevitt gave his bondsmen half a day off and went to Natchez to purchase gifts. On Christmas day, Nevitt settled debts, paying them for work on Sundays, and treated them with whiskey, gifts, and a feast. The gift usually was some kind of practical item; one year he "gave all the women a dress of callico."[80] The highpoint of the holiday was the late-night party. In 1827, watching the "frolick," Nevitt "sat up untill 2 oclock in morning to keep order with them[.]"[81] Having fortified his slaves with whiskey, Nevitt remained vigilant to prevent the frolic from getting out of hand. Despite staying up so late, the slaves continued to celebrate the next day, as he noted the day after the ball, "This day nothing but frolick[.]"[82] Unsurprisingly, it was on the day after the holiday ended that the slaves slept late, on his time rather than theirs.[83]

While his slaves looked forward to Christmas, and probably remembered it as one of the happiest times of the year, Nevitt observed the feast in part to keep his slaves content. With slaves not his own, Nevitt seemed to have no regard for whether and how they celebrated Christmas. He made this lack of concern painfully clear in his Christmas Eve entry from 1831, when, in Scrooge-like fashion, he "found the two negroes bot. on the 22nd were unsound . . . and sent them home cancelling the sale[.]" Unaffected by the transaction, Nevitt also purchased gifts for the rest of his slaves' Christmas celebration.[84]

Maintaining Public Order

While planters combined plantation discipline with rewards to control their slaves, the law, too, played an important role in keeping Mississippi's slave population under control. Courts regularly identified slaves as runaways and imprisoned them. Such was the case with Tom, whose owner recovered him by applying at the Adams County justice court in 1832.[85] Justices of the peace and jailers collected small fees for the processing and maintenance of runaway slaves committed to local jails. The bureaucratic nature of these costs is apparent in the receipt given a recovering slaveowner on his slave's return:

Fees for taking up the Negro Boy George

For taking up	$10
Mileage	7.50 = 17.50

Justice Fees

Affidavit	.75
Commitment	1.00
Affidavit for release	.75
Release	1.00 = 3.50

Jailers Fees

for commitment	1.00
Maintenance 23 days at 25 cts pr day	5.75
Release	1.00 = 7.75
Advertisement	1.00 = 1.00
	29.75[86]

In addition to such seemingly routine if distasteful business, courts dealt with other, much more interesting cases. In March 1831, John Gibbs, a free black man, appealed to William Sharkey, the chief justice of Mississippi's highest court. He had been arrested as a runaway, but "says on the contrary that he is a free man and entitled to his liberty," and therefore requested a writ of habeas corpus. Sharkey heard the testimony of the jailer who brought him in as a runaway. When no owner came forward, he ruled that Gibbs was "a free man of color and illegally detained in custody," ordering his release. Such a plight was sadly familiar for Gibbs, who had been held in jail at Louisville, Kentucky, for two years before being ruled free.[87]

Local authorities vigorously enforced Mississippi's slave code as a means of reasserting control over the state's black population. In order to retain a liquor license, grogshop owners swore in "that I will not retail, sale or barter or cause or allow to be retailed sold or bartered in my house or establishment at Washington, spiritous liquors of any kind whatsoever to any slave or slaves, except by the permission given verbally or in writing of the master owner or overseer of such slave or slaves."[88] Such restrictions were the start of a long line of alcohol restrictions designed to regulate the behavior of blacks in Mississippi.

Denying strong drinks to slaves was one matter. Running off free blacks was another. Yet after 1831, being free and black in Mississippi had become illegal. Following the trend of other states which had banned free blacks from within their borders, Mississippi passed an ordinance in December 1831 that required free blacks to "remove and quit the state." Free blacks who wished to remain in Mississippi were required to apply for a license at the local court.[89] This law was adopted in reaction to the Nat Turner insurrection, when Mississippians, along with many other southerners, turned on the presence of free blacks, "whose 'locomotive habits fit them for a dangerous *agency* in schemes wild and visionary but disquieting and annoying.'" The weekly *Natchez* argued that rather than strictly enforcing existing law, Mississippi should "strike still deeper, we would not only prevent their future emigration to Mississippi, but *compel* the removal of every negro now free."[90] The legislature was quick to oblige.

Such hasty action, which restricted Mississippi's free blacks in light of a slave uprising elsewhere, betrayed white fears that, if there was a source of social instability, free blacks were that source. Legislators were confident that slavery effectively kept its subjects under control, thus any response to the Turner insurrection properly restricted the free black population.[91]

In accordance with the new law, the constable of Warren County prosecuted free blacks such as Adam Thompson and Isaac Rogers for the crime of "being in the State of Mississippi."[92] Both acquired writs of habeas corpus for their release, but probably ended up leaving the state. The few free blacks who remained in the state did so with the aid of white friends, and they always risked expulsion. Others "benefitted" from the efforts of the Mississippi Colonization Society.[93]

The adoption of the ban on free blacks in 1831 suggests that the temperature of race relations was beginning to rise following the Nat Turner insurrection in Virginia. The 1831 Turner uprising is considered the turning point at which race relations began to grow harsher and southern politics began to grow more radical.[94] In its wake, Mississippians did not immediately give up on their legal institutions as effective methods of social control for a slave society. It was true, the *Vicksburg Register* stated, that "we repose on a volcano." Rather than making calls to extralegal activity, the *Register* called for "a strict and energetic police, and an efficient organization of the militia," vigilant but legal measures to ensure that the "volcano" did not erupt.[95] The *Register*'s use of the term "police," which at the time suggested the preservation of public order (rather than a law enforcement organization), indicates a desire to avoid the kind of turmoil that might follow the discovery of a slave uprising.[96] Other newspapers never reported on the Turner uprising, only alluding to it when calling for new laws.[97]

Mississippians continued to rely on courts and law enforcement to handle routine matters such as the disposition of runaways. A free black man such as John Gibbs could still get justice a year before the legislature made his very presence in the state illegal. A wrongly enslaved child, believed "to be the issue of white parents," could by legislative fiat be emancipated. The child, Indiana Osborne, once emancipated was "invested with all the rights, privileges, and immunities of any other free white female in this state."[98] Although in a short period of time Mississippi would question the ability of the courts to maintain the racial order, its earliest response to stories of the Virginia uprising relied on its legal machinery to control the activities of slaves and free blacks.[99]

The murder of Joel Cameron and the ensuing trial was a case in point. On May 5, 1832, three Warren County slaves, Daniel, Job, and Edmund, assaulted their master, Joel Cameron, with a club, killing him. Rather than a summary execution at the hands of a vigilance committee, the county attorney prosecuted the three slaves for murder and gave them a trial. Such a move suggests a faith in a public order that could control the most violent of slaves, a faith that is even more surprising in light of the charge that another slave, Sam, "did voluntarily, maliciously and feloniously maintain and advise and assist" the murderers, making him an accessory.[100] In more hysterical times and even under existing law, such acts could be interpreted as evidence of conspiracy. Whether it was a conspiracy to murder or to insurrection, the legal consequences were the same. The Warren County courts gave the slaves a jury trial, which methodically convicted and condemned the slaves according to the letter and spirit of the law. Prosecutors did not allege conspiracy, and Vicksburg did not burst into hysteria. Indeed, owing to the support of the jurors "as well as many other respectable citizens," Sam received a pardon from Governor A. M. Scott.[101] Mississippians did not view the Turner uprising as an immediate threat, and thus made few changes in their own slave regime.

A great deal of this sense of security among the white population may have stemmed from a pattern among large planters to present themselves to slaves as a friend in a high place. The assertion was most commonly made as planters intervened between slaves and overseers. Overseers weighed the cotton and chastised slaves who had not picked enough. They meted out punishments even if the planter determined what that punishment was. Often the overseer handled the work of monitoring slave religious meetings. In performing these duties, the overseer's job was to do the planter's dirty work. The planter's image may well have been quite positive in the slave quarters when considered alongside that of the overseer. Slaves commonly welcomed absentee planters visiting the plantation from their homes. Those who did not work under the direct supervision of their masters turned to them for help when conditions became unbearable.[102] Large planters encouraged the development of adversarial, even hostile, relations between overseers and slaves. One overseer's instructions read, "your experience & good sense has taught you that familiarity with slaves will not do, an overseer ought to have but little conversations with negroes under his care & that only to tell them what to do & then see that it is obeyed[.]"[103]

Planters encouraged such tense relations, but in most circumstances the overseer did little more than their planters' bidding. Indeed, overseers kept their employers well informed of events on their plantations. An overseer who reported a low crop return explained, "I have pushed the hands harde[r] and later and they cannot get weight[.] William is runaway."[104] Thomas Adams, a longtime overseer for J. L. Trask, reported on plantation operations regularly. When, for instance, two slaves had run away, Adams wrote to advise, "I think you had better advertise them as you can write better than I can."[105] Usually, Adams's reports to Trask were rather mundane dispatches, only occasionally reporting excitement, such as in April 1830, when the slave Bill "lost the skift [sic] and all of the cotton seeds" at the beginning of planting season. The current pulled the boat under, and Bill fortunately "got on a log and floated to shore."[106] Most dispatches reported normal operations, how much cotton each slave picked, the gin's operation, and conflicts with neighbors.[107] They illustrate that absentee planters knew very well what happened at their plantations.

By creating a circumstance in which the slaves felt there was some degree of justice on plantations—determined, as it was, by their masters—the planters established a sense of security for themselves. Dissatisfied slaves, they figured, would come to their owners for help. At the very worst, they might turn on a particularly cruel overseer, perhaps even a master such as Joel Cameron. There was little chance of their turning on the entire white population. After all, the masters thought, they had positioned themselves as a friend in a high place. Indeed, the swift justice handed out to rebels such as those who killed Cameron demonstrated the futility of more violent dissent. To create a sense among the slaves that there existed a certain system of justice, masters relied upon the state to control the slaves. Slaves played the system to their advantage, when they could, not necessarily because they freely accepted the masters' system of justice, but because the only other option seemed to be a more brutal and chaotic brand of domination.

The acquisition of the "right" slave for housework often made the purchase experience of the house slave as demeaning as that of any other slave bought and sold. Planters commonly tried out cooks, maids, and valets before finalizing the transaction.[108] Masters seemed oblivious to the effect that such transactions might have. Such erratic personnel changes must have been most disturbing to the slaves involved.

Even though planters wealthy enough to own personal slaves to serve as cooks, valets, and coachmen purchased and sold them as regularly as they did field hands, they placed a premium on such skilled and trusted slaves. Joseph Ingraham observed a sense of elitism among coachmen at a slave sale in Natchez. The slave coachmen were discussing the bondsman who was about to be sold. One denied knowing him, saying, "he field nigger; I nebber has no 'quaintance wid dat class," but predicted the slave would go for five hundred dollars, having been purchased for seven hundred himself.

The second slave, with "a contemptuous glance," responded that he went for eight hundred fifty dollars, adding, "I tink dat you was more 'spectable" than that. When the field hand sold for seven hundred, the first coachman "consoled himself with the reflection that the buyer was 'a man what made no more dan tirty bale cotton; while my master make tree hun'red, and on[e] of de firs' gemmans too'!" Ingraham wondered at the slaves, "one, proud that his chain weighs down a few more gold pieces than that of his fellow, while the latter in no less degree mortified at the deficiency in weight of his own."[109]

Even such exaggerations suggest that the planters who owned such valued slaves imparted their sense of superiority to them. The workload of a coachman, a valet, or even a cook was much lighter than the labor required of field hands, reinforcing such self-perceptions. As the price of slaves skyrocketed in the early 1830s owing to the increasing price of cotton, the price of personal servants as well as skilled mechanics went up proportionately. Ingraham reported that body servants went for one thousand dollars, and "good mechanics sometimes sell for two thousand dollars, and seldom less than nine hundred."[110] Still, their status did not always confer security.

This system of plantation control, however disingenuous, seemed an ideal arrangement to the planters. The planters continued as usual, having their overseers do the dirty work of management while their slaves tended the drudgery of staple production. The bond between master and slave was quite limited, and often not even extended to the supposedly favored house slaves who tended to the personal needs of the family. Indeed, house slaves often faced the same kind of degradation that most other slaves faced.

Mississippi's use of a formal legal system for restricting race relations should not lead to the conclusion that the slaves had access to a just system. The fact that planters often intervened underscored how erratic the system truly was. It does reflect an absence of hysterical behavior concerning black-on-white crime. Mississippi residents felt confident that a proper enforcement of racial restrictions would prevent possible insurrections.[111]

The faith that white Mississippians had in their systems of law and of slavery to keep the peace rested on the fact that they had no reason to believe either would fail. Nat Turner led an insurrection in Virginia, they thought, because of some flaw in Virginia's legal or racial codes, and perhaps the existence of a large free black population. White Mississippians detected no such shortcoming in their system. The few free blacks in Mississippi were being run off in short order. Throughout the early 1830s, white opinions about slaves and slavery remained much the same. Mississippians made it quite clear in their speeches, correspondence, and even business decisions that slavery was a necessary evil on the one hand, and a chiefly economic system on the other. Sargent S. Prentiss was sincere when he wrote to his family in Maine in 1831 that "slavery is a great evil," but "a necessary evil."[112] This necessity was rooted in economic growth, and in the planter desire to maintain social order in a biracial society. It was no time for hysteria, or radicalism, just continued vigilance. Such a calm and reasoned reaction to the violence at Southampton, Virginia, seems excessively rational for Mississippi, a state whose more recent history has been one of sustained racial hysteria, peppered liberally with violence. The rationality of this response reflects the fact that Mississippi had not seen outright slave insurrection in decades. During those years, both planters and slaves played a role in defining the boundaries of slavery in Mississippi. However, the opening of new Choctaw lands, the Flush Times of the 1830s, and an expansion of the plantation world would all contribute to a transformation of the patterns of interaction between masters and slaves.

Chapter Six

THE TRANSFORMATION OF MISSISSIPPI

You have doubtless your curiosity highly excited concerning the insurrectionary movement in this state. But let me set you entirely at rest by telling you that the times are quite as orderly & peaceable here now as in any community in the U. States. It is true, that an insurrection was projected, fairly detected, and the leading characters, both white and black taken up and tried before a selected committee of thirteen men, including a chairman, condemned & hung—in all I know not how many.

— James Slade to William Slade, August 22, 1835,
William Slade Papers, Box 2, Perkins Library, Duke University

The spectre of Negro rebellion presented an appalling world turned upside down, a crazy nonsense world of black over white, an anti-community which was the direct negation of the community as white men knew it.

—Winthrop Jordan, 1968, *White Over Black*, 114

NEW FRONTIERS IN CENTRAL MISSISSIPPI

The twenty-six organized counties in Mississippi's southern half had been relatively densely settled by the late 1820s. While some stretches of wilderness remained, they had become fewer and more distant from one another. The 1822 relocation of the state capital to Jackson, near the geographical center of the state, underscored the state's expansion eastward from the Natchez district. By 1830, Adams County, long the economic and once the political locus of the state, no longer led in cotton production. Mississippi had ceased being merely the Natchez District.

The only limitation on white settlement to the north was the Choctaw and Chickasaw control of the lands. In the early 1830s, the most significant presence was the Choctaw, whose lands bordered on areas of Mississippi settled by whites. The Choctaw had the largest population of any of the "Five Civilized Tribes" of southeastern Indian groups, and they controlled millions of acres in central Mississippi.[1] Their removal would open adjacent lands for settlement by whites and also stand as a victory and an example to other southeastern Indians.

The Choctaw saw their lands taken away from them in a slow process, a series of legitimate and illegitimate treaties, federal and state laws, swindles, and betrayals. Much of the land settled by whites in Mississippi had been expropriated from the Choctaw. However, in these earlier exchanges, the Choctaw preserved their tribal homeland, giving up uninhabited but economically and culturally significant borderlands. They also received something in exchange, whether it was lands, forgiven debts, or cash.[2]

The key to the final removal of the Choctaw was the presence of mixed-blood children. As the first generation reached maturity, they became increasingly problematic. No matter which culture they had been raised in, they held position in both. Such was especially the case with the sons of Choctaw women from powerful matrilineages. A man with one-half, or even one-quarter Choctaw heritage could become a chief, owing to his mother's lineage. Other factors affected who became a chief and who did not; however, some mixed-bloods sought to assimilate the nation into white society. They rejected the traditional subsistence of farming, hunting, and later, herding, to adopt slavery and grow staple crops for the market. The mixed-blood leader Greenwood Leflore owned 250 acres cultivated in cotton; other assimilated Choctaw planters had similarly large places.[3] While only two percent of the Choctaw owned slaves, ninety-four percent of slaveowners in the Choctaw nation had English names, reflecting who among the Choctaw took to slavery.[4] The mixed-bloods' efforts to acculturate the nation implied a willingness to adopt Mississippi's slave system. Despite the efforts of mixed-bloods to assimilate, full-blooded Choctaw traditionalists offered strong resistance.

While the Choctaw debated the virtues of tradition and assimilation, white authorities in the state and national governments looked for ways to obtain their lands "legally." The Indian Removal Act of 1829 empowered the federal government to negotiate or force the removal of all southeastern Indians to a western Indian Territory. Turning up the heat, in 1830 Mississippi extended state sovereignty over the Choctaw.[5] This legislation essentially subjected them to Mississippi law, which would be administered by the state. Choctaw leadership had abandoned the traditional rule of family vengeance in favor of a formal legal system. It is clear that the goal of the law was to dissolve Choctaw sovereignty, and not to foster some sort of acculturation. This extension of sovereignty was a radical change from the previous agreement, which allowed tribal justice to punish Choctaw offenders. Any attempt to challenge the law was a crime.

For the Choctaw, the removal question suddenly became one of how rather than when. The nation could not survive its loss of sovereignty; they would be forced to exchange their homeland for their legal existence. Leflore negotiated a treaty at Dancing Rabbit Creek that probably acquired for the Choctaw the most they could get, including annuities, education funds, removal expenses, as well as lands west of the Mississippi. Leflore profited from this treaty as well, securing more lands for himself and other assimilated mixed-bloods. No leader who signed away his people's homeland could be popular, and Leflore, having come to power by criticizing an earlier treaty, knew that. He resigned as chief and remained in Mississippi, watching his own plantation operation grow prosperously.[6]

The huge cession of land in central Mississippi, as well as that in the north, by the Chickasaws' signing of the treaty of Ponontoc under circumstances similar to the Choctaws', created a vast new frontier. Mississippi had a new region whose lands were ripe for settlement, cotton cultivation, and plantation slavery. Counties that did not even exist in 1830 by mid-decade held sizeable slave majorities.[7] Governments, legal systems, even communities, had not been entirely established; wilderness enveloped the occasional plantation, and bandits roamed the roads and backwoods. Such conditions served to reverse the moderating trends in race relations, as this frontier of previously untilled lands, which would produce huge cotton crops, revived the avarice not seen in Mississippi since the first cotton boom a generation earlier. In such an atmosphere, it is hardly surprising that a small slave conspiracy precipitated a major transformation.

MYTH AND CONSPIRACY: JOHN MURRELL

During the 1830s, an era of anti-masons, anti-papists, and the money power, the fear of conspiracies was common in the United States. Americans seemed to fear all kinds of real and imagined enemies plotting against them.[8] Such fears were more potent in the newly opened regions of central and northern Mississippi. On this new frontier, planters arrived with their communities of slaves and plans to expand the cotton kingdom. Little in the way of a white community existed in the early years of the 1830s, for the arriving planters settled in isolated locales and knew few of their neighbors. Towns such as Livingston, the first center of Madison County, popped up briefly to provide meeting places and opportunities to market cotton, supplies, and newly arrived slaves. After a day's business, the frontiersmen adjourned to camps, or perhaps taverns, and engaged in late-night storytelling. Enough people had been held up or attacked to spin tales of banditry. Virtually overnight, the exaggerated exploits of an outlaw turned folk hero became frontier legend. The growth of mythology on the frontier provided entertainment while reinforcing a sense of caution among the parvenus of the cotton kingdom.[9] This type of concern was in many ways the basis for organizing communities. Yet the fears remained, heightened by racial anxieties of planters who realized they were surrounded by a potential enemy in their slaves. By the mid-1830s, seventy percent of the county's inhabitants were slaves. The racial insecurities of the white settlers could be seen in the claim that there were fifty slaves for every white man in Madison County.[10] In this atmosphere where white Mississippians were concerned over conspiracies, fearing the wilderness, and surrounded by a black majority, a few slaves decided to overthrow their masters and become free.

Madison County, Mississippi, in 1835 stands as an episode where the frontier mythology of the white settlers clashed with their fear of the slave majority and the very real discontentment of their slaves.[11] Central to this incident is a legend loosely based on the actions of John Murrell. This legend found its way into print, giving it a kind of authority not always conferred to the spoken word.[12] It named hundreds of gamblers, swindlers, horse and slave thieves, and others in the margins of society as conspirators. Claiming that a gang of "land pirates," under the leadership of the slave thief Murrell, planned to incite slaves across the South to insurrection, the story went on to explain that the uprising would serve merely as a diversion, allowing the thieves to plunder southern towns and plantations of their wealth.

A brief retelling of the Murrell legend provides us with an account that makes for great storytelling, yet seems quite unlikely. The Tennessee farmer Virgil Stewart published a pamphlet in 1835 claiming to have uncovered the plot during an adventure that began when he left Jackson, Tennessee, searching for a neighbor's runaway or stolen slaves. On the road, Stewart encountered the story's nemesis, John Murrell, who within a short time shared with Stewart his adventures as a highwayman and slave thief. Murrell recounted stories of making a living by killing travelers for their money, and stealing slaves and selling them, only to have them run away to him for resale. In his storytelling, Murrell "appeared to dwell with peculiar and fiendish delight" upon "the same gloomy topics of robbery and murder." Stewart, the whole time, attempted "to keep somewhat in rear of his companion," fearing possible death at Murrell's hands. Meanwhile he claimed to document the discussions by scrawling notes on small slips of paper, his fingernails, hands, and any other place where he might write.[13]

According to Stewart, Murrell had taken to a life of crime as revenge against a justice system that had humiliated him by imprisonment and public whipping. Such humiliation made Murrell "look upon the American people as my common enemy. They have disgraced me, and they can do no more." He intended to spend the remainder of his life "as their devoted enemy." Convinced that Stewart was a kindred villain, Murrell recruited him for his band of thieves and promised to fill him in on their scheme and induct him into the group.[14]

The land pirate's word alone was hardly enough to convince Stewart, much less his readers, of Murrell's honor among thieves. As the two men approached a slave, Murrell demonstrated his ability to recruit partners in crime from the slave quarters. The fictional interchange illustrates the racial fears on which Stewart played as he concocted his story:

> Murel. *Well old man, you must have a d——d hard master, or he would not send you to the mill this cold day.*
> Negro. *Yes, maser, all of um hard in dis country.*
> Murel. *Why do you stay with the d——d villain, then, when he treats you like a d——d dog?*
> Negro. *I can't help um, maser.*

Here, we see Murrell treating the slave as an equal upon first contact. He sympathized with the slave's hard lot, and suggested that the slave might exercise his will to change his life. Next, Murrell recommended a way for the slave to help himself and Murrell:

> Murel. *Would you help it if you could?*
> Negro. *Oh! yes, maser, dat I would.*

> Murel. *What is your name, old man?*
> Negro. *My name?——Clitto, maser.*
> Murel. *Well, Clitto, would you like to be free and have plenty of money to buy land and horses and everything you want?*
> Clitto. *O! yes maser, dat Clitto so want um.*
> Murel. *If I will steal you, and carry you off, and sell you four or five times, and give you half of the money, and then leave you in a free state, will you go?*
> Clitto. *O! yes, maser, Clitto go quick.*

In telling this section of the story, Stewart attempted to portray Murrell, for southern audiences, as a fundamental threat to white society. Murrell encouraged the slave, portrayed in racial stereotype, to take control of his own life by putting an end to the hard life of bondage. In response, Clitto expressed a desire to free himself. Murrell then proposed a plan of action for the slave to free himself where both would profit by defying the social mores of the South. The next portion of this fictional conversation suggests Stewart's primary goal was to write a terrifying tale, for it portrays Murrell challenging all social conventions.

> Murel. *Well, Clitto, don't you want a dram? (taking out his flask of liquor and offering to Clitto.)*
> Clitto. *Thankey, master, arter you.*
> Murel. *O! no, Clitto, after you. (Clitto drinks, and then Murel after him.)*
> Murel. *Well, Clitto, have you no boys that you would like to see free.*
> Clitto. *O! yes, maser.*
> Murel. *Now, Clitto, if you was to hear a pistol fired at the head of the lane some night, do you think you will be sure to come to me, and bring three or four boys with you?*
> Clitto. *O! yes maser, Clitto come this night.*
> Murel. *I am in a hurry now, Clitto, and cannot carry you off at this time; but you have the boys ready, and you shall not be with your d——d old task master much longer, to be cuffed about like a dog. I am a great friend to black people. I have carried off a great many, and they are doing well—all got homes of their own, and [are] making property—you look out, and when you hear the pistol fire, come with the boys and I will have horses ready to push you. Good bye, Clitto, until I see you again.*[15]

As presented in the story, Stewart's Murrell was a dangerous radical, one who reversed southern social conventions, *and* professed his friendship with slaves. Having been stripped of his honor by society, he now rejected its definition of honorable behavior. Murrell drank with a slave he did not own, a violation of the law and the social code of the South. Many southerners believed alcohol was a source of trouble among slaves. Slaves whose inhibitions and rage had been loosened by liquor, southern whites believed, might show disrespect, fight, or worse yet, rebel.[16] Indeed, Murrell insisted over Clitto's objections that Clitto drink before him from his flask. This expression of equality, and even deference, by a white man for a slave was just the sort of trouble that the social conventions Murrell flaunted were intended to prevent. After this exercise of establishing a familiarity, even an equality, with a slave, Murrell pronounced himself a "great friend to black people." Most readers of the story would understand this incident as a kind of exaggeration of the Murrell character: a slave thief who fraternized with the slaves. In almost any other context, except one in which planters felt outnumbered and vulnerable, the description of Murrell would be understood as an illustration of his badness but hardly as a threat to their survival.[17]

Having "proven" Murrell, for the sake of his story, a ruthless villain, Stewart continued, describing Murrell's plan. The outlaw planned to canvass the region to gain widespread support among the slave population. "The grand object," he explained, was "to excite a rebellion among the negroes of the slaveholding states." The rebellion taking place every where at the same time" would mobilize the defense of the planters, but since "many places will be entirely overrun by the negroes," the white South would withdraw into a defensive position. As patrols and militias organized and then fought insurgent slaves, Murrell and his men would have a window of opportunity to plunder the towns and plantations of their wealth.

While insurrection and plunder were the end goal, the gang first had to organize their plan with a network of supporters. Murrell wanted to "find the most vicious and wicked disposed" slaves on the large plantations. He or one of his men would then "poison their minds by telling them how they are mistreated, and that they are entitled to their freedom as much as their masters, and that all of the wealth of the country is the proceeds of black people's labor; we remind them of the pomp and splendor of their masters, and then refer them to their own degraded situation, and tell them that it is power and tyranny which rivets their chains of bondage, and not because they are an inferior race of people."[18]

In this summary of his organizational plan, Murrell, as reported by Stewart, touched on perhaps every fear possibly conceived by slaveholding southerners. First, the gang's slave contacts were to be the most prone to rebellion. Then, to touch on the class consciousness of the planters, he suggested that power, and not race, put the slaves in their position. Offering this summary of the position of the slaves to a potential rebel was anathema to everything the slave South stood for.[19] As with the conversation with Clitto, these comments served to reinforce the storyline of Murrell as a bad man. There had been concerns of abolitionists who said the same kinds of things about slaves, so why not portray a land pirate telling the slaves the same thing William Lloyd Garrison would if given a chance? Murrell is a kind of trickster, presented as a subversive or even countercultural figure, not a genuine threat but a heel in a melodramatic tale.[20]

To explain why Murrell's plans had not been discovered, Stewart depicted Murrell's efforts to maintain secrecy when recruiting his slave representatives. First, the gang would swear each slave accomplice to secrecy and then explain the plan. Murrell's gang developed "a long ceremony for the oath, which is administered in the presence of a terrific picture painted for the purpose, representing the monster who is to deal with him should he prove unfaithful in the engagements he has entered into."[21] They would then give him instructions, including a speech to their fellow slaves, which told them "how successful the West India negroes have been in gaining their freedom by frequent rebellions."[22] This swearing of secrecy in an elaborate ritual where moral vengeance is threatened for those who betray their obligations bears a striking resemblance to the popular images of the Masonic lodge.[23] Ritualistic mystery added one more element to play on the most current fears of his audience. In addition, at least some whites in Mississippi must have been aware of the secret gatherings slaves held late at night, propagating their Afro-Christian faith, and perhaps continuing West African traditions of initiation into secret societies.[24]

The gang was to incite rebellion on Christmas night of 1835. With discipline loosened over the holidays, slave populations could be called together with ease. Slave leaders, with money provided by the gang, would "procure spirits to give them a few drams," and once intoxicated, call them to fight for their liberty. Here again, Stewart played on the white fear of the intoxicated slave, for apparently southern whites deemed sober slaves less likely to rebel. The insurgents would use a few stockpiled guns, as well as clubs, axes, knives, and whatever else was handy to kill planter families in the night "when all are sleeping."[25]

Completing his fictional initiation into the world of frontier crime, Stewart described Murrell leading him into a swampy area in western Arkansas. Murrell introduced and recommended Stewart to the gang, making a speech on his behalf. After Murrell's introduction, the "counsellors" approached and introduced themselves, then "gave him the two degrees, and the signs by which they were distinguished."[26] The story of a conspiracy shrouded in mystery captured and at the same time lampooned all the fears of Americans on the frontier. Murrell's clan, as they called themselves, was a mysterious organization distinguished by signs and secret handshakes. This group consisted of social outcasts, mainly highwaymen and thieves, loners who had no roots. Unnamed outsiders, whether frontier scoundrels, Masons, or foreigners, terrified Americans, for they had no commitment to the larger society and did not share its values. On the frontier, where there was little sense of community, only shared values could unite planter society, which made the possibility of renegades in their midst sufficiently disturbing.[27]

Thanks to Stewart's efforts, a court imprisoned Murrell in Tennessee. Stewart's testimony convinced a jury to convict Murrell for slave-stealing. His self-promotion through the sale of his book on Murrell prevented the fear of such an insurrection from fading quietly.

Slave Conspiracy in Madison County

Planters unlikely to share the news of Nat Turner with the slaves were equally unlikely to tell them the story of John Murrell. The villain Murrell would be a hero to the slaves, which is perhaps the appeal of the story in white society. It seems unlikely that the story was told to be believed. Murrell had been convicted for theft, not conspiracy. Even so, in the isolated hills of the Choctaw cession, the rumors of a slave thief inciting rebellion surely kept some awake late at night. By June 1835, the fears about the story had reached a boiling point in Madison County, Mississippi. Stewart had recently traveled through the neighborhood selling his pamphlet.[28]

Outnumbered by discontented and uprooted slaves, planters certainly had something to fear. All planters knew that their slaves were unhappy, yet they punished slaves who expressed discontent. In response, slaves learned to express a kind of deference, hiding their true feelings behind a smiling face. Their expressions of discontent were reserved to moments not often recorded. When alone, the slaves in Mississippi discussed their unhappiness, and occasionally plotted to bring it to an end. A planter's widow overheard some of these conversations, and the planters of Madison County who investigated her report erroneously associated these slaves with Stewart's rumor.

Slavery and Frontier Mississippi

In late June 1835, the widowed mistress of the Latham plantation at Beattie's Bluff, on the Big Black River, overheard the discussions of her slaves concerning their plan. Hearing a "house-girl" ask, "is it not a pity to kill such * * * *?" piqued the woman's interest. A man's voice responded "that it was, but it must be done, and that it would be doing a great favour, as it would go to heaven, and escape the troubles of this world." Filled with terror, the woman told her son, who questioned the slave girl. Thinking "all of it was overheard," the girl recounted the conversation, completing, for the record, her question: "Is it not a pity to kill such a pretty little creature as this?" referring to the child in her care. Even more frightening was the slave girl's statement that there was to be an insurrection and that the slaves "intended killing all the whites." When examined, the other household servants admitted knowledge of the conspiracy.[29]

A vigilance committee convened at Livingston and began examining slaves implicated in this plan. Initial questioning of a slave belonging to William P. Johnson turned up no white men in the planning of this insurrection. It seems unlikely that Johnson's slave knew of any involvement of whites, for his interrogators chastised him severely, yet were unable to even feed such a confession to him.[30] His interrogation did reveal that the plan "was confined to the negroes of a few plantations, and principally within the knowledge of *negro preachers* (generally considered to be the greatest scoundrels among negroes), who were supposed to be the originators of it, as has been the case in all negro conspiracies."[31]

The initial findings of this committee are telling. The report made no effort to hide that the slaves were coaxed with the lash to answer their questions. While the planters on the committee attempted to find white instigators, thereby linking the plot to Stewart's claims, the first interrogation turned up no white men. Under the lash, the slave recalled that slave ministers were the originators of the plan. In its report, the committee made two revealing comments about slave ministers. First, the report characterized slave preachers as scoundrels, no doubt because they had the power and influence among the slaves that, from a white point of view, only a master should have. Also, the committee's statement that preachers were always responsible for the slave insurrection plans indicates that the committee expected to hear confirmation.[32] The existence of an insurrection plan is likely; that slave preachers led it is less certain.

These initial interrogations set the stage for a larger round of vigilance committee meetings. Planter Jesse Mabry led the interrogation, and his version tells of a brutal process of interrogation and punishment. The slaves' confessions suggest that at least some of the answers were the product of leading questions and harsh whippings. Following a lead offered by two female slaves, Mabry questioned Joe, who reportedly spoke of the conspiracy. After initial denials of any knowledge, Mabry "called for a rope, and tied his hands," threatening Joe and possibly punishing him. Joe agreed to talk if Mabry would not punish him. "He said he knew what we wanted, and would tell the whole, but that he himself had nothing to do with the business." Joe apparently knew exactly what the committee wanted, for he told of speaking with Mabry's slave, Sam, who informed him that the slaves would "rise and kill all the whites on the 4th, and that they had a number of white men at their head." They would march south, recruiting more slaves and killing whites as they went.[33]

The next day, Mabry examined Jim, a slave belonging to a Mr. Saunders. Mabry wrote that Jim "would not, for some time, make any confession; but at length agreed that, if I would not punish him any more, he would make a full confession, and proceeded to do so."[34] On the interrogations went, each slave initially denying any knowledge, then changing his mind as examiners threatened further physical punishment. One can visualize, in reading this account, initially defiant men reduced to quivering masses, begging for mercy and promising to tell the inquisitor whatever he wanted to hear.

Because Mabry's letter provokes such imagery in the mind's eye, the critic is forced to question the validity of the testimony. It is difficult to tell which answers originated with the slaves and which answers were fed to them, much less the extent of the slaves' discussions of rising up in rebellion. Jim's testimony "that it was their intention to slay all the whites, except some of the most beautiful women, whom they intended to keep as wives" suggests that the slaves had discussed some kind of plan. Jim's explanation that "he and his wife had already had a quarrel in consequence of his having told her his intentions" indicates the possibility that the statement originated from him.[35] To consider the possibility that interrogators wanted to hear this testimony, and drew it out of Jim, we must also consider the possibility Jim initiated the statement himself. Perhaps he knew that the planters were not going to spare any lives and decided that his testimony would touch on their greatest fear. Perhaps the conversations he described did occur. If he did quarrel with his wife over the matter, then the conspiracy was indeed widespread: here was a man and woman debating the future of their marriage once their enslavement was over.[36]

Nonetheless, the testimony convinced the committee. Following "two days of patient and scrutinizing examination of the negroes implicated at Beattie's Bluff," the committee reported that "their guilt was fully established, not only by their own confessions, but by other facts and circumstances, which could leave no doubt on the mind." The committee painstakingly questioned each slave, "separate and apart from the rest, neither knowing that another was suspected or in custody" but all "implicating the same *white men*, and the whole of their statements coinciding precisely with each other."[37] The men on the committee uncovered their evidence easily, for they knew what they had been looking for all along.

The statements taken in this second round of interrogations are less reliable than the initial statements. First, they began to implicate white men. The initial witness refused to do so, even under duress as indicated in the committee report. The interrogators preferred to extract confessions implicating white men, for they would be able to sleep better knowing that the slave population was content as long as white troublemakers stayed away. Assertions that their statements "precisely" coincided with each other, even though their interrogations were separate, suggest that the inquisitors asked leading questions. Once on this track, the examining committee found evidence to prove their suspicions, evidence that was in total agreement, and evidence that conformed to the Murrell story.

Frontier Hysteria

Having determined the specifics of the plan and identified the principal instigators, the vigilance committee's next obligation was to administer punishments. Questions rose concerning the possibility that "the laws were incompetent to reach their case" because the courts did not recognize slave testimony, forming a crack in white Mississippi's previously unchallenged faith in their legal system's ability to control slaves.[38] The committee called a town meeting in Livingston, which in turn "chose from among the assemblage thirteen of their fellow-citizens, who were immediately organized, and styled a 'Committee of Safety.' "[39] On Independence Day, the citizens hanged the two supposed white leaders of the uprising, steam doctors Joshua Cotton and William Saunders, "at the side of the old jail, suspended from the grating of the window."[40] Nine slaves also died on the Fourth. At the makeshift gallows, apparently hoping to either buy some time or instill fear

The Transformation of Mississippi

in the citizens, Cotton confessed that he was in league with Murrell and named several other steam doctors involved.[41]

News of Cotton's confession, the conspiracy, and the vigilance committee contributed to a general sense of hysteria in Madison County. It was almost as though white settlers were looking for a reason to lay down the law, a new law in which the slaves would not only be subordinate, but utterly subject. One resident wrote that "on the third and fourth the excitement exceeded anything I ever saw." The Columbus, Mississippi, *Press* declared that "a deeper laid scheme of villainy, was never brought to light.... Language fails to express the indignation, the horror, with which we must look upon such fiends [i.e. white instigators], for men they can hardly be called." Governor Hiram Runnells issued a proclamation calling on Mississippians to organize militia patrols to restore order.[42] Other localities formed vigilance committees of their own.

The punishments continued in and around Livingston. On July 6th, Livingstonians, before banishing two white men, aged 72 and 60, administered, respectively 50 and 150 lashes in a procedure called "slicking." The victim of this practice was tied to four pegs on the ground and "received the stripes from different hands."[43] In Clinton, Mississippi, Vincent, a mulatto slave, was hanged by the local committee of vigilance after a crowd of citizens demanded that the whipping prescribed by the committee was not sufficient punishment.[44] Several towns along the river killed or banished gamblers and other outlaws.[45] Of the ten white men implicated at Madison, only two escaped with their lives.[46] The sources give rough estimates of the slave body count, as between ten and twenty hanged.

The reaction to the discovery of the slave plot and Cotton's confessions seem outsized. In response to the alleged conspiracy, virtually every town in the neighborhood publicly whipped or executed potential threats. This type of upheaval is more common among underclasses lashing out at elites than vice versa. Yet Madison County barely had an elite. The white settlers, because of their isolation, their sense of being outnumbered, and their thorough awareness of the hard lot their slaves faced, saw a real threat in the Murrell story. Even as the slaves in late-night conversations discussed overthrowing the masters, planters anticipated with great fear the moment when they discovered who might be inciting the slaves to insurrection. They lashed out in a rebellion of their own, but they were not turning the social order over, rather they were shoring it up, and expanding it deeper into the wilderness.[47] In doing so, they crushed the older appearances of stability favored by the Natchez elite, revealing their fears, and acting on them. A new, more reactionary pattern of keeping order would emerge, one that by its violence reflected fear and insecurity rather than stability. However, the newly formed elite would continue to think themselves a continuation of the planter society established by the nabobs in Natchez. They considered themselves upper crust and, upon attaining a level of prosperity, would surround themselves in plantation luxury. A visitor to Livingston only a few weeks after the uprising observed Stewart's newly celebrated status. While still "attended with armed friends wherever he goes," Stewart was nonetheless "complemented with dinner and balls in every town."[48] The newly formed high society of central Mississippi had already found its first dignitary.

TRANSFORMATIONS

The reverberations of this affair on Mississippi's society were long lasting and significant. During the 1830s, the entire South began to reassess slavery, attempting to resolve the dilemma of enslaving an entire segment of its population in an institution it regarded as evil. Various events, from Nat Turner's insurrection and the nullification crisis to the emergence of the abolitionist movement, put southerners on notice that, if slavery was an evil institution and they did nothing to ameliorate it, internal strife or external interference would bring about some sort of change. The South, consciously or not, reexamined its stance on slavery in the 1830s, redefining slavery in moral terms that southerners could abide.

In this context, the slave conspiracy, combined with the Murrell rumor, precipitated Mississippi's participation in the regional transformation, involving wholesale changes in attitude and in law concerning slavery in Mississippi. In reassessing their position on slavery, Mississippians followed a pattern of response to social instabilities. Nonetheless, they responded to events on their own soil in ways that they had not responded to previous crises in other states.

Among the first to react to this incident were Mississippi's white evangelical Christians. One of the storm centers of hysteria, Clinton, held a public meeting that declared slavery "a blessing both to master and slave," and called on clergy in Mississippi "to take a stand upon this subject, and that their further silence in relation thereto, at this crisis, will in our opinion, be subject to serious censure."[49] Evangelical ministers, who had waffled on slavery for a decade, now took a stand in its support. The evangelical acceptance of such demands resulted in a "sanctification" of slavery.[50]

The shift in opinion toward slavery is visible in the opinions of Mississippi's public officials as well. As late as 1831, the Whig politician Sargent S. Prentiss had been critical of slavery, characterizing it as an evil, however necessary. Recounting the hysteria in 1835, Prentiss backed away from the "necessary evil" justification, defended the mob hysteria, and stated that the conspiracy's suppression "ought certainly to serve as a warning to the abolitionists, not only of their own danger but of the great injury they are doing to the slaves themselves."[51] At the next legislative session, Prentiss would take a leading role in condemning abolitionists and defending slavery.

Mississippi even began to rename landmarks in ways that suggested a new attitude regarding slavery. The slave market outside Natchez, established in 1834, initially bore the name "niggerville," a name derogatorily descriptive of the business undertaken there, but a strikingly unusual name for Natchez, a town dominated by the state's genteel elite. Yet shortly after opening, the market took on a new identity taken from the description on the land title: Forks of the Road.[52]

Such transformations in opinion, while significant, gain greater power when they enter the realm of public discourse and policy. The calm and reasoned reactions of the society carry more weight than private correspondence or even hangings, and are less likely to be reconsidered. Indeed, the reasoned, official, and public response to this affair represents the sober second thoughts of Mississippi's society on this insurrection, and its relation to slavery.

In his message for the legislative session beginning in January 1836, the first such assembly to follow the July affair, Acting Governor John Quitman raised this uprising, and the associated issue of slavery, as an important question requiring official resolution. Quitman, like Prentiss and many others in the state, blamed the uprising on the rhetoric of the emerging abolitionist movement in northern states.[53] While he noted that Mississippians "feel confident of the ready means we possess, of suppressing insurrection," he believed that "we cannot be insensible to the fact, that such unhallowed interference may . . . produce partial scenes of violence and bloodshed." Such agitation had already "disturbed the public tranquility, subjected the master to the care and anxiety of stricter vigilance, and induced a curtailment of the innocent enjoyment of the slave."

More important than assigning blame, Quitman's message virtually framed the question that Mississippians faced in the wake of the insurrection.

"The morality, the expediency, and the duration of the institution of slavery," he stated, "are questions, which belong exclusively to ourselves."[54] In announcing that such questions need be addressed by Mississippians (and only Mississippians), Quitman implicitly called on the legislature to address these questions as well. No longer was the view of slavery as a necessary evil the accepted canon; change was at hand. The governor's call for a resolution asking free states to suppress the activities of abolitionists seems only a secondary consideration to his reassessment of the morality of slavery.

The legislative reports accompanying the requested resolutions reveal a transformation in thought about slavery in Mississippi. The Senate report decried the abolitionists' "injustice of demanding our surrender of this right [of slavery], and that too without compensation." Northern reformers, the committee said, "assume first—that slavery is a sin against heaven," and on that basis claim "a right or obligation . . . to wrest from us as morally contraband, this species of property." The committee report continued, "the issue . . . thusly presented, is utterly false." In no uncertain terms, the report stated that "it is a question exclusively with ourselves," and as such, no answer need even be mentioned.[55] The committee report from the House echoed that from the Senate, asserting that "our institutions are our own, and so long as we see fit to continue them, we recognize the right of no power or person on earth to interfere in any manner with them."[56] The transition was complete. This portrayal of slavery as a right, and one having no moral consequences, sharply contrasts with a joint resolution adopted by the General Assembly a decade earlier declaring that "however great may be the national evil of slavery and however much we may regret it, circumstances over which we have no control have rendered it inevitable."[57]

In the light of such changes in attitude, the law of slavery did not go untouched. As Quitman had mentioned, planters had taken it upon themselves to become more vigilant. Localities adopted stricter codes concerning slave activity as well. The town of Woodville restricted slaves from making Sunday visits to town in 1836.[58] The Mississippi legislature also established separate criminal courts "for the trial of slaves and free persons of color" in each county.[59] In an effort to get slaveowners to take responsibility for the actions of their chattel, the House declined to pay for executed slaves.[60]

In 1837, Mississippi undertook an even more significant revision of the slave code. The constitution of 1832 had prohibited the introduction of slaves into the state for the purpose of sale. This prohibition was intended at the time to limit the expansion of slavery, still considered a necessary evil. The ban lost its teeth in a United States Supreme Court decision that required enabling legislation to enforce it.[61]

In 1837, the legislature revisited the issue by passing a law banning the import of slaves as merchandise. The revised prohibition was not a recognition that slavery was an evil, but an indication that Mississippians located the source of slave disturbances outside their "native" slave population. Governor Charles Lynch felt that the "experiment ... has not been fully and fairly made." He called on the legislature to act, for as long as they did not, "there exists no penalty to be enforced," suggesting that such importations, to his mind, posed a genuine threat.[62] At the special session of the Mississippi legislature held in spring of 1837, both houses passed, with little fanfare, Section 89 of the Mississippi slave code, banning "the business of introducing or importing slaves into this state as merchandise." The legislature required that four newspapers publish the new legislation during the weeks following its passage, no doubt to ensure that ignorance of the law would not be a defense.[63]

The effectiveness of this law is no doubt questionable. As the slave population grew at a rate of over ten thousand slaves a year during the 1830s, it seems unlikely that slave merchants had no hand in this growth after 1837.[64] Natchez planters often circumvented the ban by purchasing slaves across the Mississippi River at Vidalia. Such activity was hardly called for, as the Natchez slave market at Forks of the Road continued its thriving business. Nonetheless, owing to this ban, the leading slave-trading firm in the Natchez area, Franklin & Armfield, liquidated their partnership.[65] While this law was honored only in the breach, it reflects an attempt among Mississippi's white elites to shield their slave population from the ideas of potentially rebellious slaves imported from other states.

These varying manifestations of a social softening accompanying a legal hardening of slavery together illustrate the emergence of slavery in its mature, late antebellum form. The insurrection's impact on the perception of slavery in Mississippi can be seen throughout white society. This change in perception motivated a change in the reality of slavery in Mississippi. Such changes in opinion and law indicate that the "great reaction," which throughout the South simultaneously tightened the boundaries of slavery and increased the humanitarian interest in slaves' well-being, reached Mississippi in the wake of this affair. As the morality of slavery no longer was even in question—both houses of the legislature in no uncertain terms silenced such concerns—planters began to build a way of life around this institution.

Slavery and Frontier Mississippi

The transformation of Mississippi began as a reaction to the Madison County ordeal, but most of the changes are not direct consequences of the Murrell story or the slave conspiracy. Rather, they reflect the permanency of Mississippi's new attitude toward slavery and toward race. With the passage of time, these new values would inform the actions of most of Mississippi's slaveowners, providing for them, even if not for their slaves, a way to make sense of their world.

Conclusion

Mississippi, the Closed Society

The politicians who enunciated the first defense of a new racial code set the pattern for a new society in Mississippi. Over time Mississippi has been referred to as the "lynching state," the "Magnolia jungle," and the "Closed Society." John Quitman's declaration that Mississippi's internal issues are "questions, which belong exclusively to ourselves," was of course the kind of rhetoric that made him a fire-eater.[1] But the legislature's acceptance of his call to reassess—and ultimately dismiss—the moral consequences of slavery marked a transformation in race relations, the effects of which would be felt for over a century.

The horrors of Madison County were not the last visited on Mississippi owing to white hysteria or black insurrection. They were indeed only the first of many atrocities committed by radical and insecure whites. In the 1840s, whites in Natchez conducted an "Inquisition," punishing its free black population for their own insecurities.[2] And in 1861, Adams County planters interrogated and hanged fifty or more slaves who had plotted an uprising that would aid arriving Union armies.[3] By the Jim Crow era, mob violence against blacks was widely accepted in the white community.[4] Hysteria became a way of life as racial violence became sickeningly commonplace.

When the opportunity arose for courts to reassert some kind of order in Mississippi's society, the results were strangely skewed. In 1851, the murder of William Johnson, a prominent and wealthy free black man from Natchez, demonstrated that race more than wealth or social position defined the place of blacks. His murderer, Baylor Winn, who was suspected of being a mulatto, proved his "whiteness" to the court, immunizing himself from the testimony of black witnesses.[5] But neither blacks nor dissenting whites could be guaranteed justice in Mississippi's courts.[6]

The transformation of Mississippi runs strikingly parallel to events in colonial South Carolina. When slaves in black-majority regions of the colony rose up in rebellion, the whites responded with brutal suppression. They revamped the slave code and established a reactionary social system that had little room for dissent.[7] Virtually every aspect of public and private life in both

Conclusion

states was in some way defined by the racial code. Ultimately, South Carolina and Mississippi were the first and second states to secede in defense of slavery.

Mississippi's transformation to radicalism was not the first change it made. Rather, it was one of the last. In its early generations, Mississippi's slave society had been remarkably flexible. Despite social conventions that divided them, masters and slaves had a shared identity as pioneers. But the nation's westward movement, which included blacks and whites, and the forced emigration of the Choctaw and the Chickasaw from central and northern Mississippi revived a boomtown mentality in Mississippi that fostered the settlement of lands in the entire absence of communities to support the settlers. As slaves developed new communities, their masters, who felt isolated from former homes and other settlements, grew suspicious of all strangers. White strangers and black slaves became targets of scrutiny, and victims of planter fear. Antebellum Mississippians never let go of such suspicion. While our hindsight tells us the ways in which Mississippi's race relations evolved, the outcome was never inevitable.

Appendix A

Slaves Purchased by John Randolph, Charleston, South Carolina, February–March 1830

Name	Age	M/F	Seller
Gllick	27	M	John Ashe
Abigail	34	F	Boyle
Rudy[a]	29	F	Boyle
Harry	18	M	Britton Branch
April	27–30	M	Britton Branch
Bib?	21	M	Bryant Branch
Sarah	35	F	Ann Coburn
Toby	35	M	George Cox
Robert	28	M	George A. Fisher
Jim	26	M	Mrs Fourgeaud
Eve	18	F	J. W. Gray
Susan	40	F	J. W. Gray
Patsy	60	F	J. W. Gray
Adam	20	M	J. W. Gray
Jim	20	F	J. W. Gray
Martha	21	F	Hanahan
Kit	14	M	B. Jenkins
Dryden	14	M	B. Jenkins
Bristo	14	M	B. Jenkins
Abraham	14	M	B. Jenkins
Bass	19	F	Miss Keith
Jenny	17	F	Miss Keith
Abner	26	M	Francis Lance
Susannah	15	F	Peter May

Appendix A

Abraham	@14	M	Hugh McDonald
John	25	M	Hugh McDonald
Caroline[b]	@40	M	Henry O'Hara
Amy	@30	F	Henry O'Hara
Peggy	27	F	Pellay
George	26	M	Pellay
Diana	16	F	Pellay
Sally/Isaac[c]	22	F	Pellay
Brister	40	M	Mrs Rodgers
Charles	@30	M	James Sanford
Harvey	14	M	James Williams

Source: Bills of sale in Slaves & Slavery collection, Natchez Trace Collection, Barker Texas History Center, University of Texas at Austin, Oversize Box 2.325/V48.

a With two children, Phillis and Nancy.
b "African marks on each side of his face."
c Mother & child.

Appendix B

Locust Grove Plantation, ca. 1833

Extended Families and Families with Children

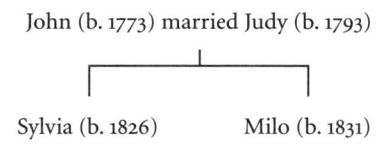

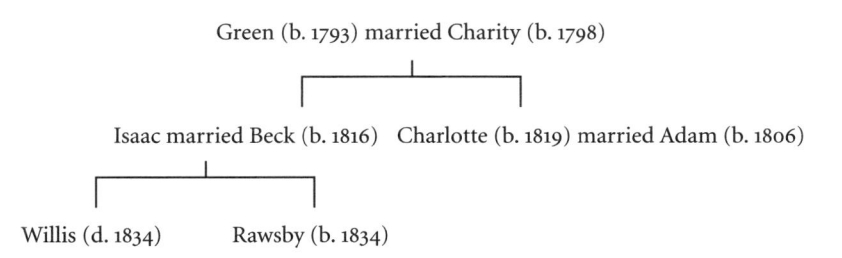

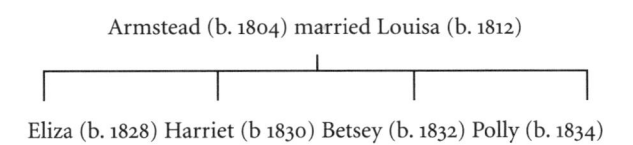

Matt (b. 1808) married Betsy (b. 1808)
|
Adam (b. 1824)

John (b. 1773) married Judy (b. 1793)
|
Sylvia (b. 1826)   Milo (b. 1831)

Green (b. 1793) married Charity (b. 1798)
|
Isaac married Beck (b. 1816)   Charlotte (b. 1819) married Adam (b. 1806)
|
Willis (d. 1834)   Rawsby (b. 1834)

Armstead (b. 1804) married Louisa (b. 1812)
|
Eliza (b. 1828) Harriet (b 1830) Betsey (b. 1832) Polly (b. 1834)

Appendix B

Leven (b. 1806) married Mary (b. 1810)

Sarah Ann (b. 1827) Andrew (b. 1829) Emiline (b. 1831) Pleasant (b. 1833)

(Parents Unknown)

Peter (Jacob) married Peggy (b. 1815)   Kitty (b. 1817) married Tillman

Jack   Tillman (b. 1834)

(Unknown) married Marie (d. 1825)

Henry (b. 1824)   Lewis (b. 1825)

(Unknown) married Easter

Walker (b. 1814) married Elisabeth (b. 1834)   Lewis (b. 1813) married Silsy (b. 1816)

Hagar (b. 1834)

Jacob married Mary

Wesley   Thomas

Darcus married Caroline

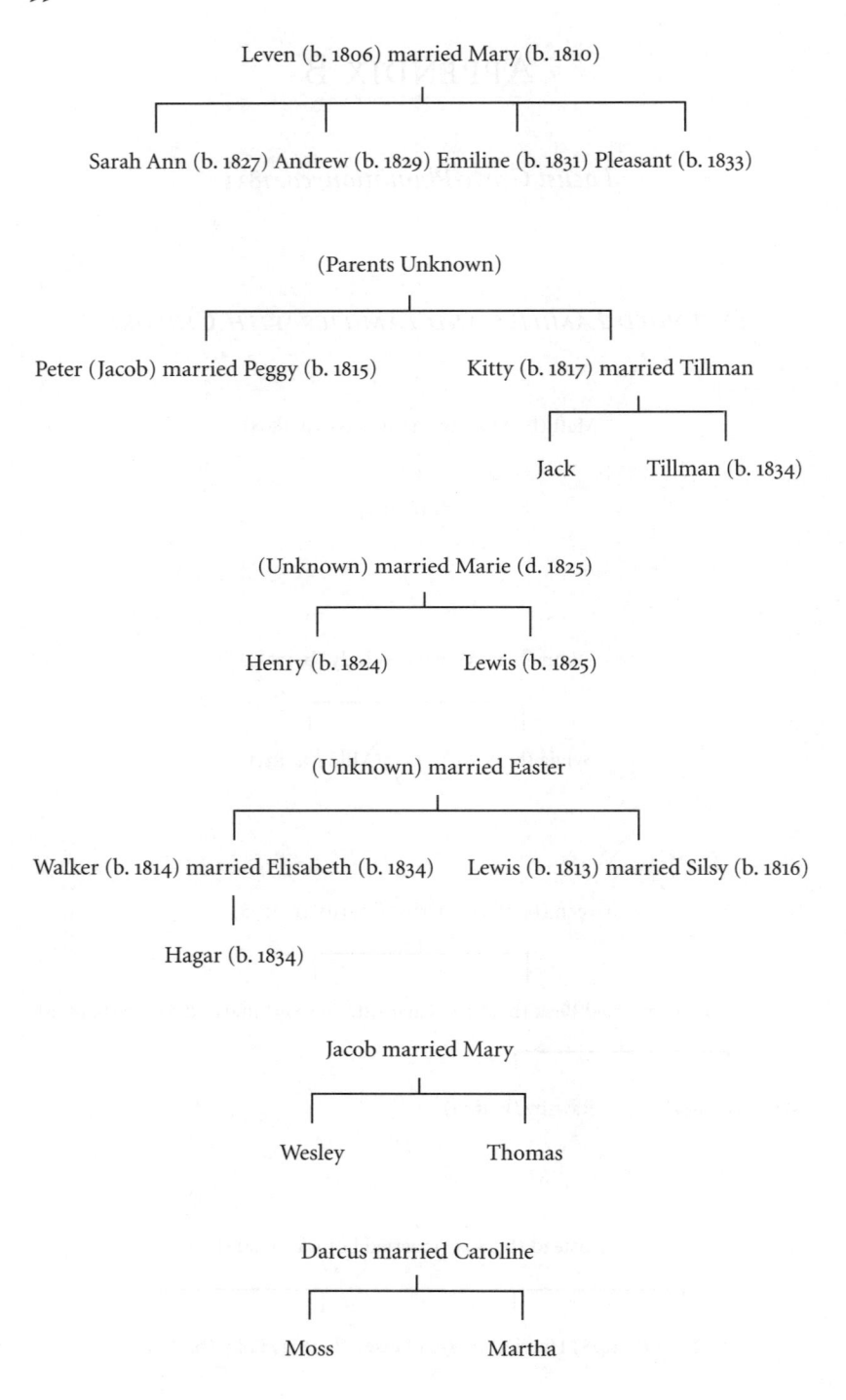

Moss   Martha

Appendix B

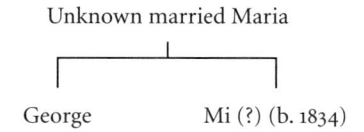

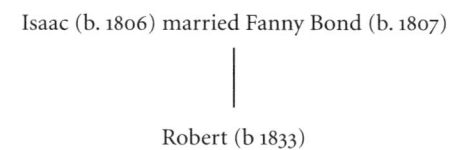

Unknown married Maria
┌──────────┴──────────┐
George   Mi (?) (b. 1834)

Isaac (b. 1806) married Fanny Bond (b. 1807)
                    |
              Robert (b 1833)

CHILDLESS COUPLES

Warren (b. 1772) -m- Ellen (b. 1793)
Sam (b. 1798) -m- Fanny (b. 1798)
Henry (b. 1805) -m- Belinda (b. 1801)
Old Billy (b. 1763, d. 1829) -m- Amy
Bill (b. 1790) -m- Delphy (b. 1796)
Rose (b. 1791) -m- Phillis (b. 1783, d. 1831)
Rose (b. 1791) -m- Jim [in 1833]
Maryann -m- Lewis
Edmund -m- Nancy

UNATTACHED

Frank
Uriah
Chatherine
Nancy
Caroline
Maryann
Ned Bell
Charles (b. 1819)
Alfred (b. 1810)
Aaron
Allen
Mac
Fanny

m = Married (b.) = Born | = Children; (d.) = Died

Notes

Introduction

1. [Ingraham], *The South-West, by a Yankee*, vol. 2 (New York: Harper & Brothers, 1835): 185–186.
2. D. Clayton James, *Antebellum Natchez* (1993; Baton Rouge: Louisiana State University Press, 1968): 83–84, 86.
3. For interpretations of colonial contact as the creation of a new world, see James Merrell, *The Indians' New World: The Catawbas and Their Neighbors from European Contact through the Era of Removal* (Chapel Hill: University of North Carolina Press, 1989); and James Axtell, *The Indians' New South: Cultural Change in the Colonial Southeast* (Baton Rouge: Louisiana State University Press, 1997).
4. Charles Sackett Sydnor, *Slavery in Mississippi* (1933; Gloucester, Ma.: Peter Smith, 1965), viii.
5. David M. Oshinsky, *"Worse than Slavery": Parchman Farm and the Ordeal of Jim Crow Justice* (New York: Free Press, 1996): 22. Similarly, Neil McMillen studied several generations of race relations in a cross-sectional framework in *Dark Journey: Black Mississippians in the Age of Jim Crow* (Urbana: University of Illinois Press, 1989).
6. An exhibit at the Old Capitol Museum in Jackson, Mississippi, illustrates the pattern of population decline among Native Americans in the years following European contact. Also see note 8 below.
7. Those studies that I have been influenced by the most include Winthrop D. Jordan, *White Over Black: American Attitudes toward the Negro, 1550–1812* (1968; New York: Norton, 1977); Peter H. Wood, *Black Majority: Negroes in Colonial South Carolina from 1670 to the Stono Rebellion* (New York: Norton, 1974); Michael Mullin, *Africa in America: Slave Acculturation and Resistance in the American South and the British Caribbean, 1736–1831* (Urbana: University of Illinois Press, 1992); Daniel C. Littlefield, *Rice and Slaves: Ethnicity and the Slave Trade in Colonial South Carolina* (Baton Rouge: Louisiana State University Press, 1981); Gwendolyn Midlo Hall, *Africans in Colonial Louisiana: The Development of Afro-Creole Culture in the Eighteenth Century* (Baton Rouge: Louisiana State University Press, 1992). Most recently, Ira Berlin and Philip Morgan have published massive interpretations of colonial slavery. However, of the two, only Berlin connected the lower Mississippi valley to the broader history of slavery in the English colonies. See Berlin, *Many Thousands Gone: The First Two Centuries of Slavery in North America* (Cambridge: Harvard University Press, 1998), and Morgan, *Slave Counterpoint: Black Culture in the Eighteenth-Century Chesapeake and Lowcountry* (Chapel Hill: University of North Carolina Press, 1998).
8. These studies include Patricia Kay Galloway, *Choctaw Genesis, 1500–1700* (Lincoln: University of Nebraska Press, 1995); Daniel H. Usner Jr., *Indians, Settlers, and Slaves in a Frontier Exchange Economy: The Lower Mississippi Valley before 1783* (Chapel Hill: University of North Carolina Press, 1993); Christopher Morris, *Becoming*

Notes

    Southern: The Evolution of a Way of Life, Vicksburg and Warren County, 1770–1860 (New York: Oxford University Press, 1995).
9. Ingraham, *South-West*, vol. 2, 183.

Chapter One

FRENCH SLAVERY IN COLONIAL NATCHEZ

1. On the unique nature of the Natchez hierarchy, see Ian W. Brown, "Natchez Indians and the Remains of a Proud Past," in *Natchez Before 1830*, ed. Noel Polk (Jackson: University Press of Mississippi, 1989): 8–9. Primary accounts of Natchez ceremony can be found in Antoine Le Page du Pratz, *The History of Louisiana*, ed. Joseph G. Tregle Jr. (London, 1774; facsimile reprint, Baton Rouge: Louisiana State University Press, 1975): 332–343; and Richebourg Gaillard McWilliams, trans. and ed., *Fleur de Lys and Calumet, being the Pénicault Narrative of French Adventure in Louisiana* (Baton Rouge: Louisiana State University Press, 1953): 90–96. Hereafter cited as *Pénicault Narrative*.
2. Quoted in Brown, "Natchez Indians", 20.
3. On the process of consolidation, see ibid., 20–21; Brown, "An Archaeological Study of Culture Contact and Change in the Natchez Bluffs Region," in *La Salle and His Legacy*, ed. Patricia Kay Galloway (Jackson: University Press of Mississippi, 1982): 179. On diseases, see Galloway, *Choctaw Genesis*, 134–143.
4. Patricia Woods, "The French and the Natchez Indians in Louisiana: 1700–1731," *LH* 19 (fall 1978): 416.
5. Jack D. Elliot Jr., "The Fort of Natchez and the Colonial Origins of Mississippi," *JMH* 52 (August 1990): 165.
6. Woods, "The French and the Natchez," 414. Father Paul du Ru quoted in same.
7. McWilliams, ed., *Pénicault Narrative*, 83.
8. Several works discuss the French goals in settling the Mississippi valley, and especially Natchez, including Woods, "The French and the Natchez," 418–419; Woods, *French-Indian Relations on the Southern Frontier, 1699–1762* (Ann Arbor: UMI Research Press, 1980): 55–63; Elliot, "Fort of Natchez," 164–165; Usner, *Indians, Settlers, and Slaves*.
9. On Choctaw society, authority structures, and matrilineage, see Charles Hudson, *The Southeastern Indians* (Knoxville: University of Tennessee Press, 1976): 202–205, 229, and passim; also Galloway, *Choctaw Genesis*.
10. Grayson Noley, "The Early 1700s: Education, Economics, and Politics," in *The Choctaw Before Removal*, ed. Carolyn Keller Reeves (Jackson: University Press of Mississippi, 1985): 32.
11. An excellent discussion of the cultural differences between the French and the Choctaw is Patricia Galloway, " 'The Chief Who Is Your Father': Choctaw and French Views of the Diplomatic Relation," in *Powhattan's Mantle: Indians in the Colonial Southeast*, ed. Peter H. Wood, Gregory A. Waselkov, and M. Thomas Hatley (Lincoln: University of Nebraska Press, 1989): 254–278. Galloway suggests that the inability of the French to conduct diplomatic negotiations effectively with the Choctaw was rooted in the differing social construction of male authority in the two cultures.
12. Usner, *Indians, Settlers, and Slaves*, 18–19.

13. On Chickasaw slaving raids, see Galloway, "Henri du Tonti du Village des Chacta, 1702: The Beginning of the French Alliance," in *La Salle and His Legacy*, 159.
14. A good discussion of Choctaw slavery, as well as Choctaw interaction with African slaves, is Stephen M. Rosecan, "Valuable Captives: Louisiana Slaves among the Choctaw Indians during the Early 1730s" (Master's thesis, University of Mississippi, 1996), especially pp. 29–40, 53–64. The Natchez probably had concepts of slavery, but in the thorough, albeit confused, descriptions of their social structure written by French visitors, little mention of slavery is made. General discussions of slavery among southeastern Indians are in Hudson, *Southeastern Indians*, 253–255.
15. Hudson, *Southeastern Indians*, 254
16. The issue of Indians' perceptions of racial distinctions is discussed in James H. Merrell, "The Racial Education of the Catawbas," *JSH* 50 (August 1984): 363–384; and Perdue, *Slavery and the Evolution of Cherokee Society* (Knoxville: University of Tennessee Press, 1979), chapter 3. Southeastern Indians did perceive the differences between themselves and outsiders as racial distinctions, but initially they made little distinction between Europeans and Africans. See Nancy Shoemaker, "How the Indians Got to Be Red," *AHR* 102 (June 1997): 625–644.
17. In 1717, the French proprietor of Louisiana, Antoine Crozat, transmitted the colonial charter to the Company of the West, headed by the Scots investor John Law. Shortly thereafter the concern was renamed the Company of the Indies. See Elliot, "Fort of Natchez," 167.
18. In reparation for the "murder" of four French traders, the French demanded that the Natchez construct a fort. See Elliot, "Fort of Natchez," 166–167; also Woods, "The French and the Natchez," 418–420.
19. Woods, "The French and the Natchez," 423; Elliot, "Fort of Natchez," 172. Daniel Usner estimates only 105 settlers lived in Natchez in 1726, alongside 65 black slaves and 9 Indian slaves. *Indians, Settlers, and Slaves*, 48.
20. These issues are debated in two essays, James J. Cooke, "France, the New World, and Colonial Expansion," 81–92, and Glen R. Conrad, "Reluctant Imperialist: France in America," 93–105, both in *La Salle and His Legacy*.
21. James D. Hardy Jr., "The Transportation of Convicts to Colonial Louisiana," *LH* 7 (summer 1966): 207–220.
22. René Le Conte, "The Germans in Louisiana in the Eighteenth Century," trans. Glenn R. Conrad, *LH* 8 (winter 1967): 67–84.
23. Over a decade before the introduction of slaves to Natchez, French officials had already discussed plans to develop Louisiana with slaves by trading Indians for Afro-Caribbean slaves. While discussed and authorized, such plans never went into operation. Ultimately French Louisiana would get its slaves directly from the Atlantic trade. See Louis XIV to DeMuy, June 30, 1707, in *Mississippi Provincial Archives: French Dominion* (Hereafter cited as *MPAFD*), Dunbar Rowland, Albert Sanders, and Patrick Kay Galloway, eds., vol. 3, 53, for authorization of such exchanges.
24. Hall, *Africans in Colonial Louisiana*, chapter 2, especially 29–34.
25. These distinctions are illustrated in Phillip D. Curtin, *Economic Change in Precolonial Africa: Senegambia in the Era of the Slave Trade* (Madison: University of Wisconsin Press, 1975): 34–35; and James F. Searing, *West African Slavery and Atlantic Commerce: The Senegal River Valley, 1700–1865* (Cambridge: Cambridge University Press, 1993): 49.
26. Curtin, *Economic Change*, 35. A more thorough and subtle discussion of royal slaves in Senegambia is Searing, *West African Slavery*, 38–43.

Notes

27. Curtin, 115.
28. du Pratz, *History of Louisiana*, 376–377.
29. Daniel H. Usner Jr., "From African Captivity to American Slavery: The Introduction of Black Laborers to Colonial Louisiana," *LH* 20 (winter 1979): 33.
30. Hall, *Africans in Colonial Louisiana*, chapter 3.
31. The cultural context for this resignation provided the framework in which slaves complied with their enslavement. Even as they took on the external demeanor of subordination, they did not necessarily internalize the fact of their subordination. See Bertram Wyatt-Brown, "The Mask of Obedience: Male Slave Psychology in the Old South," *AHR* 93 (December 1998): 1228–1552.
32. The French commented on these differences at the time. See Searing, *West African Slavery*, 50. Although as a matter of custom the French had abandoned slavery, civil law and Christian tradition provided the grounds for legal enslavement.
33. Curtin illustrates the distinction between slave as property and slave as obligation in *Economic Change*, 34.
34. Slavery in the Louisiana colony may have been similar to Caribbean slavery, but it was in fact almost foreign to France. Having abandoned slavery centuries earlier, the French took pride in the claim "there are no slaves in France," even as they reintroduced the practice in the New World. Whatever qualms they may have had were easily overcome, as they established brutal and strikingly efficient slave operations in the Caribbean. Sue Peabody, *There Are No Slaves in France* (New York: Oxford University Press, 1996).
35. Dawson Phelps, trans., "Narrative of the Hostilities Committed by the Natchez against the concession of St. Catherine, October 21, November 4, 1722," *JMH* 7 (January 1945): 3–10.
36. Minutes of the Superior Council, September 16, 1723, *MPAFD* vol. 3, 375–376.
37. Minutes of the Council of War, January 7, 1724, ibid., 387
38. Memoir on Louisiana, the Indies and the commerce that can be carried on with them, 1726, ibid., 510–524. The two major slaveowners in Natchez were Mr. Le Blanc (a company representative) and Mr. Kolly (a partner with Hubert).
39. Committee of Louisiana to Directors of the Company, November 8, 1824, ibid., vol. 2, 399.
40. Minutes of the Superior Council of Louisiana, April 7, 1725, ibid., 427.
41. Minutes of the Superior Council of Louisiana, March 23, 1725, ibid., 421.
42. Superior Council of Louisiana to Directors of the Company of the Indies (Abstract), August 28, 1725, ibid., 492, 494.
43. When the council appointed Sieur Du Tisné in 1725, he was immediately characterized as "not at all suited to command." Memoir from the Council of Louisiana to the Council of the Company of the Indies, April 23, 1725, ibid., 459. Several years later the actions of the commander Sieur de Chepart precipitated a major uprising among the Natchez, as described below.
44. Périer and De La Chaise to Directors of the Company of the Indies, January 30, 1729, ibid., 639.
45. Périer to [Abbe Raguet], May 12, 1728, ibid., 573.
46. du Pratz, *History of Louisiana*, 79.
47. Ibid., 80.
48. Périer to Maurepas, March 18, 1730, *MPAFD* vol. 1, 63.
49. Périer to Maurepas, December 5, 1729, ibid., 54.

50. Hall devotes an entire chapter to Bambarra resistance in *Africans in Colonial Louisiana*, 96–118. Her interpretation is somewhat problematical. While the evidence of resistance is convincing, Hall relies on French characterizations of these slaves as Bambarras when their ethnicity may have been a French designation. Curtin's discussion of the difficulty of interpreting the term "Bambarra" from the sources is a good antidote to Hall's generalizations. See *Economic Change*, 178–179. A more skeptical treatment of Bambarras in French Louisiana is Peter Caron, " 'Of a nation which the others do not Understand': Bambara Slaves and African Ethnicity in Colonial Louisiana, 1718–60," *Slavery and Abolition* 18 (1997): 98–121.
51. Beauchamp to Maurepas, November 5, 1731, *MPAFD* vol. 4, 82.
52. This discussion of the Natchez-slave dialogue and the decision-making process among the slaves is informed by James C. Scott, *Domination and the Arts of Resistance: Hidden Transcripts* (New Haven: Yale University Press, 1990).
53. Périer to Maurepas, March 18, 1730, *MPAFD* vol. 1, 65. It is quite possible that these slaves were Bambarra, as it was common in Senegambia for captured Bambarras to escape and return to their previous master. See Curtin, *Economic Change*, 115.
54. Diron d'Artaguette recorded that "about fifty negroes" had been recovered, while Périer claimed they recovered "one hundred of our negroes." D'Artaguette later wrote that le Seur and the Choctaw brought back "one hundred and fifty negroes and negresses whom they took from the enemy." The precision with which the officials recorded the number of French women and children, and the absence of any in counting the slaves is most probably rooted in both the value they placed on each as well as the fact that the Choctaw retained the slaves, awaiting payment for the revenge they exacted. D'Artaguette to Maurepas, February 10, 1730, *MPAFD* vol. 1, 61; Périer to Maurepas, March 18, 1730, ibid., 68; d'Artaguette to Maurepas, March 20, 1730, *MPAFD* vol. 1, 78.
55. Périer to Maurepas, March 18, 1730, *MPAFD* vol. 1, 68.
56. While the Choctaw may have been surprised by the support that the Natchez received from the slaves, the French must have been even more surprised. As a show of colonial strength intended to impress Indians and French colonists alike, Governor Périer sent a band of company-owned slaves to slaughter the Chaouachas. The intent was to demonstrate that the French were in the region to stay, but this decision also displayed his trust in company slaves. While these slaves were not strangers to the idea of acting as a Janissary force, it seems that the governor was a bit less comfortable in using slaves this way. He reported his concern that such actions "might on the contrary cause our negroes to revolt as we see by the example of the Natchez," and thus limited the military use of slaves to this one raid. Périer to Maurepas, March 18, 1730, *MPAFD* vol. 1, 64.
57. French and Choctaw forces killed most of the Natchez and captured the survivors, shipping them off to Caribbean slavery. The few who remained slowly joined the neighboring Chickasaw. See Usner, *Indians, Settlers, and Slaves*, 75.
58. Richard White's *The Middle Ground: Indians, Empires, and Republics in the Great Lakes Region, 1650–1815* (New York: Cambridge University Press, 1991) describes the emergence of a middle ground connecting European/Native frontiers. While White first used the term "middle ground" in his study of the Great Lakes region, in *The Roots of Dependency: Subsistence, Environment, and Social Change among the Choctaws, Pawnees, and Najavos* (Lincoln: University of Nebraska Press, 1938): 36, he suggested that French-Choctaw economic activity "was not so much the

Notes

triumph of one or the other, or even a compromise, as a series of exchanges which took place in the interstices between the two cultures."

59. Descriptions of these demands and exchanges can be found in Périer to Maurepas, March 18, 1730, *MPAFD* vol. 1, 68; Lusser's Journal, March 16, 1730, ibid., 110; and du Roullet's Journal, March 29, 1730, ibid., 179.
60. Galloway, "The Chief Who Is Your Father," 254–278.
61. Lusser's Journal, March 10, 1730, *MPAFD* vol. 1, 103.
62. du Roullet's Journal, April 27, 1730, ibid., 180.
63. du Roullet to Périer, March 16, 1731, ibid., vol. 4, 66. Such abuse was not surprising, as the slaves had no social protection within Choctaw society. See Rosecan, "Valuable Captives," 53–64.
64. du Roullet to Périer, March, 16, 1731, *MPAFD* vol. 4, 67.
65. Périer to Ory, November 15, 1730, ibid., 54.
66. Michael Mullen discusses suicide as a form of resistance to slavery in *Africa in America*, 69. Also see John Blassingame, *The Slave Community: Plantation Life in the Antebellum South*, rev. ed. (New York: Oxford University Press, 1979): 7.
67. du Roullet to Périer, March 16, 1731, *MPAFD* vol. 4, 66–67.
68. du Roullet's Journal, May 10–23, 1731, ibid., vol. 1, 186–187.
69. Jesse O. McKee and Jon A. Schlenker, *The Choctaws: Cultural Evolution of a Native American Tribe* (Jackson: University Press of Mississippi, 1980: 27–28, 33–34); du Roullet's Journal, July 21, 1731, *MPAFD* vol. 1, 187.
70. Daniel Littlefield refers to a Savanna, Georgia, runaway slave who had arrived from a French settlement on the Mississippi River via the Chickasaw trade. See *Rice and Slaves*, 134.
71. While there is little evidence concerning such bands in the wake of this uprising, examples in nearby locales tend to justify speculation that a group could survive. The French discovered fifteen African and Indian fugitives near Natchez in 1727. On a much larger scale, the maroon community living in the swampy lowlands south of New Orleans survived for years. In South Carolina, British colonists discovered "an outlaw band composed of a Spaniard, and Indian, a Negro and a mulatto, known to have made forays against whites and Indians alike." See Usner, *Indians, Settlers, and Slaves*, 58; Hall, *Africans in Colonial Louisiana*, 205–235; and Wood, *Black Majority*, 263.

Chapter Two

Resettlement of the Natchez Region

1. Bienville and Salmon to Maurepas, May 12, 1733, *MPAFD* vol. 3, 592.
2. Some may have served as interpreters, for the linguistic skills of first-generation slaves has been noted elsewhere. Ira Berlin emphasizes the value of linguistic and other specialized skills in "charter generation" slaves at far-flung outposts of the emerging Atlantic commercial system. See "From Creole to African: Atlantic Creoles and the Origins of African-American Society in Mainland North America," *WMQ*, 3d ser., 53 (April 1996): 251–288; Berlin, *Many Thousands Gone*, especially chapter 8 on the "charter generation" in the lower Mississippi valley.

Notes

3. On the deerskin economy, see Usner, *Indians, Settlers, and Slaves*, chapter 8.
4. On the transformations that accompanied the British takeover, see ibid., chapter 4; Usner, "American Indians on the Cotton Frontier: Economic Relations with Citizens and Slaves in the Mississippi Territory," *JAH* 72 (September 1985): 297–317.
5. See Usner, "American Indians on the Cotton Frontier"; also Morris, *Becoming Southern*.
6. There has been very little study of the British colony of West Florida. Most works have focused on the economy of the region. See Clinton N. Howard, *The British Development of West Florida, 1763–1769* (Berkeley and Los Angeles: University of California Press, 1947); and Robin F. A. Fabel, *The Economy of British West Florida, 1763–1783* (Tuscaloosa: University of Alabama Press, 1988). Other works have looked at the region during the American Revolution. See J. Barton Starr, *Tories, Dons and Rebels: The American Revolution in British West Florida* (Gainesville: University Press of Florida, 1976); and Robert V. Haynes, *The Natchez District and the American Revolution* (Jackson: University Press of Mississippi, 1976).
7. Monfort Browne to the Earl of Hillsborough, July 6, 1768, Mississippi Provincial Archives: English Dominion (microfilm) (Hereafter cited as MPAED) (mf), vol. 3.
8. Phillip Pittman, *The Present State of the European Settlements on the Mississippi* (London, 1770; reprint, Gainesville: University of Florida Press, 1973): 37.
9. Peter Chester to Hillsborough, September 26, 1770, MPAED (mf), vol. 4.
10. See the discussion of this plan in Governor George Johnstone to Secretary John Pownell, (extract) in MPAED (mf), vol. 1.
11. Browne to Earl of Shelburne, February 1, 1768, MPAED (mf), vol. 3.
12. During his first visit to Natchez, Montfort Browne befriended the "Tinnicaws," a group whom earlier British expeditions had found difficult to deal with. He reported that "I would now nearly as soon depend upon them as Our Friends the Chickasaws." He also treated with the Choctaws. Brown to Hillsborough, July 6, 1768, ibid.
13. On the economic impact of Indian trade with Europeans, see White, *The Roots of Dependency*, especially chapter 1 on the declining population, and chapter 4 on the effect of British trade on the Choctaw economy.
14. According to Richard White, the Choctaw borderlands provided military security and ample hunting grounds. *Roots of Dependency*, 31–32. See also Jay Gitlin, "Crossroads on the Chinaberry Coast: Natchez and the Creole World of the Mississippi Valley," *JMH* 54 (November 1992): 365–384.
15. Elias Dunsford to [unknown], February 6, 1770, MPAED (mf), vol. 4.
16. James, *Antebellum Natchez*, 14–15.
17. See the summary of land grants along the Mississippi River in Appendix 1 of Howard, *British Development of West Florida*.
18. John McIntire to [Gov. Peter Chester], July 19, 1770, MPAED (mf), vol. 4.
19. Daniel Huey Deposition to Peter Chester, August 26, 1770, ibid.
20. Edward Mease, "Narrative of a Journey Through Several Parts of the Province of West Florida in the years 1770 and 1771," in ibid. The bracketed letters are my reading of the document, which was damaged.
21. Chester to Earl of Dartmouth, May 16, 1773, ibid.
22. "A Description of West Florida with the State of Its Settlements by Lieutenant Governor Dunsford," January 15, 1774, ibid., vol. 6.
23. Bernard Romans, *A Concise Natural History of East and West Florida* (New York: n.p., 1775): 104, 105, 190–192. Romans's rejection of white, or indentured, servitude,

Notes

is probably rooted in a fear of the sizeable landless white population that would result once significant numbers of indentures were completed.

24. In this respect, Natchez more closely resembled Boston, which had been depopulated by epidemics from Indian-European contacts predating the Puritan settlements, than Jamestown, where the Powhattan Confederation was effective at limiting the extent of English settlement.
25. Fabel, *Economy of British West Florida*, 329–338, discusses the sources of the slave trade. Fabel concludes on page 338 that "the sources of slaves in West Florida were amazingly diverse. Although the paucity of official import lists is frustrating, the slaves of West Florida who were not already there when the British first arrived came from Spanish Louisiana, Jamaica, Charleston, East Florida, the Windward Islands, West Africa, and possibly elsewhere!"
26. Romans included a lengthy discussion of these crops and many others in *Natural History*, 117–145, and passim. Montfort Browne pointed out a similar diversity of potential staples. See Browne to Hillsborough, July 6, 1770, MPAED (mf,) vol. 3.
27. Morton Rothstein, "'The Remotest Corner': Natchez on the American Frontier," in *Natchez Before 1830*, 94. Spain never executed a formal embargo on Anglo-American exports, but fearing such a ban, planters avoided crops that involved significant investments.
28. Dunbar is the subject of several studies, including ibid.; James R. Dungan, "'Sir' William Dunbar of Natchez: Planter, Explorer, and Scientist, 1792–1810," *JMH* 24 (October 1961): 211–228.
29. On Dunbar's migration, see Bernard Bailyn, *Voyagers to the West: A Passage in the Peopling of America on the Eve of the Revolution* (New York: Alfred A. Knopf, 1986): 489.
30. William Dunbar Diary in Eron Rowland, ed., *Life Letters and Papers of William Dunbar: Pioneer Scientist of the Southern United States* (Jackson: Mississippi Historical Society, 1930), May 27, 1776, p. 23. Hereafter cited as Dunbar Diary.
31. Ibid., May 27, 1776, p.23
32. Two useful descriptions of the frontier economies in this region are James, *Antebellum Natchez*, 19–20; and Morris, *Becoming Southern*, 12–20.
33. B. L. C. Wailes, *Report on the Agriculture and Geology of Mississippi: Embracing a Sketch of the Social and Natural History of the State* (Washington: E. Barksdale, 1854): 141–142.
34. Dunbar Diary, June 14, 1777, p. 47.
35. Ibid., November 8, 1777, p. 52.
36. Ibid., June 12, 1776, p. 25; April 23, 1777, p. 46. Slaves killing and eating alligators illustrates their familiarity with the landscape of the South, owing to parallels in environment and wildlife. An African who had killed and eaten crocodiles in his homeland would see nothing amazing in this feat.
37. Ibid., June 8, 1776, p. 24; January 8, 1777, p. 40.
38. Ibid., January 24, 1780, p. 70; July 20, 1776, p. 28.
39. Ibid., January 24, 1780, p. 70; June 9, 1776, p. 25; January 7, 1777, p. 40. See also July 30, 1776, p. 30; March 29, 1777, p. 46, passim. Other entries record Dunbar's receiving new slaves for sale. See, for instance, January 4, 1777, p. 40; January 15, 1777, p. 43, passim. Economic exchanges were the basis for the formation of communities along the lower Mississippi valley. See Morris, *Becoming Southern*, 11–22.

Notes

40. Dunbar Diary, July 29, July 30, August 3, 1776, p. 29–30; May 12, 1777, p. 46–47; August 27, 1777, p. 50.
41. Ibid., November 21, 1777, p. 532; November 24, p. 54; February 23, 1778, p. 59.
42. Ibid., December 12, 1777, p.55; September 18, 1777, p. 51. Dunbar recorded similar festivities on January 2, 1778, p. 56–57.
43. These ideas are influenced by Scott, *Domination and the Arts of Resistance*.
44. Dunbar Diary, July 12, 1776, p. 26–28.
45. John Fitzpatrick to John Stephenson, July 2, 1776, in Margaret Fisher Dalrymple, ed., *The Merchant of Manchac: The Letterbooks of John Fitzpatrick, 1768–1790* (Baton Rouge: Louisiana State University Press, 1978): 204–205.
46. Fitzpatrick to Miller, Swanson & Co., May 8, 1773, in Dalrymple, ed., *Merchant of Manchac*, 147.
47. Fitzpatrick to Robert Montgomery, February 17, 1779, ibid., 311.
48. Fitzpatrick to Robert Montgomery, May 9, 1779, ibid., 319. Planters in the Natchez region may have viewed linguistic skill as a potential threat to the stability of the slave system. Such linguistically talented slaves usually were of great value in the Atlantic world, and played a role as cultural brokers, which benefitted their masters and gained for them a greater degree of autonomy than was enjoyed by most slaves. See Berlin, *Many Thousands Gone*.
49. Fitzpatrick to Jesse Lum, October 12, 1772, in Dalrymple, ed., *Merchant of Manchac*, 130–131.
50. Fitzpatrick to Peter Swanson, October 12, 1772, ibid., 131–132.
51. Fitzpatrick to Isaac Johnson, December 27, 1774, ibid., 181.
52. Fitzpatrick to Captain Cornelius Van Horn, November 23, 1776, ibid., 215.
53. Fitzpatrick to Alexander McIntosh, April 28, 1777, ibid., 245.
54. Fitzpatrick to John Stephenson, October 2, 1776, ibid., 209.
55. Although the Spaniards never entirely closed the Mississippi River to Anglo-American traffic, that traffic was heavily regulated by mercantilistic policies. Products leaving New Orleans had first to go to another Spanish port before shipment abroad. See Jack D. L. Holmes, "Indigo in Colonial Louisiana and the Floridas," *LH* 8 (fall 1967): 337.
56. Fabel summarizes this issue concisely in *Economy of British West Florida*, 34–35.
57. Peter Chester to Lord George Germain, November 27, 1778, MPAED (mf), vol 8.
58. Peter Chester to Lord George Germain, March 25, 1778, ibid., vol. 7. See also Starr, *Tories, Dons and Rebels*, chapter 3; and Haynes, *Natchez District and the American Revolution*.
59. Dunbar Diary, May 1, 1778, p. 60–63. Also Starr, *Tories, Dons and Rebels*, 90.
60. Frey, *Water from the Rock*.
61. Memorial to the HMS *Sylph*, March 27, 1778, signed by fourteen planters, MPAED (mf), vol. 7.
62. William Barker to Bernardo de Gálvez, May 30, 1778, in Lawrence Kinnaird, ed., *Spain in the Mississippi Valley, 1765–1794: Translations of Material from the Spanish Archives in the Bancroft Library*, vol. 2 of the Annual Report of the American Historical Association for the year 1945, 2 vols. (Washington: Government Printing Office, 1946 and 1949), vol. 1, 283.
63. Chester to Germain, March 25, 1778, MPAED (mf), vol. 7. The slave count is in Haynes, *Natchez District and the American Revolution*, 73.
64. This incident, along with British efforts to shore up Natchez defenses, is described in Starr, *Tories, Dons and Rebels*, 138–140.

Notes

65. Articles of Capitulation from the fall of the Fort at Manchac, May 17, 1780, MPAED (mf), vol. 8.
66. Natchez residents to Lieutenant Colonel Dickson, October 4, 1779, MPAED (mf), vol. 8. Their thanks is to the commander who surrendered at Baton Rouge, not Manchac; however, the residents expressed appreciation that their defenders gave up before any hostilities reached Natchez.
67. Regulations Governing the Tobacco Trade in Louisiana, June 15, 1777, in Kinnaird, ed., *Spain in the Mississippi Valley*, vol. 1, 237–238.
68. John Hebron Moore, "The Cypress Lumber Industry of the Lower Mississippi Valley During the Colonial Period," *LH* 24 (winter 1983): 42.
69. Charles de Gran-Pré to Pedro Piernas, May 7, 1781, in Kinnaird, ed, *Spain in the Mississippi Valley*, vol. 1, 425–426.
70. Sale of Property belonging to English Prisoners, May 6, 1782, ibid., vol. 2, 12.
71. Juan Delavillebeuvre to Estaban Miró, April 25, 1780, ibid., vol. 1, 376.
72. Francisco Bouligny to Esteban Miró, August 22, 1785, ibid., vol. 2, 136.
73. Grand Pré to Miró, April 22, 1790, and Report of Americans Arriving at Natchez, July 5, 1788, ibid., 257, 327. In the second document, the migration of Eziikel Forman, who with his wife and four children brought 67 slaves from the United States, stands out among other records that described the arrival, over a six-month period, of 138 settlers bringing 36 slaves. Thirty of those slaves belonged to a single settler.
74. Allen Kulikoff, *The Agrarian Origins of American Capitalism* (Charlottesville: University Press of Virginia, 1992): 255–258. An example of the heavily African origins of slaves in the Mississippi valley is the succession of John Fitzpatrick, Appendix 1 of Dalrymple, ed., *Merchant of Manchac*, 450. The only slaves on this list born in the New World were the children of Fitzpatrick's African slaves.
75. Gwendolyn Hall has termed this process a "re-Africanization." See *Africans in Colonial Louisiana*, especially, chapter 9. On the alienation of Africans introduced into creole populations, see Ira Berlin, "Time, Space, and the Evolution of Afro-American Society on British Mainland North America," *AHR* 85 (February 1980): 44–78.
76. Dunbar to Diana Dunbar, May 19, 1794, William Dunbar Papers, Z114.1, Mississippi Department of Archives and History (Hereafter cited as MDAH).
77. The best easily accessible discussion of tobacco cultivation is T. H. Breen, *Tobacco Culture: The Mentality of the Great Tidewater Planters on the Eve of the Revolution* (Princeton: Princeton University Press, 1985): 46–55.
78. Dungan, "'Sir' William Dunbar," 214.
79. William Dunbar to Diana Dunbar, August 11, 1789, Dunbar Papers, Z114.1, MDAH.
80. Dunbar to Diana Dunbar, April 27, 1791, ibid.
81. Dunbar to Diana Dunbar, March 1794 and April 1, 1794, ibid. When Ross made these purchases, Rhode Island was still an important center of the Atlantic slave trade. See Jay Coughtry, *The Notorious Triangle: Rhode Island and the African Slave Trade, 1700–1807* (Philadelphia: Temple University Press, 1981).
82. Usner, *Indians, Settlers, and Slaves*, 268–286. A local trader kept track of the new settlers, chronicling the growth of settlement in the interior of the Natchez district during the 1780s and 1790s. The number of new settlers grew every year, from one and two households, respectively, in 1788 and 1789, to five in 1795, and thirteen in 1796. See George Rapalji Notebook (photocopy), Z580f, MDAH.

Notes

83. Commercial Priviledges Granted to Louisiana and West Florida, January 22, 1782, in Kinnaird, ed., *Spain in the Mississippi Valley*, vol. 2, 1–4; Miró's Offer to Western Americans, ibid., vol. 2, 269–270.
84. Wailes, *Report*, 67–73.
85. As illustrated by transactions in John Fitzpatrick's letterbooks. See Dalrymple, ed., *Merchant of Manchac*, passim.
86. Holmes, "Indigo in Colonial Louisiana," 342.
87. On the process of indigo production, see Wailes, *Report*, 135–138; also ibid., 338–339.
88. Ibid., 137.
89. Fragmentary evidence of a 1796 indigo crop suggests the profitability of the staple. Benjamin Farrar sold his crop for "$3273.4½" and after provisions, overseer's salary, and shares to partners, Farrar still collected $2402.30. Record of Expenditures by Benjamin Farrar, Landry-Hume Collection, Department of Special Collections and Archives, John Davis Williams Library, University of Mississippi (Hereafter cited as UM).

Chapter Three

THE COTTON FRONTIER OF TERRITORIAL MISSISSIPPI

1. On the process of creolization in the Mississippi valley, see Hall, *Africans in Colonial Louisiana*.
2. For the conspiracy in general, see ibid., 344–374. Invoice reimbursing "Mrs. Rapalje" for the "criminal slaves of the District of Pointe Coupee," November 17, 1795, Landry-Hume Collection, UM. A similar document in the collection records the transaction in French.
3. John Steele to Samuel Steele, January 14, 1799; on John's departure, see John Steele to Samuel Steele, July 28, 1798, both in Samuel Steele Papers, Perkins Library, Duke University.
4. John Steele to Samuel Steele, May 2, 1799, ibid.
5. John Steele to Samuel Steele, May 24, 1799, ibid.
6. John Steele to Samuel Steele, December 12, 1799, ibid.
7. John Steele to Samuel Steele, November 15, 1799, ibid.
8. James, *Antebellum Natchez*, 110, 210, 244.
9. William Charles Cole Claiborne to James Madison, December 20, 1801, Dunbar Roland, ed., *Mississippi Territorial Archives* (Nashville, 1905): 364. (Hereafter cited as *MTA*).
10. Bill of sale, October 7, 1807, in Slaves and Slavery Collection, Box 2E775, Natchez Trace Collection, Barker Texas History Center, University of Texas at Austin (Hereafter cited as NTC).
11. One description of the early patterns of cotton cultivation in Mississippi is John Q. Anderson, ed., "The Narrative of John Hutchins," *JMH* 20 (January 1958): 5.
12. Jack D. L. Holmes, "Cotton Gins in Spanish Natchez, 1795–1800," *JMH* 31 (August 1969): 160.
13. Lewis Cecil Gray, *History of Agriculture in the Southern United States to 1860*, 2 vols. (Washington: Carnegie Institution, 1933), vol. 2, 675–680.
14. Wailes, *Report*, 155, and passim.

Notes

15. See Wailes, *Report*, 167–169. The simplicity of the design made it easy to replicate, and this simplicity rendered Whitney's efforts to protect his patent unsuccessful. See Joyce Chaplin, *Anxious Pursuit: Agricultural Innovation and Modernity in the Lower South, 1730–1815* (Chapel Hill: UNC Press, 1993): 307–319. Jack D. L. Holmes suggests two possible origins of the gin in Mississippi. See "Cotton Gins," 161–162.
16. Quoted in Holmes, "Cotton Gins," 160.
17. Even so, until the middle 1830s most gins were custom-made, rather than mass-produced. See Algernon Smith, *The Story of the Continental Gin Company* (Birmingham: Continental Gin Company, 1952): 9–10.
18. Paul A. Fryxell, *The Natural History of the Cotton Tribe* (College Station: Texas A & M University Press, 1979): 162–177. Fryxell identifies the four slave species as *G. hirsutum, G. barbadense, G. herbaceum*, and *G. arboreum*.
19. On the introduction of Mexican cotton, see John Hebron Moore, *Agriculture in Antebellum Mississippi* (New York: Bookman Associates, 1958): 31–34; also Moore, *Emergence of the Cotton Kingdom in the Old Southwest: Mississippi 1770–1860* (Baton Rouge: Louisiana State University Press, 1988): 11–14. Lewis Gray in *History of Agriculture*, and Moore, in his earlier work, identified the Mexican strain as a separate species owing to the herbal taxonomy of their time. Since the publication of their studies, it has been determined that the Mexican strain was, in fact, *G. hirsutum*, and not a separate species. See Fryxell, *Cotton Tribe*, 171.
20. See, for instance, Moore, *Agriculture*, chapter 2.
21. The cotton plant is by nature a perennial. Thus, the previous year's plants need to be cleared from the fields. In ideal tropical conditions, cotton can be planted once, and harvested annually. But even temperate Mississippi freezes every year, and the cotton plants die in the fields. On the annual habituation of perennial cottons, see Fryxell, *Cotton Tribe*, 173–176, 186. Prior to the invention of the gin, Caribbean cotton planters cultivated cotton trees as perennials. See the illustration in Wailes, *Report*, plate opposite page 141.
22. Wailes, *Report*, 170.
23. Ibid., 150.
24. Ibid., 151. Later in the antebellum era, some planters began to adopt seed drills. See Gray, *History of Agriculture*, vol. 2, 701.
25. John W. Monette, "The Cotton Crop," an essay appended to Joseph H. Ingraham, *The South-West, by a Yankee* (New York: Harper & Brothers, 1835): 281.
26. William Pearson, interview by the author, Sumner, Mississippi, October 6, 1995.
27. See Wailes, *Report*, 151; also Monette, "Cotton Crop," 282.
28. Wailes, *Report*, 151–152. The process of "dirting" continues today. Planters still plough their fields shortly after the plants sprout to kill grasses and weeds. See Linda Hallam, "A Year in the Land of Cotton," *Southern Living* (September 1996): 84–89, for a description of modern cotton cultivation in Mississippi.
29. Wailes, *Report*, 184.
30. Ibid. It would seem that the delayed harvest of corn was only practiced by those who grew small crops of cotton, as a large crop would not have been completely in until the start of winter, well after the corn was ready.
31. Ibid., 154. The sharpness of the boll's locks, a fact little noted by historians or contemporary observers, became apparent to me during a visit to the Sumner, Mississippi, plantation of Frank Michener on October 6, 1995.
32. Gray, *History of Agriculture*, vol. 2, 702.

33. Monette, "Cotton Crop," 285.
34. Wailes, *Report*, 154.
35. Monette, "Cotton Crop," 287.
36. Ibid., 286.
37. Wailes, *Report*, 154.
38. Ibid., 169–170.
39. Ibid., 173–175. Gray, *History of Agriculture*, vol. 2, 705, discusses the varying weights of bales.
40. Monette, "Cotton Crop," 290.
41. Mark M. Smith has suggested that planters and slaves adapted to modern conceptions of time as quickly as industrial societies. Rather than becoming time conscious, Smith argues that the slaves became "time obedient." See "Time, Slavery and Plantation Capitalism in the Ante-Bellum American South," *P&P* 150 (February 1996): 142–168; "Old South Time in Comparative Perspective," *AHR* 101 (December 1996): 1432–1468; and *Mastered by the Clock: Time, Slavery, and Freedom in the American South* (Chapel Hill: University of North Carolina Press, 1997).
42. Gray, *History of Agriculture*, vol. 2, 689, and Moore, *Agriculture*, 25, both make this assertion.
43. On mechanization in the twentieth century, see Jack Temple Kirby, *Rural Worlds Lost: The American South, 1920–1960* (Baton Rouge: Louisiana State University Press, 1987), chapters 1 and 2.
44. For the relationship between rice culture and African traditions, see Wood, *Black Majority*, chapter 2; Littlefield, *Rice and Slaves*, chapter 4; Charles Joyner, *Down by the Riverside: A South Carolina Slave Community* (Urbana: University of Illinois Press, 1985), chapter 2; Berlin, *Many Thousands Gone*, chapter 6; Morgan, *Slave Counterpoint*, chapter 3.
45. While not steeped in African tradition, this relationship nonetheless was resistant to the emerging mercantile world. See Breen, *Tobacco Culture*; Berlin, *Many Thousands Gone*, chapter 5; Morgan, *Slave Counterpoint*, chapter 3.
46. Michael Mullin presents these issues in comparative perspective in *Africa in America*.
47. Some accounts of modern cotton cultivation, which is a highly mechanized process, still characterize it as a very traditional undertaking. For instance, Linda Hallam, in "A Year in the Land of Cotton," describes the tractors, seed drills, spindle pickers, crop dusters, insecticides, and defoliants involved in cotton planting. Still, because planters rely on the seasons, she characterizes cotton cultivation as a nearly romantic, agrarian undertaking.
48. Sea Island cotton cultivation may be an exception. See Gray, *History of Agriculture*, vol. 1, 551, and *passim*.
49. Monette, "Cotton Crop," 287.
50. This is not to suggest one system was milder than the other. The differences between these two labor systems in terms of household economies are explored in Mullin, *Africa in America*, 126–158.
51. On this transformation in Mississippi, see Michael Wayne, *The Reshaping of Plantation Society: The Natchez District, 1860–1880* (Baton Rouge, 1982; reprint, Urbana: University of Illinois Press, 1990). More generally, see Eric Foner, *Nothing but Freedom: Emancipation and Its Legacy* (Baton Rouge: Louisiana State University Press, 1983).
52. While cotton production may not have been as relentless as mill work, its constancy forced a divergence from traditional agricultural senses of time. See Mark Smith,

Notes

"Time, Slavery and Plantation Capitalism." Few slavery historians emphasize the relationships between cotton and the Industrial Revolution. James Oakes, however, has implicitly noted the significance of this connection throughout *Slavery and Freedom: An Interpretation of the Old South* (New York: Alfred A. Knopf, 1990). It is also important to note that the seasons could have a major impact on cotton mills in the early nineteenth century, as they were usually powered by rivers that flooded and ran low according to variable rains and spring thaws. Neither is modern by twentieth-century standards, but both were by contemporary standards.

53. The Revolutionary ideology very clearly affected Virginia's slaves. See Douglass R. Egerton, *Gabriel's Rebellion: The Virginia Slave Conspiracies of 1800 and 1802* (Chapel Hill: University of North Carolina Press, 1993); James Sidbury, *Ploughshares into Swords: Race, Rebellion, and Identity in Gabriel's Virginia, 1730–1810* (New York: Cambridge University Press, 1997).
54. Jordan, *White Over Black*, 398.
55. Ibid., 403–414.
56. Andrew Elicott to Timothy Pickering, September 24, 1797, in Clarence Edwin Carter, ed., *Territorial Papers of the United States*, vol. 5 (Washington: Government Printing Office, 1937): 5.
57. "An Act for the Government of the Mississippi Territory," in ibid., 20–21. Even the foreign trade ban seems to have been ignored.
58. Jordan, *White Over Black*, 403–406, discusses the tightening of slave laws throughout the South during the years surrounding the turn of the nineteenth century.
59. *Statutes of the Mississippi Territory* (Natchez: Peter Isler, 1816) (hereafter cited as *Turner's Digest*): 163, 223, 382.
60. Egerton, *Gabriel's Rebellion*, and Sidbury, *Plowshares into Swords*, both describe the conspiracy and its ideology. On the reaction to the uprisings throughout the country, see Jordan, *White Over Black*, 395–396.
61. Circular letter to Slave-Holders from Governor Sargent, November 16, 1800, MTA, 311–312.
62. Address to Militia Officers, January 12, 1801, ibid., 324–326.
63. Dungan, "'Sir' William Dunbar," 218.
64. *Mississippi Messenger*, October 1, 1805.
65. On these agricultural innovations, see Moore, *Agriculture*, chapter 3. William Dunbar previously had used cottonseed oil for lamps. Forty-five hundred years earlier, Nubians had cultivated cotton for the seed, which they used as feed for their livestock. They apparently discarded the fiber. See Fryxell, *Cotton Tribe*, 168.
66. William Dunbar to Isaac Briggs, B. L. C. Wailes Papers, Z76.00S, Box 1, MDAH.
67. Joyce Chaplin draws similar conclusions about South Carolina and Georgia at the same time. See *Anxious Pursuit*. On resistance to agricultural innovation in later years, see Lacey Ford, *Origins of Southern Radicalism: The South Carolina Upcountry, 1800–1860* (New York: Oxford University Press, 1988). John Hebron Moore suggests in *Emergence of the Cotton Kingdom* that in late antebellum years Mississippi planters were quite willing to adapt technological innovations. However, high rates of soil exhaustion both before and after the Civil War indicate the limits of such an assertion.
68. Various secondary sources discuss early Natchez's cosmopolitan nature. See especially the essays in *Natchez before 1830*, ed. Noel Polk (Jackson: University Press of Mississippi, 1987).

69. On the commodification of people implicit in slavery, see Walter Johnson, *Soul by Soul: Life Inside the Antebellum Slave Market* (Cambridge: Harvard University Press, 1999), especially chaters 1 and 4.
70. William Dunbar to Col Morehouse, March 22, 1806, in Rowland, ed., *Papers of Dunbar*, 333. A planter's reputation could also be questioned if a purchaser was disappointed with the slave. Stephen Minor, disappointed with a slave woman for reasons unclear, demanded that the seller, Giles Harding, "just take back the woman and give me my money," and suggested that if there was not a speedy refund, perhaps Harding was already aware of the problem. See Stephen Minor to John Minor, May 10, 1811, Minor Family Papers, *Records of Antebellum Southern Plantations from the Revolution through the Civil War* (microfilm), Series J, part 6, reel 1. (Hereafter cited as *Records*).
71. Unknown to John Willis, May 23, 1811, Barnes-Willis Family Papers, Box 2E530, NTC.
72. See, for instance, John B. Willis to William Willis, November 20, 1812, Barnes-Willis Family Papers, Box 2E530, NTC; also Bill of sale, July 16, 1803, in Slaves and Slavery Collection, Box 2E775, NTC, in which a ten-month-old boy was sold to balance a larger transaction. It is likely that the child was not formally exchanged. My thanks to Light T. Cummins for clarifying the nature of this transaction.
73. Abijah Hunt to Unknown, June 12, 1805, Abijah and David Hunt Papers, Z0230, Box 1, MDAH.
74. Indenture, March 3, 1808, Gladys Crial Evans Collection, G14, Box 1, UM.
75. The newspapers cited throughout this chapter contained dozens of advertisements for entire plantations for sale. For a discussion of the expense and effort involved in establishing plantations on the Georgia frontier, see Alan Gallay, *The Formation of a Planter Elite: Jonathan Bryan and the Southern Colonial Frontier* (Athens: University of Georgia Press, 1989): 94–99.
76. *Natchez Mississippi Messenger*, November 26, 1807. Emphasis in the original.
77. Dunbar to Tunno and Price, February 1, 1807, in Rowland, ed., *Papers of Dunbar*, 351–352.
78. William Dunbar to John Vaughan, December 15, 1806, in Rowland, ed., *Papers of Dunbar*, 349.
79. (Natchez) *Mississippi Republican*, June 8, 1814.
80. George Rapalje to Benjamin Farrar, April 16, 1808, Landry-Hume Collection, UM.
81. E. P. Thompson, *The Making of the English Working Class* (New York: Vintage, 1966), discusses the breaking of machines as a protest against modernization. He refers to it in terms of mob activity; however, in the slave quarters it was probably less organized.
82. Even between 1810 and 1813 there was some sort of transformation. The richest source cited here is the *Natchez Mississippi Messenger*, while a few years later, the advertisements in the *Natchez Mississippi Republican* and the *Washington Republican* (later the *Washington Republican and Natchez Intelligencer*) were fewer and less descriptive despite the growth in Mississippi's population during this period. Michael Mullin summarizes the transformation in runaway advertisements in *Africa in America*, 234.
83. Scholars have studied runaway slave advertisements with considerable success. Peter H. Wood, Daniel C. Littlefield, and Michael Mullin all suggest the value of such advertisements as well as their limitations. See Wood, *Black Majority;* Littlefield, *Rice and Slaves;* and Mullin, *Africa in America*. These sources do not

Notes

constitute a census of runaways, but instead suggest which slaves planters valued, and also which slaves the planter considered most dangerous.

84. *Mississippi Messenger*, March 25, 1806, September 26, 1806, July 28, 1807. Despite the memorable punishment meted to the fictional slave Kunta Kinte in the popular novel *Roots*, nothing indicates that these slaves were disfigured by vengeful masters. As the territorial legislature neither prescribed nor banned such punishment, it probably did not cross the minds of planters. Alex Haley, *Roots* (Garden City: Doubleday, 1976): 244.
85. The owner of "Saul, or Solomon" describes frost as the cause for missing toes. See *Mississippi Messenger*, May 19, 1807.
86. Jon Sensback, *A Separate Canaan: The Making of an Afro-Moravian World in North Carolina, 1763–1840* (Chapel Hill, UNC Press, 1998): 1–2, describes the effects of the Guinea worm on a slave purchased by Moravian colonists in Salem, North Carolina, in 1771.
87. *Mississippi Messenger*, September 2, September 26, October 28, 1806; June 2, September 1, 1807.
88. Quote in ibid., August 12, 1806. Additional examples of scars from whipping include ibid., June 17, September 2, 1806; July 21, 1807; *Washington Republican*, December 15, 1813; and *Mississippi Republican*, July 26, 1816.

    Scholarship on planter treatment of slaves still remains somewhat divided. In efforts to quantify abuse, Robert Fogel and Stanley Engerman as well as Eugene Genovese suggest that whippings were not common, at least based on available evidence. On the other hand, Kenneth Stampp, James Oakes, and most recently William Dusinberre have emphasized the abusive and incredibly arbitrary nature of slave punishments. See Fogel and Engerman, *Time on the Cross: The Economics of American Negro Slavery*, 2 vols. (Boston: Little, Brown, 1974); Genovese, *Roll, Jordan, Roll: The World the Slaves Made* (New York: Pantheon, 1974); Dusinberre, *Them Dark Days: Slavery in the American Rice Swamps* (New York: Oxford University Press, 1996); Oakes, *Slavery and Freedom*; Stampp, *The Peculiar Institution: Slavery in the Antebellum South* (New York: Knopf, 1956). In many ways, chapter 4 of Stampp's *The Peculiar Institution* remains the best statement on the abusive discipline planters exercised over their slaves.
89. *Mississippi Messenger*, May 12, September 2, 1806; March 24, September 22, 1807; February 25, June 2, 1808; and *Mississippi Republican*, March 1, 1816.
90. *Mississippi Messenger*, January 28, 1806; and *Mississippi Republican*, August 13, 1817.
91. Shane White and Graham White, "Slave Hair and African American Culture in the Eighteenth and Nineteenth Centuries," *JSH* 56 (February 1995): 45–76.
92. *Washington Republican and Natchez Intelligencer*, February 5, 1817.
93. *Mississippi Messenger*, September 16, 1806, includes an advertisement for Dave, who, it reported, was previously called George.
94. Ibid., October 7, 1806; March 29, 1807; March 24, May 13, 1808.
95. Ibid., January 28, June 17, September 16, 1806; July 14, 1807; *Mississippi Republican*, February 23, April 20, 1814. Michael Mullin has raised speech disorders as a manifestation of the psychological impact of abuse on slaves in *Africa in America*, 232.
96. *Mississippi Messenger*, October 22, 1805; October 7, 1806; May 26, 1807; *Washington Republican and Natchez Intelligencer*, April 9, 1813; January 22, 1817.
97. *Mississippi Republican*, May 4, 1814.

98. Stephen Minor to John Minor, April 18, 1811, in Minor Papers, *Records*, Series J, part 6, reel 1.
99. David Holmes to James Wilkinson, July 22, 1812, in Clarence E. Carter, ed., *Territorial Papers of the United States* vol. VI (Washington: Government Printing Office, 1937): 299.
100. David Holmes to David Pannell, July 23, 1812, in Carter, ed., *Territorial Papers*, vol. VI: 301.
101. James Williams to Benjamin Farrar, September 23, 1814, Landry-Hume Collection, UM.
102. William Kenner to Stephen Minor, December 6, 1813, in Minor Papers, *Records*, Series I, part 3, reel 12.
103. *Turner's Digest*, 192–193.
104. Ibid., 238–239, 359–360.
105. Willis Vick to William Willis, no date, Barnes-Willis Papers, Box 2E530, NTC.
106. Sylvia Frey has noted the tension between reinvigorated plantation operations and the growth of slave assertiveness in the years following the Revolution. See *Water from the Rock*, chapter 7, especially 222–232. More to the point, as Frey argues in chapter 8, in the decades that followed, planters, recognizing their shared humanity with their slaves, reordered the slave society, fearing the moral implications of the brutal practices in which they engaged.
107. *Turner's Digest*, 199.
108. David Daswell to George Rapalje, April 12, 1813, Landry-Hume Collection, UM.
109. J. Warner to John Willis, January 7, 1814, Barnes-Willis Papers, Box 2E530, NTC.
110. Daniel Barnett to William McAlpine, August 26, 1815, Daniel Barnett Papers, Box 2E552, NTC.
111. H. A. Huntington to William Christie, February 4, 1817, in William Hughes Family Papers, Z60, Box 1, MDAH.
112. On the impact of evangelicalism on master-slave relations, see Frey, *Water from the Rock*, chapter 8, especially 276–283; also Gallay, *Formation of a Planter Elite*, 161–166. In the process, of course, evangelical religion abandoned its antislavery stance. See chapter 5 below.
113. Jordan, *White Over Black*, 365–368.
114. Two studies that address the acculturation of individuals are Michael Mullin, *Africa in America;* and Sydney W. Mintz and Richard Price, *An Anthropological Approach to the Afro-American Past: A Caribbean Perspective* (Philadelphia: Institute for the Study of Human Issues, 1976).
115. Frey, *Water from the Rock*, 238, suggests that reforms were in response to "the collective action of slaves."
116. Planter appeals to sentiment began to appear at the same time that antislavery opponents appealed to sentiment in their own reformism. See Jordan, *White Over Black*, 368–372.
117. See for instance the discussion between Isaac Guion and his sons, Frederick and John. Isaac issued friendly greetings from the slave Hannibal, but his discussions of other slaves in the same letters were much less sentimental. Isaac Guion to Frederick and John Guion, April 22, 1816; September 15, 1816, both in Guion Family Papers, *Records*, Series J, part 6, reel 1.
118. An entirely different question is whether the slaves believed the pretense. The answer probably differed with each slave, but since the masters held the power, the

Notes

slaves followed their lead in a kind of public drama of planter "humanity" and slave docility. Once this "understanding" is worked out, a process of constant negotiation begins, which will be explored in chapter 5. See, more generally, Scott, *Domination and the Arts of Resistance*.

Chapter Four

SLAVES IN THE WESTERN MIGRATION

1. Isaac Farnsworth to James Farnsworth, January 27, 1827, Isaac Farnsworth Papers, Perkins Library, Duke University.
2. [Joseph Holt Ingraham], *The South-West, by a Yankee*, 2 vols. (New York: Harper & Brothers, 1835), vol. 2, 195–197.
3. See Johnson, *Soul by Soul*, chapter 6.
4. In addition to *Soul by Soul*, other studies that have focused on the slave trade include Frederic Bancroft, *Slave-Trading in the Old South* (Baltimore: J. H. Furst, 1931); Michael Tadman, *Speculators and Slaves: Masters, Traders, and Slaves in the Old South* (Madison: University of Wisconsin Press, 1991); Stephen Deyle, "The Irony of Liberty: Origins of the Domestic Slave Trade," *JER* 12 (spring 1992): 37–62. In their emphasis on the trade, however, these studies overlook other forms of slave migration. Other scholars focus on the effects of the migration more than the migration itself. Herbert Gutman, *The Black Family in Slavery and Freedom, 1750–1925* (1976; New York: Vintage, 1977); Blassingame, *The Slave Community*; Ann Patton Malone, *Sweet Chariot: Slave Family Household Structure in Nineteenth-Century Louisiana* (Chapel Hill: University of North Carolina Press, 1992). Allan Kulikoff has provided a framework for further investigation in chapter 8 of *Agrarian Origins of American Capitalism* (Charlottesville: University Press of Virginia, 1992).
5. Kulikoff, *Agrarian Origins*, chapter 8.
6. For the early limitations on new settlements and migration to the Southwest, see Thomas D. Clark and John D. W. Guice, *Frontiers in Conflict: The Old Southwest, 1795–1830* (Albuquerque: University of New Mexico Press, 1989).
7. E. A. Andrews, *Slavery and the Domestic Slave-Trade in the United States* (Boston: Light and Stearns, 1836): 104, 146–147.
8. Linda Brent [Harriet Jacobs], *Incidents in the Life of a Slave Girl*, ed. Walter Teller (1861; New York: Harcourt Brace, 1973): 14. Jacobs's descriptions are contemporary to those by Andrews. For a later description of slave pens in Virginia and the District of Columbia, see Solomon Northup, *Twelve Years a Slave* (1853; Baton Rouge: Louisiana State University Press, 1975): 21–40.
9. Andrews, *Slavery and the Domestic Slave Trade*, 137. Another visit to Franklin & Armfield's stockade is described in E. S. Abdy, *Journal of a Residence and Tour in the United States of North America*, 3 vols. (London: John Murray, 1835), vol. 2, 179–180.
10. [Jacobs], *Incidents*, 53.
11. Andrews, *Slavery and the Domestic Slave Trade*, 78, 150, 80. As revealed in the correspondence of Rice Ballard, Franklin & Armfield's operation was not nearly so humane.

Notes

12. Carol Wilson, *Freedom at Risk: The Kidnaping of Free Blacks in America, 1780–1865* (Lexington: University Press of Kentucky, 1994), especially chapter 1.
13. G. W. Featherstonaugh, *Excursion through the Slave States, From Washington on the Potomac to the Frontier of Mexico*, 2 vols. (London: John Murray, 1844), vol. 1, 120. Emphasis in the original.
14. Ibid., vol. 2, 122.
15. At times the overland trip faced delays owing to weather conditions, forcing the slaves and their escorts to camp out and wait. Samuel Alsop, a migrating planter who agreed to escort a coffle to Mississippi for Franklin & Armfield, reported that the weather held up the departure. He used the event of this delay to return "Old James," a forty-two-year-old slave whom he found "will not suit me." Samuel Alsop to Rice Ballard,—6, 1834, Rice Ballard Papers, Southern Historical Collection, University of North Carolina, Box 1, SHC.
16. Featherstonaugh, *Excursion*, vol. 2, 122.
17. Deposition of Samuel Scomp, Philadelphia, Pennsylvania, June 30, 1826, in John Blassingame, ed. *Slave Testimony: Two Centuries of Letters, Speeches, Interviews, and Autobiographies* (Baton Rouge: Louisiana State University Press, 1977): 180–181.
18. Peter Hook interview, 1826, in ibid., 182
19. Wilson, *Freedom at Risk*, chapter 2.
20. Wendell Holmes Stephenson, *Isaac Franklin: Slave Trader and Planter of the Old South, With Plantation Records* (Baton Rouge: Louisiana State University Press, 1938): 52.
21. Ibid., 40–41.
22. One other instance was the 1841 *Creole* incident, in which the slaves in transit from Richmond to New Orleans rebelled, took control of their ship, and successfully requested asylum from British authorities in Nassau.
23. Isaac Franklin to Ballard, February 28, 1831, Rice Ballard Papers, Box 1, SHC.
24. Ingraham, *South-West*, vol. 2, 29–30.
25. Ibid., 193.
26. Isaac Franklin to Ballard, April 29, 1832, Ballard Papers, Box 1, SHC.
27. Ballard to Isaac Franklin, December 2, 1832, ibid.
28. Isaac Franklin to Ballard, December 8, 1832, ibid.
29. James Franklin to Ballard, April 24, 1833, ibid.
30. James Franklin to Ballard, May 7, 1833, ibid. The term "one-eyed man" in the traders' correspondence has dual meaning: both a half-blind fool, as used here, and a euphemism for the penis. See Edward Baptist, " 'Cuffy,' 'Fancy Maids,' and 'One-Eyed Men': Rape, Commodification, and the Domestic Slave Trade in the United States," *AHR* 106 (December 2001): 1619–1650.
31. Isaac Franklin to Rice Ballard, November 1, 1833, Rice Ballard Papers, Box 1, SHC. Also, see Johnson, *Soul by Soul*, 155.
32. Featherstonaugh, *Excursion*, vol. 2, 317.
33. Adam Hodgson, *Remarks During a Journey Through North America in the Years 1819, 1820, and 1821; in a Series of Letters* (New York: Samuel Whiting, 1823): 145.
34. Michael Tadman and Walter Johnson contend that slave traders account for a majority of the slaves in the Southwest. See *Speculators and Slaves*, and *Soul by Soul*. While by the 1850s this assertion may have been the case, it seems to be less likely in the early years of migration. Some planters started anew on the frontier, but many eastern planters had large slave populations that would have been more valuable on new land than their old land would have been with fewer slaves.

Notes

35. Silas Caldwell to James Polk, January 2, 1835, in John Spencer Bassett, *The Southern Plantation Overseer as Revealed in His Letters* (Northampton: Smith College, 1925): 44.
36. Caldwell to Polk, Feb. 10, 1835, ibid., 49–50.
37. Susan Dabney Smedes, *Memorials of a Southern Planter*, ed. Fletcher M. Green (New York: Alfred A. Knopf, 1965): 34–35.
38. Sarah Sparkman to her sister, October 20, 1835, in Michael Mullin, ed., *American Negro Slavery: A Documentary History* (Columbia: University of South Carolina Press, 1976): 213.
39. Johnson, *Soul by Soul*, chapter 7.
40. Sarah Sparkman to Richard T. Brownrigg, November 4, 1835, Mullin, *American Negro Slavery*, 214–215.
41. Sarah Sparkman to Mary Brownrigg, January 4, 1836, ibid., 215.
42. Phebe Brownrigg to Amy Nixon, September 13, 1835, in Blassingame, ed. *Slave Testimony*, 22.
43. Various primary sources suggest this labor regimen; most easily accessible is Smedes, *Memorials*, 49–51; and Bassett, *Plantation Overseer*, 48–49. Joan Cashin's discussion of the work regimen of women on the frontier is strikingly different and informative. *A Family Venture: Men and Women on the Southern Frontier* (New York: Oxford University Press, 1991): 69. See also Steven F. Miller, "Plantation Labor Organization and Slave Life on the Cotton Frontier: The Alabama-Mississippi Black Belt, 1815–1845," in *Cultivation and Culture: Labor and the Shaping of Slave Life in the Americas*, ed. Ira Berlin and Phillip D. Morgan (Charlottesville: University of Virginia Press, 1989): 155–169.
44. Smedes, *Memorials*, 44.
45. Hodgson, *Journey*, 125–126.
46. Samuel Cobon to Abram Barnes, June 25, 1828, Barnes-Willis Papers, Box 2E529, NTC. Cobon witnessed the following transactions: male 22 years, $520; male 18 years, $526; male 21 years, $355; male 18 years, $385; male 25 years, $341; male 15 years, $330; male 14 years, $331; male 14 years, $389; female 16 years, $251; female 15 years, $290; male 55 to 60 years, $150. Cobon added that "those in the above list which went low, were very unlikely & those which went so very high were the finest I have ever saw, and were bought by person[s] living here."
47. Cobon to Barnes, July 10, 1828, ibid.
48. Bery Smith to Barnes, May 19, 1816, ibid.
49. Stephen C. Archer to Richard T. Archer, July 3, 1833, Archer Family Papers, Box 2E562, NTC.
50. John Faulkner to William Fitzhugh Powell, September 4, 1835, William C. Fitzhugh Powell Papers, Perkins Library, Duke University.
51. Smith to Barnes, August 24, 1816, Barnes-Willis Papers, Box 2E529, NTC.
52. Smith to Barnes, October 5, 1816, ibid.
53. The following paragraphs are based on bills of sale for slaves purchased by John Randolph in February and March of 1830 located in the Slaves and Slavery Collection, Box 2.325/V48, NTC. Appendix 1 lists the vital information of these transactions. The typicality of this purchase is certainly open to debate; the very survival of such a run of records makes it atypical.
54. Of course the estimation may have been a bow to ignorance. Three other slaves' ages were listed as "about," although they were round numbers, thirty and forty. Another slave's age was listed as twenty-seven to thirty, illustrating similar uncertainty.

Notes

55. Steven Miller has suggested that planters buying slaves in the east tended to purchase very young slaves with their most productive years ahead of them, along with a few older slaves to tend to housework. "Plantation Labor Organization," especially 157–160.
56. In his statistical analysis of the slave trade, Michael Tadman ferreted out the planter migration from the trade by focusing on the gender ratio (for which traders had no preference) and the ages of the slaves (traders preferred slaves in their prime years).
57. On this process, see chapter 5 below.

Chpater Five

Defining the Boundaries of Enslavement

1. Complaint, April 17, 1834, Slaves and Slavery Collection, Box 2E773, NTC.
2. This incident is retold in Bertram Wyatt-Brown, *Southern Honor: Ethics and Behavior in the Old South* (New York: Oxford University Press, 1982): 462–493.
3. Several scholars have attempted to lay out explanations for this type of power struggle. See Genovese, *Roll, Jordan, Roll*; Scott, *Domination and the Arts of Resistance*; and Christopher Morris "The Articulation of Two Worlds: The Master-Slave Relationship Reconsidered," *JAH* 85 (December 1998): 982–1007.
4. Studies that emphasize the domination of slavery include Stampp, *The Peculiar Institution*; Orlando Patterson *Slavery and Social Death: A Comparative Study* (Cambridge: Harvard University Press, 1982); Oakes, *Slavery and Freedom*; and Peter Kolchin "Reevaluating the Antebellum Slave Community: A Comparative Perspective," *Journal of American History* 70 (December 1983): 579–601.
5. On the planters' mindset, see Genovese, *The World the Slaveholders Made: Two Essays in Interpretation* (New York: Pantheon, 1967).
6. See Jeffrey Robert Young, *Domesticating Slavery: The Master Class in Georgia and South Carolina, 1670–1837* (Chapel Hill: University of North Carolina Press, 1999), especially chapter 5.
7. Studies that illustrate the subversive nature of slave culture include Genovese, *Roll, Jordan, Roll*; Blassingame, *The Slave Community*; Lawrence Levine, *Black Culture and Black Consciousness: Afro-American Folk Thought from Slavery to Freedom* (New York: Oxford University Press, 1977); and Joyner, *Down by the Riverside*.
8. See the discussion of Locust Grove plantation below.
9. Samuel Townes to John and G. F. Townes, quoted in Cashin, *A Family Venture*, 103.
10. John W. Monette, "The Cotton Crop," an essay appended to Ingraham, *South-West*, vol. 2, 287.
11. Mississippi participated in this movement with the construction of a penitentiary in Jackson. See Oshinsky, "*Worse Than Slavery*," 6–7.
12. Monette, "Cotton Crop," 288.
13. Chaplin, *Anxious Pursuit*, outlines planter justification of slavery as a humane practice. Such a definition recognized the humanity of its subjects while proclaiming their humane treatment by masters.
14. A language of dominance involves the use of certain euphemisms to reframe the discussion. See Scott, *Domination and the Arts of Resistance*, 53–55.

Notes

15. Moore, *Emergence of the Cotton Kingdom*, 16.
16. William Kenner to Benjamin Farrar, January 6, 1819, Landry-Hume Collection, UM.
17. George Green & Son to William Newton Mercer, May 31, 1833, ibid. This is one of several similar letters in the collection.
18. Isaac Farnsworth to Joseph Farnsworth, September 12, 1830, Isaac Farnsworth Papers, Perkins Library, Duke University.
19. John Faulkner to William Powell, September 4, 1835, ibid.
20. While a few planters had established plantations along the rivers that create the delta, settlement did not begin to penetrate the region until the 1850s. See James Cobb, *The Most Southern Place on Earth: The Mississippi Delta and the Roots of Regional Identity* (New York: Oxford University Press, 1992), chapter 1, and especially pp. 7–9 for early settlement.
21. "Nabob" is a corruption of the Hindi word "nawab," which means nobleman. In Britain, nabobs were colonial officials who made fortunes in India and returned to luxurious lives in England. Beyond its use to describe the Natchez elite, the term is obscure in the United States. My thanks to Anne Hardgrove for explaining this word's origins.
22. The ideal of plantation self-sufficiency bore little resemblance to reality. Still, planters desired the appearance of self-sufficiency, which bolstered their sense of personal, economic, and political independence.
23. Winthrop D. Jordan, *Tumult and Silence at Second Creek: An Inquiry into a Civil War Slave Conspiracy* (Baton Rouge: Louisiana State University Press, 1993), describes the Natchez plantation world at its maturity. Quote from p. 9. Two other works that have influenced this discussion are Polk, ed., *Natchez before 1830*; and James, *Antebellum Natchez*.
24. John Dick to Benjamin Farrar, January 15, 1822, Landry-Hume Collection, UM.
25. On the fluidity of society during this era, see James, *Antebellum Natchez*, passim. For an example of entry into the primary class of planters, see Robert May, *John Quitman: Old South Crusader* (Baton Rouge: Louisiana State University Press, 1985). A prominent free black businessman in Natchez was William Johnson. See William R. Hogan and Edwin A. Davis, *William Johnson's Natchez: The Ante-Bellum Diary of a Free Negro* (Baton Rouge: Louisiana State University Press, 1951). These examples do not illustrate widespread patterns; however, they demonstrate that the possibility existed.
26. Randy J. Sparks, *On Jordan's Stormy Banks: Evangelicalism in Mississippi, 1773–1876* (Athens: University of Georgia Press, 1994), is the best study of religion in antebellum Mississippi. Chapter 2 discusses the religious differences between elites and plain folk, a difference which extended to the slaves as well.
27. Joseph Johnson to George Comer, December 23, 1831, B. L. C. Wailes Papers, 76.00S, Box 1, MDAH. This letter is reprinted in John Hebron Moore, ed., "Two Documents Relating to Plantation Overseers of the Vicksburg Region, 1831–1832," *JMH* 16 (January 1954): 31–36.
28. On the Awakening's arrival to the frontier, see chapter 1 of Sparks, *On Jordan's Stormy Banks*. General studies of this revival include Christine Heyrman, *Southern Cross: The Beginnings of the Bible Belt* (New York: Alfred A Knopf, 1997); John B. Boles, *The Great Revival, 1787–1805: The Origins of the Southern Evangelical Mind* (Lexington: University Press of Kentucky, 1972); and Dickson D. Bruce, *And They*

Notes

      All Sang Hallelujah: Plain-Folk Camp-Meeting Religion, 1800–1845 (Lexington: University Press of Kentucky, 1974).

29. Ibid., 60–62.
30. Ibid., 66–67, 69. A broader discussion of the tensions between early evangelicalism and slavery is David T. Bailey, *Shadow on the Church: Southwestern Evangelical Religion and the Issue of Slavery, 1783–1860* (Ithaca: Cornell University Press, 1985): 116–120.
31. Randy Sparks, relying on Winans's memoir, argues that Poindexter "blamed his defeat on Winans and the evangelicals." However, in reporting the election returns, the *Port Gibson Correspondent* showed no count of votes cast for Winans. Poindexter lost to Christopher Rankin, and by a rather large margin of 2,204 votes. See Sparks, *On Jordan's Stormy Banks*, 70; *Port Gibson Correspondent*, September 13, 1822; also Ray Holder, *William Winans: Methodist Leader in Antebellum Mississippi* (Jackson: University Press of Mississippi, 1977): 68–70.
32. Sparks, *On Jordan's Stormy Banks*, 70–71. On segregation within churches, see Bailey, *Shadow on the Church*, 192–193. The law was so quickly revised that the offending sections were never printed in the 1824 compilation of Mississippi law. See *Revised Code of the Laws of Mississippi* (Natchez: Frances Baker, 1824): 376, 380, 381. Mississippi's secular press paid little attention to this conflict.
33. *Code of Mississippi* (Jackson: Price and Fall, 1848): 534.
34. Sparks, *On Jordan's Stormy Banks*, 72–75, quote on p. 75. More general discussions of the compromise between evangelicalism and slavery include Bailey, *Shadow on the Church*; Anne Loveland, *Southern Evangelicals and the Social Order, 1800–1860* (Baton Rouge: Louisiana State University Press, 1980), chapters 7 and 8; and Mitchel Snay, *Gospel of Disunion: Religion and Separatism in the Antebellum South* (Cambridge: Cambridge University Press, 1993). On the emergence of the colonization movement, see Sydnor, *Slavery in Mississippi*, 203–238.
35. There is very little direct evidence of a folk religion among the slaves, which to some degree affirms the assertions made here. The effectiveness of "hidden transcripts" or traditions of resistance to dominant culture rests in good part on the ability to keep it hidden. See Scott, *Domination and the Arts of Resistance*, 23–28, 108–135. There are several fine studies of the folk religion among slaves, including Albert Raboteu, *Slave Religion: The "Invisible Institution" in the Antebellum South* (New York: Oxford University Press, 1978); Eugene D. Genovese, *Roll Jordan, Roll*; and Charles Joyner, *Down by the Riverside*, chapter 5.
36. In 1835, Mississippi's white population voiced in no uncertain terms their suspicion of slave preachers. See chapter 6 below.
37. C. C. Goen, *Broken Churches, Broken Nation: Denominational Schisms and the Coming of the Civil War* (Macon: Mercer University Press, 1985); Snay, *Gospel of Disunion*, chapter 4.
38. Much of this evidence is in George Rawick, *The American Slave: An Autobiography*, 39 vols. (Westport, Conn.: Greenwood Press, 1974). Evidence specific to the time period under consideration here is unavailable. I chose not to use the WPA narratives to avoid projecting backward in time.
39. Locust Grove Plantation Slave Ledger, C-9, UM. This ledger is an unusual document for several reasons, but perhaps most notably because it tells a great deal about the identities and lives of the slaves, yet has few clues as to the plantation's location or owner. Clippings from Natchez newspapers suggest that Locust Grove was an Adams County plantation, but this assumption is by no means certain.

Notes

40. Isaac's name appears next to the names of others purchased in 1832, but the date of his purchase is not clear. Appendix B organizes the ledger's data into a family tree.
41. Sally McMillen, *Motherhood in the Old South: Pregnancy, Childbirth, and Infant Rearing* (Baton Rouge: Louisiana State University Press, 1990), chapter 7.
42. Starks to Ballard, February 5, 1833, Ballard Papers, Box 1, SHC.
43. John Nevitt Diary (typescript), May 2, 1831, *Records*, Series J, part 6, reel 3.
44. Ibid., October 11, 1831.
45. Ibid., October 12, 1831.
46. Ibid., January 13, 1827.
47. Ibid., January 9, 1827.
48. Ibid., March 3; March 13, 1826.
49. Ibid., January 19, 1827.
50. Ibid., February 26, 1827.
51. Ibid., March 16, 1827.
52. Ibid., April 3, 1827.
53. Daniel Willis to Abram Barnes, March 12, 1825 in Barnes-Willis Family Papers, Box 2E529, NTC.
54. M. Ashbrook to Mrs. Rapalje, March 12, 1821, in Ellis-Farrar Papers, *Records*, Series I, part 3, reel 10.
55. Nevitt Diary, August 25, 1827.
56. Ibid., June 11, 1827. Many planters insured their gins. See the letter accompanying John Minor's 1826 policy renewal, William Kenner to John Minor, December 12, 1825, Kenner Papers, *Records*, Series I, part 3, reel 13.
57. Several years earlier his gin burned, also attributable to an "incendiary." *Natchez Mississippi Republican*, October 31, 1822.
58. Nevitt Diary, April 4, 1830.
59. Ibid., August 27, 1830.
60. Ibid., April 26, 1831.
61. Planters were much more aware of slave theft than is the common perception; however, they seemed willing to attribute missing supplies to slave theft and leave it at that if no culprit could be apprehended. However, slave thefts could cause difficulties between masters and their business associates. New Orleans merchant Jos. Saul informed Benjamin Farrar that missing stores from a supply recently delivered "must have been purloined by the servants or some body. My son John counted every article and for fear of mistakes I examined them after him." Jos. Saul to Benjamin Farrar, Oct. 25, 1819, Landry-Hume Collection, UM.
62. Nevitt Diary, April 21, 1826.
63. Ibid., August 28, 1827.
64. Ibid., December 4, 1827.
65. Ibid., March 2, 1828.
66. Ibid., September 9, 1829.
67. Ibid., January 3, 1828.
68. Ibid., July 24, 1830.
69. Ibid., June 11, 1830. Emphasis in the original.
70. Ibid., February 5, 1831.
71. Thomas Hill to James Wilkins, April 8, 1826, James Campbell Wilkins Papers, Box 2E545, NTC.
72. Nevitt Diary, January 10, 1830.

Notes

73. Ibid., July 14, 1828.
74. Ibid., August 25, 1828. Such proceedings were not very unusual. See the Warren County Jury Summons of November 1833 in Slaves & Slavery Collection, Box 2.325 V48, NTC.
75. Ibid., March 8, 1829. Nevitt also had an ownership conflict with a "Mr. P. Sistoff," who had taken the slave Willis. Sistoff "refused to give him up saying he had a right to the negro being the owner &c &c[.]" While the two settled their ownership claims in court, Nevitt recovered Willis "and put him in Jail for safe keeping[.]" No outcome is mentioned. Ibid., August 23, 1830.
76. Ibid., August 17, 1827.
77. Ibid., January 25, November 22, December 13, 1828; October 5, 1829.
78. Ibid., July 4, 1827.
79. Nevitt hoped to establish a kind of reciprocity with them, which would create a middle ground between master and slave. This reciprocity can be viewed as paternalism, but it is probably better understood as an exchange in which both parties defined their needs in terms that appealed to the interests of the other. See Morris, "The Articulation of Two Worlds."
80. Nevitt Diary, December 17, 1829.
81. Ibid., December 27, 1828.
82. Ibid., December 27, 1829.
83. See ibid., December 30, 1829, when he noted that the slaves slept "until 8 oclock in the morning," late by any agricultural standard.
84. Ibid., December 24, 1831.
85. Affidavit, June 24, 1832, in Slaves and Slavery Collection, Box 2E773, NTC.
86. Receipt, no date, in ibid. Several other receipts that follow this form are located in this collection.
87. Affidavit, March 10, 1831, in ibid. Similar affidavits and petitions can be found in this collection.
88. Affidavit, June 7, 1832, in Slaves and Slavery Collection, Box 2E777, NTC.
89. *Code of Mississippi* (1848): 533.
90. *Natchez*, November 11, 1831.
91. Similar fears and legislation followed slave conspiracies in Virginia and South Carolina. See Jordan, *White Over Black*, 406–414. Mississippi did consider shutting down the slave trade, but lobbying efforts by the slave trader Isaac Franklin appear to have convinced legislators that slaves were not the problem. See letters from Franklin to Ballard, February 28, 1831, and October 26, 1831, Ballard Papers, Box 1, SHC.
92. Arrest warrants, May 26, 1832, in Slaves and Slavery Collection, Box 2E775, NTC.
93. Sydnor, *Slavery in Mississippi*, chapter 9.
94. On the Nat Turner insurrection, see Henry Irving Tragle, *The Southampton Slave Revolt of 1831: A Compilation of Source Material* (Amherst: University of Massachusetts Press, 1971); Stephen B. Oates, *The Fires of Jubilee: Nat Turner's Fierce Rebellion* (New York: Harper & Row, 1975); and Kenneth S. Greenberg, ed., *The Confessions of Nat Turner and Related Documents* (Boston: St. Martin's Press, 1996).
95. *Vicksburg Register*, September 16, 1831.
96. Christopher Tomlins, *Law, Labor, and Ideology in the Early American Republic* (New York: Cambridge University Press, 1993), chapter 2, asserts the significance of the older meaning of "police."

Notes

97. The *Natchez* never reported the uprising, although it covered race riots in Providence, Rhode Island, in September of 1831. See *Natchez*, November 4, 1831.
98. William McCain, ed., "The Emancipation of Indiana Osborne," *JMH* 8 (April 1956): 98.
99. With the passage of time, white Mississippians would grow increasingly frustrated with the law's inability to control slaves completely. See Christopher Waldrep, *Roots of Disorder: Race and Criminal Justice in the American South, 1817–80* (Urbana: University of Illinois Press, 1998), chapter 3.
100. Indictment, May 1832, in Joel Cameron Papers, Box 2E553, NTC. Cameron owned these slaves in a partnership with Alexander McNutt.
101. Pardon, June 9, 1832, ibid. Bertram Wyatt-Brown suggests that hysteria regarding potential slave uprisings broke out in a nearly cyclical fashion based on the mood of the white society. The issue remains, however, that in light of Nat Turner's uprising, Mississippians were *not* hysterical. Wyatt-Brown, *Southern Honor*, chapter 15.
102. For example, see unknown to J. A. Trask, June 19, 1827, in Trask-Ventress Papers, Z607m (microfilm), reel 2, MDAH.
103. Joseph Johnson to George Conner, December 23, 1831, B. L. C. Wailes Papers, Z7600s, Box 1, MDAH.
104. J. Ford to [unknown], October 12, 1828, Landry-Hume Collection, UM.
105. Thomas C. Adams to J. L. Trask, August 27, 1818, in Trask-Ventress Papers, Z607m (microfilm), reel 1, MDAH.
106. Thomas C. Adams to J. L. Trask, April 4, 1830, ibid.
107. These are the subjects of letters from Adams to Trask written on, respectively, October 16, 1831, November 15, 1831, and November 30, 1832, ibid. For the correspondence between an overseer and an absentee planter from a slightly later period, see Bassett, *Plantation Overseer*.
108. Examples of masters trying out slaves can be seen in Stephen C. Archer to Richard T. Archer, July 28, 1833, ibid.; Ann Farrar to William Mercer, April 15, 1825, Landry-Hume Collection, UM; James Smylie to Aurelia Montgomery, March 13, 1836, Montgomery Papers, Z537f, MDAH.
109. Ingraham, *South-West*, vol. 2, 30–32.
110. Ibid., 244.
111. This faith in the law and in communities' ability to administer it is illustrated in the certification of several slaves belonging to a planter moving away from Vicksburg. "So long as they remained in this country [they] were under good character & *they were not removed for any crime*[.]" Certification of slaves, August 9, 1830, in Slaves and Slavery Collection, Box 2E775, NTC. Emphasis in the original.
112. George L. Prentiss, *A Memoir of S. S. Prentiss*, 2 vols. (New York: Charles Scribner, 1881), vol. 1, 107.

Chapter Six

The Transformation of Mississippi

1. Ronald N. Satz, "The Mississippi Choctaw: From the Removal Treaty to the Federal Agency," in Samuel J. Wells and Roseanna Tubby, eds., *After Removal: The Choctaw in Mississippi* (Jackson: University Press of Mississippi, 1986): 3–5.

2. Several works have discussed the removal of the Choctaws. Arthur H. DeRosier Jr., *The Removal of The Choctaw Indians* (Knoxville: University of Tennessee Press, 1970), is the chief book-length study. See also Samuel J. Wells, "Federal Indian Policy: From Accommodation to Removal," in Reeves, ed., *The Choctaw Before Removal*, 181–213; Jesse O. McKee and Jon A. Schlenker, *The Choctaws: Cultural Evolution of a Native American Tribe* (Jackson: University Press of Mississippi, 1980): 50–64, 74–98. For a broader context, see White, *Roots of Dependency*, 34–146.
3. On Leflore, see R. Halliburton, "Chief Greenwood Leflore and His Malmaison Plantation," in Wells and Tubby, eds., *After Removal*, 56–63; more generally, see White, *Roots of Dependency*, 133.
4. Statistics from White, *Roots of Dependency*, 134; Arthur H. DeRosier Jr. succinctly explains the Choctaws' antipathy to plantation slavery in "Pioneers with Conflicting Ideals: Christianity and Slavery in the Choctaw Nation," *JMH* 21 (July 1959): 185–188.
5. *Code of Mississippi* (Jackson: Price and Fall, 1848): 136. The five sections of the act abolished Choctaw government, granted them citizenship, extended state law over the Choctaws, validated their marriages, and abolished the office of chief.
6. Accounts of Leflore's involvement in the removal include Samuel Wells, "The Role of Mixed-Bloods in Mississippi Choctaw History" in Reeves, ed, *The Choctaw Before Removal*, 51–53; Halliburton, "Chief Greenwood Leflore," 59–61. Quite a few full-blooded Choctaws remained in Mississippi as well. They preferred to become subject to Mississippi law, and hold onto their homelands, despite the loss of the borderlands. Most eked out a subsistence in traditional ways, supplementing their livelihood through contract labor. Their descendants still live in central Mississippi today. Unlike Leflore and the other assimilateds who remained, they never became involved in slave ownership. Clara Sue Kidwell, "The Choctaw Struggle for Land and Identity in Mississippi, 1830–1918," in Wells and Tubby, eds., *After Removal*, 64–93; also Kidwell, *Choctaws and Missionaries in Mississippi, 1818–1918* (Norman: University of Oklahoma Press, 1995) 159–175.
7. See maps 3 and 4 in chapter 4, especially the counties in central Mississippi.
8. On conspiracy theories throughout American history, see Richard Hofstader, *The Paranoid Style in American Politics and Other Essays* (New York: Alfred A. Knopf, 1965): 3–40. For a discussion of such fears as relates specifically to slavery and abolition, see David Brion Davis, *The Slave Power Conspiracy and the Paranoid Style* (Baton Rouge: Louisiana State University Press, 1969).
9. Edward Baptist provides one example of such frontier lore in "Accidental Ethnography in an Antebellum Southern Newspaper: Snell's Homecoming Festival," *JAH* 84 (March 1998): 1355–1383. Baptist makes the important point that the entertainment value of folklore involved poking fun at elites and social conventions.
10. By 1837, Madison County was 76 percent slave. See 1837 Census, printed in Jackson, Mississippi, May 12, 1837. The 50 to 1 estimate is in "Proceedings at Livingston," in H. R. Howard, comp., *History of Virgil A. Stewart and his Adventure in Capturing and Exposing the Great "Western Land Pirate" and his Gang, in Connection with the Evidence; Also of the Trials, Confessions and Execution of Murrell's Associates in the State of Mississippi During the Summer of 1835, and the Execution of Five Professional Gamblers by the Citizens of Vicksburg, on the 6th July, 1835* (New York: Harper & Brothers, 1836): 233.

Notes

11. The principal studies of this event are Edwin A. Miles, "The Mississippi Slave Insurrection Scare of 1835," *JNH* 42 (January 1957): 48–60; and Davidson Burns McKibben, "Negro Slave Insurrections in Mississippi, 1800–1865," *JNH* 34 (January 1949): 73–90. More recent studies of this incident have used it as a window through which to observe aspects of the Mississippi frontier society. These include Laurence Shore, "Making Mississippi Safe for Slavery: The Insurrectionary Panic of 1835," in Orville Vernon Burton and Robert C. McMath Jr., eds. *Class, Conflict, and Consensus: Antebellum Southern Community Studies* (Westport: Greenwood Press, 1982): 96–127; and Christopher Morris, "An Event in Community Organization: The Mississippi Slave Insurrection Scare of 1835," *JSoc.H* 22 (fall 1988): 93–111 (which I find the more convincing of the two). Finally, James Lal Penick, *The Great Western Land Pirate: John A. Murrell in Legend and History* (Columbia: University of Missouri Press, 1981), is concerned more with the Murrell legend than the Madison County conspiracy; however, the plot plays a major role in the development of that legend.
12. The Murrell story is remarkable for its longevity. Mark Twain briefly retold the Murrell story in *Life on the Mississippi* (1883; New York: Bantam, 1981): 143–147. As evidence of the persistence of the Murrell myth, in 1997, a Mississippi native and colleague in graduate school corrected my pronunciation of his name, but assured me that I told the story accurately.
13. Howard, *History of Virgil A. Stewart*, 29. This and Augustus Q. Walton, *A History of the Detection, Conviction, Life and Designs of John A. Murel, the Great Western Land Pirate; together with his system of Villany, and Plan of Exciting a Negro Rebellion also, a Catalogue of the Names of Four Hundred and Fifty-Five of his Mystic Clan of Fellows and Followers and a Statement of their Efforts for the Destruction of Virgil A. Stewart, the Young Man who Detected Him. To Which is Added a Biographical Sketch of V. A. Stewart* (Cincinnati: n.p., n.d.), are the chief sources for Stewart's fictional adventure. In the initial telling Murrell represented the crimes as his brother's actions, but quickly revealed them as his own.
14. Howard, *History of Virgil A. Stewart*, 35, 46–7, 60, 66–67. Quote on p. 60. Murrell apparently had been whipped and imprisoned for horse-stealing. A full treatment of the historical Murrell, including his encounters with the law, can be found in Penick, *The Great Western Land Pirate*, 9–32.
15. The entire conversation is in Walton, *History of Murel*, 36–39. A similar version of the same conversation is in Howard, *History of Virgil A. Stewart*, 51–52.
16. Denise Herd, "The Paradox of Temperance: Blacks and the Alcohol Question in Nineteenth Century America," in *Drinking: Behavior and Belief in Modern History*, ed. Susanna Barrows and Robin Room (Berkeley and Los Angeles: University of California Press, 1991): 354–371, argues that the white paranoia concerning slave drunkenness was a means of locating the rebellious nature of normally contented slaves in an outside source, liquor.
17. This mode of storytelling is part of a style of folklore common on the southern frontier but rarely recorded. See Baptist, "Accidental Ethnography." Laurence Shore suggests that initially Stewart's story "was considered a joke wherever it was distributed," "Making Mississippi Safe for Slavery," 108. As will become clear, for a brief moment the story's content was no laughing matter for white southerners.
18. Walton, *History of Murel*, 40.

Notes

19. While planter ideology remains a subject of debate among historians, it is instructive that the modern discussion centers on questions of race, class, and power—the same issues Stewart raised in Murrell's fictional plan.
20. In this respect, Murrell is similar to the trickster Snell in Baptist, "Accidental Ethnography."
21. Howard, *History of Stewart*, 56.
22. Walton, *History of Murel*, 40–41.
23. Only a decade earlier the Masons in New York were held accountable for the disappearance of a local stonemason, William Morgan, who revealed their secrets. Paul Johnson, *A Shopkeeper's Millennium: Society and Revivals in Rochester, New York, 1815–1837* (New York: Hill and Wang, 1978): 66–68.
24. Mullin, *Africa in America*, 67–68, describes the significance of oath-taking in slave communities.
25. Howard, *History of Stewart*, 57, 61.
26. Ibid., 92.
27. In the years that followed this incident, Mississippi planters would often look for outsiders influencing slave insurrections. In "An Old South Morality Play: Reconsidering the Social Underpinnings of the Proslavery Ideology," *JAH* 77 (December 1990): 860, Michael Wayne suggests that the slavery defense involved identifying outside instigators, whether or not they existed, and lynching them to reassert planter hegemony. Jordan, *Tumult and Silence at Second Creek*, 137–139, discusses the suspicion of "socially marginal white men" who provoked slave discontent.
28. Penick, *Great Western Land Pirate*, 108.
29. "Proceedings at Livingston," 223–225. This pamphlet was originally published in Jackson in 1836, and later was appended to H. R. Howard's edition of Stewart's adventure. Citations here come from the later edition.
30. The *Philadelphia Gazette* reported that the committee gave him "six hundred lashes, before he would discover anything; then he informed them that the blacks were to rise on the 4th of July." While the figure of six hundred lashes, and two hundred given to another slave, are probably exaggerations, they attest to the brutality of the interrogations. Reprinted in *The Liberator*, August 1, 1835.
31. "Proceedings at Livingston," 227. Emphasis in the original.
32. The possible threat that slave preachers posed to plantation society is discussed in Genovese, *Roll, Jordan, Roll*, 255–279. Genovese suggests that slave preachers presented little threat of insurrection because most did not have the messianic zeal necessary for such a movement. On the other hand, other slave conspiracies have employed religious mysticism to recruit supporters. See the discussion of evangelicalism and slavery in chapter 5.
33. "Proceedings at Livingston," 230.
34. Ibid., 231.
35. Ibid., 232.
36. The wording of Jim's statement—"keep[ing women] as wives" rather than ravishing or seducing plantation women—indicates that Jim raised the issue first. Laurence Shore suggests this aspect of the confession brings the entire statement into question; however, I would suggest that it is evidence of the conversations going on in Madison County slave quarters prior to the discovery of the conspiracy. In addition, general and specific discussions of the sexual dimension of slave rebellions

Notes

by Winthrop Jordan indicate a greater tension in such statements, suggesting that reports, while playing on white fears, had a degree of truth in them. Finally, Diane Miller Somerville has questioned the validity of scholarly assumptions that white southerners truly feared the possibility of slaves raping white women. See Shore, "Making Mississippi Safe," 105; Jordan, *White Over Black*, chapter 4, especially 154–163; Jordan, *Tumult and Silence*, chapter 9; Somerville, "The Rape Myth in the Old South Reconsidered," *JSH* 61 (August 1995): 481–518.

37. "Proceedings at Livingston," 228.
38. Ibid., 234. More generally, see Waldrep, *Roots of Disorder*, which elaborates on growing doubts about the ability of courts and systems of law to control slaves in Mississippi.
39. Ibid., 235. In the wake of this affair, the Mississippi legislature would attempt to address the issue of slave testimony in the courts. See below.
40. *Charleston Courier*, reprinted in *The Liberator*, August 22, 1835. Steam doctors were practitioners of Thompsonian medicine, a kind of aroma therapy. They gave their patients large doses of spices, most commonly cayenne pepper, assuming that the perspiration the treatment induced would force the patient to sweat out their illness. Considered quacks by most whites, many slaves preferred their treatments to the bleedings and purgatives that masters administered to their slaves who were ill. The image of steam doctors associating with slaves made them appear even more dangerous to white society.
41. *Nashville Republican*, reprinted in *Niles' Register*, August 1, 1835, p. 377. Laurence Shore discusses Cotton's motives for confessing and agrees that there was little truth in the confession. "Making Mississippi Safe," 109.
42. Both quotations, as well as the governor's proclamation, are in *Niles' Register*, 377, 403.
43. *Charleston Courier*, quoted in *The Liberator*, August 22, 1835.
44. *Clinton Gazette*, quoted in the *Jackson Mississippian*, July 24, 1835.
45. See, for instance, the gambling riots in Vicksburg described in Morris, *Becoming Southern*, 121.
46. Joshua Cotton, William Saunders, Albe Ean, A. L. Donovan, and Ruel Blake were executed by the committee. Lee Smith was lynched shortly after being freed, William Earle committed suicide, and his brother John was released to the Committee of Safety in Vicksburg. Lastly, William Benson and Lansford Barnes were ordered off. The committee seemed convinced that these men were abolitionists attempting to overthrow the slave system. See "Proceedings at Livingston," 238–259, for the committee's actions concerning these men.
47. In a sense, Livingston's planters were turning the social order upside down, for the parvenus on the frontier were not part of the Natchez elite. However they were by no means subordinated to the nabobs either. An interpretation that also views this incident as one in which the white leadership asserted its dominance is Morris, "An Event in Community Organization." For a general discussion of this type of social upheaval, see Scott, *Domination and the Arts of Resistance*, 202–227.
48. James Slade to William Slade, August 22, 1835, William Slade Papers, Box 2, Perkins Library, Duke University.
49. Quoted in Loveland, *Southern Evangelicals and the Social Order*, 195.
50. On this transformation, see ibid., chapters 7 and 8; also Mitchell Snay, "American Thought and Southern Distinctiveness: The Southern Clergy and the Sanctification

Notes

of Slavery," *CWH* 35 (December 1989): 311–328; Snay, *Gospel of Disunion;* Sparks, *On Jordan's Stormy Banks.*
51. Prentiss, *Memoir of S. S. Prentiss,* vol. 1, 107, 161.
52. Bancroft, *Slave-Trading in the Old South,* 301.
53. The connection that Mississippians drew between the abolitionist mailing campaign that began in 1835 and this insurrection has been thoroughly discussed in Penick, *Great Western Land Pirate,* 151–157. On the 1835 abolitionist mailing campaign's effects in the South, see Snay, *Gospel of Disunion,* 19–49.
54. *Mississippi Senate Journal* (1836): 36.
55. Ibid., 147, 148.
56. *Mississippi House Journal* (1836): 196.
57. Dunbar Rowland, *History of Mississippi, Heart of the South,* 4 vols. (Chicago: S. J. Clarke, 1925), vol. 1, 547.
58. Sydnor, *Slavery in Mississippi,* 80–81.
59. *Mississippi Senate Journal* (1836): 355.
60. *Mississippi House Journal* (1836): 93–94.
61. J. F. H. Claiborne, *Mississippi as a Province, Territory and State, with Biographical Notices of Eminent Citizens,* 2 vols. (Jackson: Powers & Barksdale, 1880), vol. 1, 472, 476.
62. *Mississippi Senate Journal* (1837): 53. In the context of the Specie Circular, the capital drain that the slave trade had on Mississippi may also have motivated this restriction. However, as Bradley G. Bond has noted, Mississippians did not recognize the scope of the currency crisis until 1838. *Political Culture in the Nineteenth-Century South: Mississippi, 1830–1900* (Baton Rouge: Louisiana State University Press, 1995): 82–85.
63. *Jackson Mississippian,* May 19, 1837. The ordinance was published for four weeks in the *Natchez Mississippi Free Trader,* the *Columbus Democrat,* the *Eastern Clarion,* and the *Mississippian.* No legislative records were published for the special session that spring.
64. Bancroft, *Slave-Trading in the Old South,* 387.
65. Stephenson, *Isaac Franklin,* 62.

Conclusion

MISSISSIPPI, THE CLOSED SOCIETY

1. On Quitman's political career, see May, *John Quitman;* on fire-eaters, see Eric H. Walther, *The Fire-Eaters* (Baton Rouge: Louisiana State University Press, 1992).
2. James, *Antebellum Natchez,* 163, 177–180.
3. Jordan, *Tumult and Silence at Second Creek.*
4. McMillen, *Dark Journey;* Waldrep, *Roots of Disorder.*
5. James, *Antebellum Natchez,* 181.
6. On the antebellum origins for the crooked system of Jim Crow justice, see Waldrep, *Roots of Disorder,* chapters 2 and 3; see also Oshinsky, "*Worse than Slavery,*" 1–7.
7. Wood, *Black Majority.*

Index

abolitionism, 87, 108, 115–16
absentee planters, 68, 98
Adams, Thomas, 97
African churches, 86–87
African cultural traditions, 46–47, 54–55, 108
Alabamon Mingo, 14
Alexandria, Va., 62
alligators, 24, 134 n 36
American Revolution, 30–32
Andrews, E. A., 62
antislavery, 59
Archer, Richard, 72
Archer, Stephen, 72
Armfield, John, 63, 66, 67. See also Franklin & Armfield
arson, 53, 90, 91
asylum reform, 82
Atlantic slave trade, 33, 52, 61
Atlantic World, ix, 36, 83

Bahamas, 64
bale, 44–45
Ballard, Rice, 65, 66, 67, 89
Bambarra, 7, 11–12; problematic nature of designation, 11–12, 131 n 50
Barcly and Sackeld, 52
Barnes, Abram, 72, 73, 90
Beanland, Ephraim, 68
Beattie's Bluff, 110, 112
Bienville, Jean-Baptiste Lemoyne, Sieur de, 9, 10
borderlands, x, 19, 102
Browne, Montfort, 18
Brownrigg, Mary, 69, 70
Brownrigg, Phoebe, 70
Brownrigg, Richard, 69
Brownrigg, Tom, 70

Cahokian Civilization, viii
Caldwell, Silas, 68
Cameron, Joel, 96–97, 98
Chepart, Sieur de, 10–11
Chester, Peter, 18, 19–20
Chickasaw Indians, 5, 19, 56, 83, 102, 103, 120
Choctaw cession, 84, 100, 102, 103, 109
Choctaw chief, 4–5. See also Alabamon Mingo; Leflore, Greenwood
Choctaw Indians, viii, 4, 19, 56, 83, 84, 93, 102, 103, 120; attack on Natchez, 13; recovery of African slaves, 14; relations with French colonizers, 5; rivalry with Chickasaw Indians, 5
cholera, 66
Christianity. See religion
Christmas, 45, 93–94, 108
Claiborne, William C. C., 39
Claremont Plantation, 89–94
Clinton, Miss., 72
Clitto, 105–06
coastal slave ships, 60, 63, 64. See also Comet; Creole
Cobon, Samuel, 72
coffle, 60, 63
Colonization Society, 87, 96
Columbus, Miss., *Press*, 113
Comer, George, 86
Comet, 64
Company of the Indies, 6, 7, 9
Concise Natural History of East and West Florida. See Romans, Bernard
conspiracy. See slave rebellion
cotton, 23, 36, 37–47, 72, 81, 82, 83, 89–90, 138 n 18, 138 n 19, 138 n 21. See also Mexican cotton
cotton cultivation, 41–47, 90, 98

Index

cotton factors, 83, 84
cotton fever, 38–39
cotton gin, 36, 39–41, 44, 90, 91, 93, 98
Cotton, Joshua, 112–13
cotton kingdom, 83, 84, 104
cotton press, 44–45
cotton seed, 50
Creek Indians, 56, 57
Creole, 145 n 22
creolization, 34, 59
cult of domesticity, 80–81

Dabney, Thomas, 68, 69
De Soto, Hernando, 3–4
deerskin trade, 4, 17–18, 34
defense of slavery, 115–16, 117, 119–20
Delta (Mississippi River), 84
Dick, John, 85
disease, effect on Indians, 3
domestic slave trade, 60, 61–67, 116–17
Dunbar, William, 22–28, 34, 44, 50–53, 90
Dunsford, Elias, 20

Embargo Act, 61
English trade practices, 17–18
epidemics, 66
escape. *See* flight
European colonization, viii–ix
Evangelical religion. *See* religion
exchange networks, 17–18

"fancy girls," 66, 67
Farnsworth, Isaac, 60
Farrar, Benjamin, 31, 56, 85
Faulkner, John, 72, 84
Featherstonaugh, George, 63
Federal ban, on slave trade, 61
First Natchez War, 6
Fitzpatrick, John, 28, 29–30
"Five Civilized Tribes," 102
flight, 25–26, 27, 53–55, 75, 91–92. *See also* runaway slave, advertisements
"Flush Times," 75, 100
folk religion, 87

Forks of the Road, 65, 115
Fort Panmure, 19, 33
Fort Rosalie, 6
Foster, James, 79
Fourth of July, 93, 112
Franklin & Armfield, 62–63, 64, 67, 117. *See also* Armfield, John; Franklin, Isaac
Franklin, Isaac, 65, 66, 67, 151 n 91. *See also* Franklin & Armfield
Franklin, James, 66, 67
free blacks, 93, 95–96, 99–100
French settlers, 4, 6
French slavery, 8
frontier, 79, 82–83, 103, 109

Gabriel's rebellion, 49
gang labor, 46
Garrison, William Lloyd, 108
gender division, of slave purchases, 74
gendered division, of labor, 41
George Green & Son, 83
German settlers, 6
Gibbs, John, 96
great reaction, 117
Great Sun, 3–4
Guillard, Tacitus, 31

Haitian Revolution, 49
Hill, Thomas, 92
Holmes, David, 55
honor, 51, 79, 105, 107
house slaves. *See* personal slaves
Hubert, Marc-Antoine, 6
humanitarianism, 48, 59, 62, 64–65, 73, 78, 81, 82, 85, 147 n 13
Hunt, Abijah, 52
Hunt, Jesse, 51, 52
Hutchins, Anthony, 31
hysteria, 100, 112–14, 119–20, 152 n 101

Ibo, 52
India, 40
Indian adoption, 15, 16
Indian removal, 102–03, 153 n 6

Index

Indian Removal Act, 102
Indian slavery, 5, 129 n 23
indigo, 29, 35–36, 137 n 89
Industrial Revolution, 45–47, 50
Ingraham, Joseph Holt, vii, 65, 98–99
insurrection. *See* slave rebellion
interracial worship, 85–87
interrogation, of slaves, 110–11

Jackson, Miss., 101
Jackson, Tenn., 104
Jamaica, 23
Jefferson, Thomas, 50
Jerry (slave), 89, 92
Johnson, Joseph, 86
Johnson, William, 119
Jordan, Winthrop, 101

La Salle, René Robert Cavalier, 4
land pirates, 104–09
land boom, of 1770s, 18
language, of dominance, 82, 85
Latham Plantation, 110
Leflore, Greenwood, 102
liquor, 26–27, 95, 106–07, 108
Livingston, 104, 110, 112, 113, 114
Locust Grove Plantation, 88–89, 123–25, 149 n 39
Louisiana Slave Insurrection, 57
Lum, Jesse, 29
Lynch, Charles, 117

Mabry, Jesse, 110–11
Madison County, 103–18
Madison, James, 39
Mammy Harriet, 68, 69, 71
Manchac, British surrender at, 32
maroon societies, 16, 132 n 71
masculinity, 79
masonry, 103, 108
matrilineage, 4, 14, 102, 128 n 11
McIntire, John, 19–20
McIntosh, Alexander, 30
measles, 66

merchant firms, 17–18
messages, from slaves to family, 69–70
Mexican cotton, 40, 50
middle passage, 7–8
military slavery, 131 n 56
militia, 49, 56
Mingo. *See* Choctaw chief
Minor, John, 55
Minor, Stephen, 53, 55
Mississippi statehood, 59, 82
mixed-blood Choctaws, 102–03
modernization, 46–47, 50
Monette, John, 81
Murrell, John, 103–09, 118
mythology, 104

nabob, 81, 84, 114, 148 n 21
Nat Turner Insurrection. *See* Turner, Nat
Natchez Indians, 3–4; African slaves allied with, 13–14; destruction of, 13, 22; social structure, 3
Natchez Mississippi Messenger, 54
Natchez Rebellion (1729), 10–11, 12
Natchez (weekly), 95
"necessary evil," 85, 100, 116
Nevvitt, John, 89–94
New Orleans, Battle of, 57
Nixon, Amy, 70
nullification crisis, 114
Nutt, Rush, 50

okra, use in indigo production, 35
"one-eyed men," 67, 145 n 30
organic society, 85
Osborne, Ind., 96
overseers, 68, 97–98

Pannell, David, 56
penitentiary reform, 82
Periér, Etienne Boucher de, 10, 11
personal slaves, 98–99
plantation homes, 84–85
planter migration, 60, 61, 67–71, 72, 84
Poindexter, George, 86

161

Index

Pointe Coupée, 37
police, 85, 96, 151 n 96
Polk, James K., 68
Pollock, Oliver, 32
Port Gibson, Miss., 66; cotton, 50
Powell, William, 72
Prentiss, Sargent S., 115
"prime" slaves, 61, 74
Proclamation of 1763, 19
purchase of slaves, in Eastern states, 61, 71–74

Quitman, John, 115–16, 119

race relations, x, 8, 48, 96, 99, 103, 119–20
racial stereotype, 106
radicalism, 100, 116–18, 119–20
Randolph, John, 73–74, 121
Rapalje, George, 53
rape: of black women by slave traders, 67; of white women by slaves, 111, 155 n 36
reform movements, 57, 59, 81, 82
religion, 58–59, 85–87, 108, 114, 149 n 35
remarriage, following division of slave families, 78
Rogers, Isaac, 96
Romans, Bernard, 20–22
Ross, Alexander, 23, 26, 27, 30, 34
Roullet, Regis du, 14, 15
runaway slaves, 54–55, 94–95, 96, 97–98; advertisements, 54–55
Runnels, Hiram, 113

sabotage. *See* slave resistance
sanctification, of slavery, 115
Sargent, Winthrop, 49
Saunders, William, 112
Scott, A. M., 97
Second Great Awakening, 86
Second Natchez War, 8, 11
Senegambia, 7, 11
Senegambian slavery, 7
sex, coerced, 67
Slade, James, 101

Slade, William, 101
slave assault, on white man, 79, 96–97
slave auction, 65
slave code, 48–49, 56–58, 95, 99
slave communities: division of, 60, 69, 71, 75, 76; new, 78, 81; relocation of, 67–71
slave families, 88–89; division of, 60, 62, 67, 68, 71, 72, 73, 75, 76, 88
slave patrol, 56, 575
slave population, vii–ix, 19, 20, 33, 75, 76–77, 103, 104
slave preachers, 86–87, 110
slave purchase, preferences, 73, 74
slave quarters, 84
slave rebellion, 12, 27–28, 30, 37, 49, 55–57, 75, 76, 80, 87, 97, 103–04, 107, 109, 110, 113, 115, 118. *See also* Gabriel's rebellion; Louisiana Slave Insurrection; Turner, Nat
slave religion, restrictions on, 87
slave resistance, 25–27, 52–57, 80, 90, 91, 150 n 61. *See also* flight
slave trade, 25, 29, 30, 50, 51; positive image of, 62–63, 66. *See also* Atlantic slave trade; domestic slave trade
slave traders, 60, 62, 71, 73, 84, 117. *See also* Franklin & Armfield
slaves, freed following shipwreck, 64
"slicking," 113
Smith, Bery, 72–73
soil, 18, 35
Spanish rule, of Natchez, 32–36; planter rebellion against, 33
Sparkman, Sarah, 69, 70
Starks, L. R., 89
state capital, 101
state census (1837), 75
state sovereignty, extension of, over Indians, 102–03
Staunton (overseer), 79–80
staves, 23–24, 30
Steele, John, 38–39
Stewart, Virgil, 104–09, 114
stockade, 62, 65, 71
suicide, slave, 15

162

Sydnor, Charles Sackett, ix
Sylph, 31

task labor, 46
Thompson, Adam, 96
timber, 23–24
time, 46–47
Tobacco, 9, 33, 34
transatlantic marketplace. *See* Atlantic World
Trask, J. L., 97–98
Treaty of Dancing Rabbit Creek, 103
Turner, Nat, 95, 96, 97, 99, 114
Twain, Mark, 154 n 12

United States, 37, 48

Vick, Willis, 57
Vicksburg, 31
Vicksburg Register, 96
Vidalia, La., 117
vigilance committee, 28, 96, 110–12, 113, 119

War of 1812, 58, 60, 61
West Florida, x, 18–32
whippings, 43, 54, 57, 80, 81–82, 91
White Apple village, 10–11
Wilkinson, James, 56
Willing, James, 31–32
Willis, John, 50, 58
Willis, William, 57
Winans, William, 86
Winn, Baylor, 119
work culture, 46
work patterns, after migration west, 70, 71
work slowdowns, 80